Authoritarian Fictions

Authoritarian Fictions

The Ideological Novel
As a Literary Genre

Susan Rubin Suleiman

PRINCETON UNIVERSITY PRESS
PRINCETON, NEW JERSEY

Published by Princeton University Press, 41 William Street,
Princeton, New Jersey 08540
In the United Kingdom: Princeton University Press,
Chichester, West Sussex

Library of Congress Cataloging-in-Publication Data
Suleiman, Susan Rubin, 1939–
Authoritarian fictions: the ideological novel as a literary
genre / Susan Rubin Suleiman.
p. cm.
Includes bibliographical references and index.
ISBN 0–691–01536–8 (pbk.)
1. French fiction—20th century—History and criticism.
2. Literature and society—France—History—20th century.
3. Political fiction, French—History and criticism.
4. Authoritarianism in literature. 5. Literary form.
6. Propaganda. I. Title.
PQ671.S94   1992
843'.9109—dc20   92–30219

First Princeton Paperback printing, with a new preface, 1993

Reprinted by arrangements with Columbia University Press

Princeton University Press books are printed on acid-free
paper and meet the guidelines for permanence and
durability of the Committee on Production Guidelines for
Book Longevity of the Council on Library Resources

10 9 8 7 6 5 4 3 2 1

Printed in the United States of America

To my children
To my mother
To the memory of my father

Contents

Preface to the 1993 Edition
On Reading Yourself Later

> To read is to struggle to name.
>
> Roland Barthes (1970)

> Does naming really solve, or cure, or does it kill? The question is adamic, endemic, academic.
>
> Christine Brooke-Rose (1990)

> But orderliness has its advantages, too.
>
> Robyn Warhol (1989)

HAVING TO WRITE a preface for it, I sat down and read the book, cover to cover, including the notes. It was the first time.

This may sound strange, given the well-known narcissism of authors. But anyone who has published a book will understand what I mean. The fact is, by the time you actually hold the object in your hand, you have gone over it so many times—as individual chapters, as the completed manuscript, as galleys, as page proofs—that the last thing you want to do is *read* it. I mean the way a reader reads it, out of curiosity, for pleasure or instruction, turning the pages faster or slower, putting it down to answer the phone or run an errand, picking it up again and underlining a passage, maybe writing a note in the margin when you don't agree, or when you agree most vigorously. Occasionally, starting to nod over it: it's getting late, time to put away the book and go to bed.

Nine years and two books later, I finally took the plunge, though not without some trepidation: Would I still recognize this work as mine? Or would it feel like something from another world, another's pen (sorry, another's IBM)? Nine years, it might be objected, is not that long. True, but everything depends on which nine years. Between 1983 and 1992, the world has become radically other—both the big world of geopolitics, in which words like "Berlin Wall" or "Soviet Union" no longer designate anything existing in the present, and the apparently smaller world of academic controversies. Whoever had heard of the "multiculturalism debate" in 1983? "Politically correct" was a quaint term from the 1930s. Pornography was with us, as always—but the "debate on pornography" was barely on the horizon, and neither Mapplethorpe nor Helms (nor Dworkin nor MacKinnon) were household names. As for AIDS, most people would have defined it, if asked, as a strange new disease afflicting homosexuals and Haitians.

Even within the much smaller world of literary theory and criticism (small despite its international cast, witness David Lodge's comic inside view in *Small World*), things were different then. Books of feminist criticism or theory were relatively scarce—something hard to imagine now, like trying to remember what life was like before video stores on every corner. In France, the *Tel Quel* group, although no longer in existence (the last issue of the journal, published continuously since 1960, had appeared in December 1982), still functioned as a shorthand for a certain idea of "modernity." In the United States, Paul de Man was still alive and had not yet become a "case;" the latest rage in literature departments was "reader-oriented criticism" and the related notion (put into circulation by Stanley Fish) of "interpretive communities;" writing about postmodernism had not yet become an industry; the "new historicism" had not yet been invented; "queer theory," if it had been invented, would have sounded merely odd; structuralism had not yet become historical.

Enter *Authoritarian Fictions*: What kind of work is/was this? Where was its place in the critical-theoretical landscape of 1983, and where does it fit now?

Possibly the most succinct summing up I have read of this book is as follows: "Combining descriptive poetics with interpretive criticism, Suleiman proposes a model for the genre of the ideological novel, then reads individual texts against the model."[1] What Robyn Warhol presents, in admirably condensed fashion, as a coherent method existing on a single temporal plane—what we used to call, following the linguists, synchrony—was actually the result of a gradual evolution over time. Like most books, this one was several years in the making; it had a history. In the spirit of the current critical age, which encourages both personal writing and historical self-consciousness, I will allow myself to sketch that history here.

When I first conceived of this book in the early 1970s, structuralism—and particularly narratology, that branch of structuralism which made the systematic study of narratives its specialty—was at its glorious height. In 1966, a special issue of the journal *Communications* devoted to "L'analyse structurale du récit," "Structural Analysis of Narrative," including articles by Roland Barthes, A. J. Greimas, Claude Bremond, Umberto Eco, Christian Metz, Tzvetan Todorov, and Gérard Genette, had appeared as a veritable manifesto of the new methodology; the narratologists claimed every kind of story as their domain, from jokes and newspaper articles to fairy tales, myths, James Bond films, and "classic" fiction. A few years later, Barthes published his groundbreaking study of realist fiction, *S/Z*; Genette, after two brilliant books of essays, produced the most systematic study of narrative discourse ever in his "Discours du récit"; Greimas, reviving and streamlining Vladimir Propp's early work on the structure of fairy tales, proposed a structural semantic model so general that it could be used for every kind of story; Todorov, besides presenting the work of the Russian Formalists to French readers, published several important books on aspects of the "poetics of prose." All this by 1972, when I found myself, a young Ph.D. in modern French literature (also a young mother trying to cope with teaching, child care, and wifely obligations), starting to worry about writing my first book.

---

[1] Robyn R. Warhol, *Gendered Interventions: Narrative Discourse in the Victorian Novel* (New Brunswick: Rutgers University Press, 1989), p. 4.

My own critical training, at Harvard in the 1960s, had been varied but unsystematic: some close reading in the New Critical mode, some archetypal criticism (Northrop Frye was "in"), quite a bit of intellectual history, a taste of philology, a smattering of Marxism (via Lucien Goldmann), a whiff of psychoanalysis, and lots and lots of Sartrean existentialism and Beauvoirian autobiography, my personal passions. I wrote my Ph.D. dissertation on the novels of Paul Nizan, a close friend of Sartre's in their youth, a passionate Communist during the 1930s who had left the Party after the Hitler-Stalin pact of 1939 and been killed in the war the following year, at age thirty-five. After finishing the dissertation, I got a job as an assistant professor at Columbia, which at the time was a veritable hotbed of the new methodologies. Everyone who was anyone, it seemed, came to lecture at the Maison Française on West 113th Street. In addition, the young faculty and advanced graduate students started a study group on structuralism. That is where my real education in modern literary theory began.

It was like entering a dazzling new country. My guides were not only Barthes, Genette, Greimas, and Todorov, but those who had guided them: the Russian Formalists, the Czech structuralists, the structural linguists and anthropologists—Saussure, Hjelmslev, Benveniste, Jakobson, Lévi-Strauss. They offered a new way of looking at texts and a new language in which to describe them, methods I found difficult to master but so heady once I succeeded. Together, this way of looking and this language promised nothing less than rigor and scientific precision—the wide world of literature at last mapped and named, and thus truly understood, classified and ordered.

Thinking again about my dissertation ("Paul Nizan and the Novelist's Problem of Commitment," a very Sartrean title), I realized that I didn't want to publish it as my first book. Instead, I would start from scratch, reframe the whole question of commitment (a term covering everything from party militancy to Sartrean *engagement*) in narratological terms. I would no longer deal with a single novelist and his "problem," but with a whole category of texts and *their* problem. The *roman à thèse*, a kind of novel that indubitably existed and even flourished in France and elsewhere at certain highly polarized political moments since the nineteenth century, had such a bad reputation (to most people, it meant "annoyingly didactic novel") that no writer would claim it as their own. Nor would any structuralist critic or theorist claim it, for by then it was clear that structuralists liked to work either on "classically great" literature (even if they viewed it extremely critically, as Barthes and the *Tel Quel* group viewed realist fiction), or else on popular and mass cultural texts and genres, from Hollywood films and detective novels to comic strips. The *roman à thèse*, although practiced by writers as important, in their time, as Barrès and Bourget (two "greats" of the 1890s whom very few people read now), as well as by Nizan, Aragon, Malraux, Mauriac, and many other writers of varying degrees of fame and recognition, did not fall easily into either of those categories. All the more reason to rescue it for, as well as by, narratology. For a while, Todorov's *The Fantastic: A Structural Approach to a Literary Genre* (first published in Paris in 1970) became my bible—not because of its subject matter, since the *roman à thèse* as I define it is a realist genre, but for its method.

Oh, the reams of paper spent on charts and diagrams! Oh, the desire to name and master, oh, the "Linnean lust!" (Elizabeth Bruss's happy phrase). And, oh, the discouragement, the loss of heart and confidence, when a text I knew (intuitively *knew*) to be a *roman à thèse* didn't exactly fit my models. It took me a long time to come to terms with the understanding that gradually dawned on me: literary structures are *constructed*, not discovered in nature, or even in texts. A generic structural model is useful precisely to the degree that it allows one to see both the "pure" construction and its "impure" variants, both the "perfect fit" between text and structure, and its absence.

This understanding is not necessarily at odds with the project of narratology—indeed, one could claim that it is an essential part of it. Yet, in my own case, I would say that when

I realized it was all right—indeed, inevitable—to acknowledge impurity and difference, I was already halfway out of narratology. That means halfway in as well, of course, which may explain why, in reading the book now, I have the sense of a layered, hybrid mode of discourse—as if the author were speaking several languages in quick alternation, or even, by some quirk of a sound system, simultaneously. In fact, a literal alternation of languages had gone into the book, for I first wrote it in French (the language of structuralism, in my mind), then translated it into English and rewrote it in the process, then retranslated all the rewritings into the French version which was published simultaneously with the English one. The hybrid effect I have in mind, however, is a somewhat different thing—occurring not between French and English, but within each one.

As a start, there is the confident language of narratological description, bristling with technical terms and names and categories, some invented, others a part of a now-standard vocabulary: *extraheterodiegetic narrator, actantial configuration, syntagmatic structure, positive exemplary apprenticeship, structure of confrontation, discursive coherence, redundancy, narratee.* The highpoint of this technicity is no doubt chapter four, with its pseudo-algebraic formulas and diagrams. As these are all accompanied by definitions in ordinary prose, I ask myself whether I couldn't have simply omitted the formulas; probably, I could have. Yet, recalling the process of constructing that elaborate system, that whole exhaustive inventory of redundancies in realist fiction, I look back at my earlier self with a kind of amazement, and yes, even admiration, for surely I would not have the patience (or the desire) to undertake such a construction now. I *needed* those formulas to work out the system and so there they stay, reminders of another day.[2]

---

[2] In fact, I have found a small mistake which I here take the opportunity to correct: on page 182, the string of redundancies should read $C_4I = C_5I_2$, not $C_4I_2 = C_5I$ as it does now. There are a few more typographical errors, but they are too minor to note here, and impossible to correct in the text, which is being reprinted exactly from the 1983 edition. Hence, no updating of references either. I would, however, like to men-

An altogether different language in the book is that of the hermeneutic, reader-oriented critic—for I could hardly shut my eyes, even while pursuing my project of "descriptive poetics," to the new theoretical developments that were occurring around me. This was especially true of reader-oriented criticism, to which I myself had contributed. Somewhat to my surprise, the essay I wrote as an introduction to *The Reader in the Text*, published in 1980 by Princeton University Press, attracted a great deal of attention in the field. It was after writing that essay that I added the highly personal (and diagramless) section on "Redundancy and the Problem of Evaluation" to chapter four, which ends with a sentence that I now see as a veritable turning point: "Structural and semiotic analyses provide a method and a tool, but they are no substitute for personal engagement with a text." After that, there are no more diagrams and there is a perceptible decrease in the use of technical terms. Above all, there is the twist of chapter five, which had not been part of the original plan of the book.

Chapter five, "Subversions, or the Play of Writing," which in a sense undoes, or at least puts into question, all the careful constructions that precede it, is also the chapter in which (as at least one reviewer noted) the name of Jacques Derrida makes its single, belated appearance. Indeed, this is the self-consciously, explicitly "deconstructionist" moment of the book. As I have suggested, however, the deconstructionist impulse was present in muted form from the very first chapter, adding yet another discursive—and historical—layer to its writing. The occasional ironic remarks about the vulnerability of analytic commentary, and other similarly self-reflexive statements that punctuate the early chapters were grafted on later to their more earnest original versions. Historically, they no doubt signal the move—or my move—toward poststructuralism. I was interested to see that Christopher Norris, in his review essay in

---

tion Régine Robin's book, *Le réalisme socialiste: une esthétique impossible* (Paris: Payot, 1986), which directly took up my suggestion (chap. 5, n. 6) about applying my models for the *roman à thèse* to Soviet socialist realist fiction.

the *London Review of Books,* considered the book as a whole as an example of poststructuralism: "[Suleiman] mounts a most impressive case against the arguments of those who regard post-structuralism in any guise as a species of textual mystification devoid of political relevance."[3]

Norris suggests that the book's political relevance—perhaps one might also call it an ethical relevance—is to be found in its poststructuralist suspicion of authoritarian discourses, whether of the Right or Left, whether in literature or in politics. On the whole, I agree: the book's politics, insofar as it has one, resides in its contesting of orthodoxies. I would merely remark that in my own mind the contesting extended even to poststructuralism, which by the late 1970s had itself become, in certain quarters, a discourse of orthodoxy. Such is the fate, no doubt, of all successful methods and discourses, even those predicated on the absolute refusal of orthodoxy. That is no reason, however, for accepting them on faith. My own internal polemic, throughout the book, is not only against the authoritarianism of the *roman à thèse,* which seeks to impose a single "correct" meaning on the world as on the text, but also against the coerciveness of any critical discourse once it becomes institutionalized and, in some instances, trivialized. Hence my argument with those who, under the banner of the modern (or the postmodern), might wish to renounce the search for meaning—and, correlatively, for value—altogether. Or those who, under the banner of a certain theoretical hard-headedness, were willing at one time to do away with crucial differences—claiming, for example, that *all* novels written in the realist mode were part of a single, repressive ideology. It was precisely at such moments that narratology's fine-grained distinctions and its faith in the power of naming reasserted their usefulness.

These three major layers of discourse—descriptive poetics, hermeneutics and reader-oriented criticism, poststructural-

---

[3] Christopher Norris, "Beyond Textualism," *London Review of Books,* 19 January–1 February 1984: 18.

ism—each correspond to a historical moment in the world of literary theory and in my own evolution. But where is feminism? This is a question that will certainly occur to those who know me primarily as a feminist critic, many of whom are unaware that I have also written other kinds of work. It is a question that occurred to me, too, as I was reading this book and noting with astonishment how very little feminist consciousness it seemed to manifest. Aside from two footnotes which refer to "patriarchal culture" (chap. 1, n. 24) and to the "masculine model" of the *Bildungsroman* (chap. 2, n. 5), there is no discursive trace of feminist criticism or theory here at all. I even use, save for a few exceptions, the generalizing "he" to refer to readers, critics, and authors. True, as I stated earlier, feminist criticism was not as pervasive during the years I was writing this book as it is now. Still, I find it almost unbelievable that there should be so little of its discourse and its preoccupations present in the book. I had already written two (and published one) of my feminist critical essays during the very time that I was working on the major sections of the manuscript.[4]

How to explain this absence? Clearly, a dismissive shrugging of the shoulders ("I hadn't *really* discovered feminism yet") is not sufficient—and besides, it would be untrue, even if most of my feminist work came after this book. Nor would it be sufficient to respond that "the subject does not lend itself to feminist analysis," for in fact it does, and in some places even cries out for it: What is the relation between authoritarianism and patriarchy? Why are all the authors in my corpus of French *romans à thèse* men?

Was it that, untenured and writing a first book, I was afraid to say what I really thought and cared about? Hardly. Among my many failings, hypocrisy and excessive timidity are not preeminent: if anything, I often rush in where others

---

[4] "Reading Robbe-Grillet: Sadism and Text in *Projet pour une révolution à New York*" was written in 1975 and published in *Romanic Review* in 1977; "Writing and Motherhood" was written, in its first version, in 1979; the published version appeared in 1985, in *The (M)Other Tongue: Essays in Feminist Psychoanalytic Interpretation*, ed. S. Garner, C. Kahane, M. Sprengnether (Ithaca: Cornell University Press).

would tread more prudently. To understand the repression (if repression it was) of feminism in this book, one has to seek the explanation on a deeper level than that of career worries or conscious fears. (I had tenure at a college I was happy at by the time I finished the book.)

I shall propose an explanation, or more exactly a speculation; probably not by chance, it is psychoanalytic. (The discourse of psychoanalysis, which has been a strong element in my feminist writing, is also heavily underrepresented in *Authoritarian Fictions*.) Here is my speculation: *Authoritarian Fictions* is a deeply antipaternal book, but it is also deeply ambivalent about its own antipaternalism. Obviously, the symbolic Father is the one in question here, though I wouldn't want to dismiss too quickly the importance of flesh-and-blood fathers or their role. Insofar as the Father represents a repressive authority, whether actual or textual, the book opposes him and mocks him: it speaks from the position of a rebellious daughter, the position of the "irony of the tribe" that Hegel ascribed to Antigone. In that respect, it can be said to be feminist after all, strongly, from one end to the other. The Father, however, does not stand only for repression in our culture: he also represents language, reason, empowerment, and authority in the sense of agency and authorship. Insofar as he represents those things, no daughter who writes or seeks empowerment will find it easy to do without him. Whence the ambivalence, and whence, as corollaries, the blindspots ("What *is* the relation between authoritarianism and patriarchy?") and the absence of a self-consciously feminist discourse.

This speculation may be too too classically Freudo-Lacanian, but it's the best I can do at the moment.

It brings me, however, to the question of the mother, and to the further realization that there are no mothers to be found in *Authoritarian Fictions*. The two "feminist psychoanalytic" essays I wrote before finishing the book happened to be very much concerned with mothers; indeed, "Writing and Motherhood" was exclusively concerned with the mother as writing subject. But although I myself was a mother from the moment I wrote the first word of this book, that fact does not seem to have found a place in its writing.

There is no way to deny it: *Authoritarian Fictions* is a book of the Father, and I say that emphasizing every possible meaning of the preposition. *Of*, as in my American Heritage dictionary: *originating from, caused by, at a distance from, associated with, connected to, centering upon, characterized by, about*. The book is "of" the Father critically as well: its true intellectual fathers, I realize in retrospect, are Sartre and Barthes. Or is it Sarthes and Bartre? I feel lucky to have found them—"good enough" fathers both, for one like me. Both were profoundly opposed to discourses of authority, whether dogma or *doxa*, and both were profoundly attached to their mothers. By the time this book was published, they had both been dead for three years (they both died in early 1980). I don't know exactly what that means, but I know that in some way it is significant.

One of the dictionary definitions of the preposition "of" I did not mention above suddenly comes back to me: "So as to be separated or relieved from: *cured of*." Perhaps this book of the Father is also the book that cured me of the Father. Perhaps that is why the next project I undertook centered on "the female body in Western culture," and why, in the book after that, the mother—my ideal version of her, the laughing, playful mother—became the central figure. The title of that book may be significant: *Subversive Intent*.[5]

Where, finally, will *Authoritarian Fictions* fit into the critical and political landscape of 1993? Frankly, I don't know. I hope that this attempt at a history has been useful in providing some possible answers, which I will not try to formulate, except perhaps to suggest that the book's nonhomogeneous, discursively hybrid quality may be the very thing that makes it contempo-

[5] *Subversive Intent: Gender, Politics, and the Avant-Garde* (Cambridge, Mass.: Harvard University Press, 1990); the "intermediary" book was an edited volume, *The Female Body in Western Culture: Contemporary Perspectives* (Cambridge, Mass.: Harvard University Press, 1986).

rary, rather than a "classic." I would suggest, in addition, as some others have recently done, that hybridity may also be the best hope for the ongoing project of narratology.[6]

Need I say it? I would much rather be a contemporary than a classic. And the mother of one, too.

Belmont, Massachusetts
June 23, 1992

[6] Introducing a recent volume of "critical" narratology (as opposed to the older kind) in honor of Dorrit Cohn, Ingeborg Hoesterey writes: "Somewhat in jest . . . one might conceive of 'critical' narratology as a new Hellenism, a project merging impulses from critical theory and narratology proper into a hybrid form of critical discourse" (*Neverending Stories: Toward a Critical Narratology* [Princeton: Princeton University Press, 1991], p. 4). Mieke Bal, in a longer essay, argues for the extension of narratology to nonnarrative texts, and for its usefulness in discussing questions of ideology and history ("The Point of Narrative," *Poetics Today* 11:4 [Winter 1990], pp. 727–53). The three ten-year anniversary issues of *Poetics Today* devoted to "Narratology Revisited" (alluding to the "Narratology" issues of 1980) give an interesting overview of the state of the field today. As the "re" suggests, what was still a dynamic project ten years ago is now perceived as somewhat problematic. Christine Brooke-Rose's "Whatever Happened to Narratology?" (Summer 1990), from which my epigraph by her is taken, is perhaps the most negative view expressed—not counting, of course, the many original contributors to the 1980 issues who declined to "revisit" narratology altogether. See *Poetics Today* 11:2, 11:3, 11:4 (1990–1991).

Acknowledgments

EVERYONE KNOWS that theatrical or cinematic works are collective enterprises; in a different way, books are collective too. Although I must take sole responsibility for what is written in this book, I gratefully acknowledge the help of the many people and institutions that contributed to its making.

The American Council of Learned Societies, the National Endowment for the Humanities, and the Occidental College Mellon Faculty Research Fund provided me with financial assistance that allowed me to spend a year in France, writing and doing research in 1977–1978. In earlier years, I benefited from summer grants awarded by the Columbia University Council for Research in the Humanities.

Among the many people with whom I discussed my work at various stages were my colleagues and students at Columbia University, at Occidental College, and at Harvard University: to all of them, my warmest thanks. Louis Marin was a perceptive reader of early parts of the manuscript, as were Zeev Sternhell and Steven Englund of the chapter on Barrès. Christine Brooke-Rose was instrumental in the working out of chapter 4, which I first presented before the Faculty Seminar she organized in 1977–1978 at the University of Paris VIII. My intellectual debt to Gérard Genette and A. J. Greimas is obvious, as it is to the late and regretted Roland Barthes, who read one of my first essays and encouraged me to develop it into a book. Tzvetan Todorov provided not only intellectual inspiration through his numerous works, but friendly and much appreciated support as well. Michel Beaujour and Naomi Schor read the entire manuscript in its next-to-last version and offered generous criticism for which I am most grateful. Gerald Prince saw the manuscript develop chapter by chapter and gave unstintingly of his time and his critical intelligence—to him, my very special thanks.

For many years, Ezra Suleiman was a generous and faithful helpmate and interlocutor. For his support when I most needed it, I am very grateful. Henriette Nizan was and has remained a steadfast friend and "second mother." Sophie and Nassim R. Suleiman have encouraged and facilitated my work not like "in-laws" but like loving parents. My sister, Eve Sprotzer, has provided aid and love, in good times and bad.

My editor at the Columbia University Press, Bill Germano, has my thanks not only for his unfailing good humor and good sense, but for his implacable insistence that I stick to my schedule.

Chapters 1 and 2 first appeared, in shorter revised versions in French, in *Poétique* (November 1977 and February 1979); an earlier, shorter version of chapter 3 appeared in *Modern Language Notes* (May 1980); a shorter version of chapter 4 appeared in *Poetics Today* (Spring 1980). I am grateful to the editors of those journals for their permission to reprint.

In the last stages of preparing the manuscript, I was greatly aided by the efficient and devoted work of my research assistant, Claudia Dobkin. Of those who typed the manuscript in various stages, in French and in English, I wish particularly to thank Pierrette Andrès, Paulette Pugnaire, and Susan Fuerst.

Like every woman who has young children and who writes, I have relied on others to make the time for writing possible. I especially remember the cheerful, loving presence of Jeanne Bénichou, Karen Nordberg, and Bertha Paredes; more than mere "caretakers," they became temporary, cherished family members to my children.

My children, Michael and Daniel, lived with this book as much as I did, although they didn't always know it. What I wish them to know is that nothing has given me more pleasure, of the kind that only the union of love and work can bring, than to dedicate this book to them—together with my parents, with whom it all began.

S.R.S.
Cambridge, Massachusetts
January 1983

Note on Translations

TO FACILITATE the task of the English-speaking reader, I have given most quotations, both from novels and from critical works, directly in English, using my own translations; the page references are to the French texts. In the few instances where I have quoted from an already-existing English translation, I have given that as the reference. For recent critical works that have been translated into English, I have indicated the English title and publication data in my bibliography. In some instances, when quoting longer or stylistically pertinent passages from novels, I have given both the original and my translation in the text.

For Barthes' *S/Z* and *Essais critiques,* I have consulted with profit the translations by Richard Miller and Richard Howard. For Nizan's *Antoine Bloyé,* I have consulted the translation by Edmund Stevens (New York and London: Monthly Review Press, 1973).

Literature, as it has been understood by all the masters, is an interpretation of life. It eliminates in order to prove.

Maurice Barrès

All literature is propaganda. [. . .] Art, for us, is what makes propaganda effective, what is capable of moving men in the direction we wish.

Paul Nizan

Then comes the modern question: why is there not today (or at least so it seems to me), why is there no longer an art of intellectual persuasion, or imagination? Why are we so slow, so indifferent about mobilizing narrative and the image? Can't we see that it is, after all, works of fiction, no matter how mediocre they may be artistically, that best arouse political passion?

Roland Barthes

. . . it is the very notion of a work created *for* the expression of a social, political, economic, moral, etc. content that constitutes a lie.

Alain Robbe-Grillet

Introduction

THIS BOOK is about novels with a clear ideological message—novels that seek, through the vehicle of fiction, to persuade their readers of the "correctness" of a particular way of interpreting the world. I call such novels ideological, not in the broad sense in which we can say that any representation of human reality depends on, and in some way expresses, a more or less consciously defined ideology (in this sense, any work of fiction, indeed any work of art can be considered ideological), but in the more narrow sense in which we might call a discourse ideological if it refers explicitly to, and identifies itself with, a recognized body of doctrine or system of ideas.

There are few words in our language as frequently used (at least in some contexts), and at the same time as ambiguous, as open to contradictory interpretations, as the words "ideology" and "ideological." Raymond Williams has noted that the concept of ideology, even within Marxist thought alone (it did not originate with Marx), has been used in at least three distinct, and incompatible, senses, ranging from the neutral sense of "a system of beliefs characteristic of a particular class or group" to the polemical—and, as Williams points out, naively reductionist—sense of "false consciousness" or "illusion," which is opposed to a "positive, scientific knowledge." This last definition leads, according to Williams, to "a familiar partisan claim (of the kind made by almost all parties) that others are biased [their thought is ideological], but that, by definition, we are not."[1]

Despite my use of a term that is so closely identified with Marxist theory and criticism, this study is not Marxist in approach or allegiance. Indeed, some Marxist critics might consider my approach regrettably "formalistic," and my use of the term "ideological" vague, imprecise—or, worst of all, ideological. I am willing to run that risk. As Roland Barthes once remarked, there is no discourse, whether in criticism or any other field, that is wholly free of ideology.[2] And even as far as Marxist theory is concerned, Raymond Williams has persuasively argued that "there can be no question of establishing, except in polemics, a single 'correct' Marxist definition of ideology."[3]

My subject, then, is a novelistic genre that proclaims its own status as both overtly ideological *and* as fictional, and whose problematic mode of existence is due precisely to the combination of—or more exactly, to the friction between—those two modes of discourse. This genre has a name other than the one by which I have called it in English: it is the *roman à thèse,* and that is how I shall refer to it from now on. This name is, as we shall see in a moment, highly problematical in its own right. It has, however, the advantage of being an accepted, if ill-understood and unanalyzed, term in literary theory and criticism.

What is the generic status of the *roman à thèse,* and what significant problems does it raise for contemporary thinking about literature? In particular, what does it suggest about the nature of reading and interpretation, about the often contrasted notions of narrative authority and modernist writing, about the relation between realism and didacticism, and the relation between fictional representation and historical reality? This whole book is an attempt to reply to these questions. It will be useful, however, to summarize a few of my arguments here.

Some Problems of (the) Genre: Definitions and
Method

In ordinary critical usage, the term "roman à thèse" has a
strongly negative connotation; it designates works that are too
close to propaganda to be artistically valid. No self-respecting
writer would consent to call his novels by that name. A *roman
à thèse* is always the work of an "other." Alain Robbe-Grillet
has referred to this genre as one "despised above all others."[4]
And Maurice Blanchot began one of his essays with the question: "One may well ask why the *roman à thèse* has a bad reputation."[5] Nor is this attitude a specifically contemporary one.
Already in 1904, shortly after the term came into current
usage, a number of writers who had perhaps nothing else in
common (and some of whom wrote novels that were indubitably *romans à thèse*) agreed in their condemnation of the genre.
Replying to a questionnaire on "contemporary literary trends"
in the weekly magazine *Gil Blas*, one author wrote: "The *roman
à thèse* is on the margins of art." According to another, "the
roman à thèse can never find a durable form, for it cannot be
used by a novelist who is an artist." A third, who identified
himself as a Marxist, exclaimed: "What a mad idea it is to try
and demonstrate a thesis through the novel! Just look at Bourget."[6] As for Paul Bourget, a highly successful novelist who
was (and is, by those who still know of him) generally considered to be a writer of *romans à thèse*, he seized every opportunity to denounce the genre: "Let us condemn the [*roman*] *à
thèse*, an essentially false genre," he declared in a formal speech
before the Académie Française in 1907. But he immediately
added: "Let us not confuse it with the novel of ideas, a legiti-
mate and necessary genre."[7] His own novels and those of his
friends were, according to Bourget, *romans d'idées, romans
d'analyse,* or *romans sociaux;* the novels of George Sand, on the
other hand, or *Les Misérables,* were *romans à thèse.* (As can be
surmised, Bourget was a right-wing writer).

What were the accusations heaped upon this genre? The

chief one was that because of its desire to "prove" something, the *roman à thèse* was unfaithful to reality: instead of being based on impartial observation, the *roman à thèse* presented a distorted image of the world, an image constructed with a demonstration in mind. "To support the thesis, one must 'trump up' characters and situations, and exaggerate, slant one's observation," wrote one of the respondents to the 1904 questionnaire.[8] In a similar vein, Bourget accused the *roman à thèse* of "altering reality" ["donner un coup de pouce au réel"].[9] The issues were defined, then, in terms of "true" or "false" representation—in other words, in terms of the chief criterion of realist fiction. But as the example of Bourget indicates, the judgment that a representation is "false" or "slanted" is determined in large part by the ideas and the political or ideological allegiances of the reader. Bourget, who was a right-wing writer, considered Sand's or Hugo's observations "slanted"; consequently, their novels (or, in the case of Hugo, at least one of his novels) were *romans à thèse*. But Bourget's own novels, or those of his friend Henry Bordeaux, even while offering interpretations of reality, made an effort "not to deform reality too much";[10] they were therefore *romans d'idées*. (The crucial question, of course, is how Bourget defined, and how one *can* define, "too much" in the phrase "deforming reality too much.")

We are confronted here with a very curious phenomenon, which in itself constitutes a theoretical problem: that of a literary genre which, to borrow Gide's famous phrase about homosexual love, "does not dare to speak its name." To say about a novel that it is a *roman à thèse* is already a negative judgment, and a slur on its author. This suggests, among other things, that the perception and the naming of the genre are interpretive and evaluative acts, which indicate, prior to any commentary, a certain attitude on the part of the reader or critic. One can probably say the same thing about all genres: to name them is already to interpret them by half. But in this instance as in many others, the *roman à thèse* is particularly interesting because it offers an extreme, and therefore all the more "visible," version of a more general phenomenon.

After all this, may I affirm without apology that there are many *romans à thèse* I have read and liked? Admittedly, it has not always been a pure affection—but, in our post-Freudian age, we know that ambivalence is indissociable from love, and creates the most lasting bonds. I read one of Bourget's novels for the first time in graduate school, and disliked it intensely. At the same time, I was sufficiently caught by it to read other novels I felt intuitively to be similar to it, and to devote several years of my life to studying how such novels are made—or, to use a more expressive term, "what makes them tick."

This is not a study in subjective criticism, however. Although my personal engagement with the *roman à thèse* will be evident in many places, the kind of discourse I am aiming for is dispassionate and analytic, not polemical or confessional. This aim is not always realized, and the reader will find description veering off, from time to time, toward interpretation and personal judgment. That is part of the nature of the enterprise, however; the *roman à thèse* is an "impure" and paradoxical genre; the commentary it provokes resembles it.

The novels and novelists I shall be discussing are French, but although it could be argued that France has provided a more fertile ground for the development of the *roman à thèse* than many other countries, neither the genre nor my way of approaching it is limited to France. Some of the authors I shall mention will be familiar, at least by name, to English-speaking readers: Malraux, Mauriac, Sartre, Aragon, Zola. Others will be known only to specialists, or to those with a particular interest in French history and society: Barrès, Bourget, Drieu La Rochelle, Nizan. The interesting point is that the works of these writers have never been studied in a perspective that seeks to disengage the formal resemblances among them. One reason for this is no doubt the obvious political and ideological differences that separate "leftist" or left-wing writers like Zola, Nizan, or Sartre from "rightists" like Barrès, Bourget, or Drieu

La Rochelle. Critics and historians who are sensitive to differences in the ideological content of these writers' fiction have not thought to look for underlying formal and generic similarities. Indeed, apart from a few important literary studies with a thematic and historical orientation (such as Victor Brombert's study of the intellectual hero in French fiction between 1880 and 1955, or Micheline Tison-Braun's two-volume work on the crisis of humanism between 1890 and 1939),[11] these writers—and especially the lesser-known ones, who do not have the "classic" stature of a Sartre, a Malraux or a Zola—have elicited interest more as individuals with a problematic and sometimes tragic biography, or as examples of "intellectuals in politics," than as practitioners of a particular *kind* of writing.[12] Contemporary theorists, whether of genre or of narrative, have been singularly uninterested in their works.

There do exist a few critical studies, published quite a while ago, that discuss novels by some of these authors as "political novels" or as examples of "committed" or *engagé* literature.[13] Neither of these categories corresponds exactly, however, to the *roman à thèse*. The political novel as a generic category is at once too broad (Stendhal's *La Chartreuse de Parme* is, as Irving Howe has shown, a superb political novel, but it is not a *roman à thèse*) and too narrow (Mauriac's "Catholic novel," *Le Noeud de vipères*, is a *roman à thèse*, but not a political novel). As for "littérature engagée," it is too imprecise a term to designate a genre; furthermore, I feel it is too specifically associated with the name of Sartre, who did not invent the term but who made it current—and who, incidentally, went out of his way to distinguish "engagé" novels from *romans à thèse* (although it may once again have been a matter of rejecting the name rather than the thing itself).[14]

What seems necessary to emphasize is that a formal resemblance between certain works (even if by "form" we mean the form of content, that is, narrative or thematic structures) does not imply the identity of their specific content—political, ideological, or merely episodic; similarly, a coincidence in the specific content of two works does not necessarily indicate that they belong to the same formal category. That is why the occasional statements one finds in French literary manuals about the "similarity" between Barrès' *Les Déracinés* (1897) and Nizan's *La Conspiration* (1938), for example, are as invalid, methodologically, as the contrary statement would be—claiming that these two novels cannot be compared, given the political divergences between their authors. In the first instance, one uses a coincidence in subject matter (both novels are "about" the life of Parisian students) in order to affirm Barrès' "influence" on Nizan; in the second, one would confuse a divergence in ideological content with a formal difference.[15] In any case, what is involved here is an isolated comparison, not a discussion pertinent to literary theory.

It is precisely in terms of literary theory, however, that the *roman à thèse* is interesting. Such, at any rate, is the founding hypothesis of this book.

As a starting point, I propose the following definition: *a* roman à thèse *is a novel written in the realistic mode (that is, based on an aesthetic of verisimilitude and representation), which signals itself to the reader as primarily didactic in intent, seeking to demonstrate the validity of a political, philosophical, or religious doctrine.* This preliminary definition, although somewhat unwieldy and in need of elucidation, presents a number of advantages.

First, the definition is specific enough to provide a basis for analytic investigation, but general enough to include a number of works whose narrative and ideological content may vary greatly. This allows us to see similarities among works that may at first glance appear incompatible.

Second, the definition implies no value judgment as to the quality of individual works that belong to the genre (or, to use Tzvetan Todorov's expression, that "manifest" the genre),[16] thus making the term *roman à thèse* a descriptive, not an evaluative term. In effect, if one accepts Todorov's definition, according to which genres are the "relays by which the [individual] work enters into contact with the universe of literature,"[17] or Michael Riffaterre's definition, according to which a genre is "a structure of which [individual] works are the variants,"[18] it follows that the quality of a literary work, which is ultimately determined not by its structures but by their realization on the level of language, cannot be deduced exclusively from its generic status—unless, of course, one considers certain genres as "bad" by definition, and I see no reason to adopt such a position from the start. What one could say, following Todorov, is that the more narrowly a work conforms to the "rules of the genre," exhibiting no "deviant" or original elements, the further away it moves from Literature with a capital L[19]—or, to put it more simply, the less interesting it becomes. (As far as the *roman à thèse* is concerned, this kind of conformity would make a work closer to "pure" propaganda without "art," to cite Nizan's phrase.) It would appear, in fact, that one of the characteristics of great—or merely important—works of literature is that they lend themselves to being analyzed in terms of more than one genre, and at the same time no analysis exclusively in terms of genre is sufficient to account for them completely.

This explains one of the words in my definition that required elucidation: the word "primarily." In order for a work to be perceived as a *roman à thèse* (and let us recall that a genre always depends on the perception of the reader—as Riffaterre has strikingly put it, a genre is "a phantom form that exists only in the mind of the reader"),[20] it must signal itself as being *primarily* didactic and doctrinaire in intent. In somewhat different terms, it must possess a set of dominant traits that form a system. I shall propose, in the next chapter, a basic model to account for the dominant traits of the *roman à thèse*. For the moment, we may simply note that even in the *roman à thèse* there may be varying degrees of dominance (some novels are more strongly "à thèse" than others), and inversely that some works that are not generally perceived as *romans à thèse* may lend themselves to a (partial) reading in terms of the genre. *A la recherche du temps perdu*, for example, can be read as a *roman à thèse* propounding the doctrine of salvation through art. Such a reading would leave out too many elements of the novel to be satisfying in and of itself. It would, however, illuminate certain aspects of *A la recherche*—in particular, its well-known tendency toward didactic generalizations and theorizing—by integrating them into a general system.

One could even go further, and claim that every novel, indeed every work of fiction (in the broad sense of "representation," which would include dramatic works in prose or verse, as well as lyric and narrative poetry) can be read as expounding a "thesis," to the extent that it is always possible to extract from it a general maxim of some kind. Monroe Beardsley, for example, has proposed to call the "thesis" of a literary work (be it a poem, a novel, or whatever) any "general statement that the [work] may be said to afford, or to contain, some observation or reflection about life or art or man or reality."[21] Similarly, some sociolinguists who have studied the function of narratives in everyday conversation have shown that any story told by a speaker to a public (who may be a single person) must justify its own existence, as well as the act of its telling, by implicitly or explicitly answering the question: "So What's The Point?"[22] In the seventeenth century, French *literati* greatly admired a treatise on epic poetry by Père Le Bossu, who claimed that the *Iliad* was an illustration of the maxim: "fighting among princes ruins their own states," and who saw in the *Odyssey* a demonstration of the maxim that "a person's absence from home, or his lack of concern for what goes on there, is a cause of great disorder."[23] In our own day, we have seen commentaries on the *nouveau roman* or on modern "metafiction" which emphasize the new conception of language, or even the new conception of man in the world, that lies at the basis of this new kind of writing.[24] In a similar way, one could read the pornographic narratives of Georges Bataille as fictional works that illustrate a certain theory of eroticism and transgression and their link with the sacred.

Following this line of reasoning, one would soon have to conclude that the *roman à thèse* is everywhere and nowhere—in other words, that it is a phenomenon of *reading* (viewed from a certain angle, all works are didactic) rather than of writing. At that point, there would be no reason to try and define a *genre* called *roman à thèse,* for the concept of genre implies that there exist certain properties that texts have in common, not that (or not only that) there exist certain modes of reading—or as is commonly said nowadays, certain interpretive strategies—that can be applied to any and every text.

Despite the indubitable appeal of a theory of interpretation that puts all the emphasis on the reader, such a theory is limited by a fact I consider undeniable (and that one must consider undeniable, unless one wishes to indulge in paradox for its own sake): there exist nontrivial differences *between and among texts,* as well as between readers, or between interpretive strategies that readers deploy in order to understand a text. Novels that are *roman à thèse* have certain identifiable traits, which distinguish them from other novels and other genres.

One of these traits, and no doubt the most important one, is that *romans à thèse* formulate, in an insistent, consistent, and unambiguous manner, the thesis (or theses) they seek to illustrate. In a *roman à thèse,* the "correct" interpretation of the story told is inscribed in capital letters, in such a way that there can be no mistaking it; the *roman à thèse,* like a certain American President, likes to "make one thing perfectly clear." As Michel Beaujour has put it, in the *roman à thèse* "an authority in the text—echoing outside authority—interprets the meaning of all that gives libidinal satisfaction [to the reader]." Whence it follows that the *roman à thèse* is a "good" or "righteous" kind of novel: it "indulge[s] in a lot of intratextual transcoding in order to eliminate ambiguity and therefore delimit the range of interpretation allowed to the reader." It is because of this repressive righteousness that the *roman à thèse* is, according to Beaujour, always "on the side of the law (or at least of some law, which may be waiting in the wings to become legal)."[25] Whether its thesis is conservative or radical, defending the *status quo* or calling for its abolition, the *roman à thèse* is essentially an authoritarian genre: it appeals to the need for certainty, stability, and unity that is one of the elements of the human psyche; it affirms absolute truths, absolute values. If, in this process, it infantilizes the reader (as

Beaujour suggests), it offers in exchange a paternal assurance.[26]

The question of authority is one I shall return to again and again in this book. For now, I shall turn to some theoretical and methodological questions regarding the analysis of genres, and in particular the analysis of the *roman à thèse* as I conceive it.

According to my definition, the *roman à thèse* is part of the broader category of "novels written in a realistic mode." This inclusion presents some problems, but it also constitutes one of the most interesting aspects of the genre. As we saw earlier, the condemnations of the *roman à thèse* were formulated according to one of the traditional criteria of realism: exactitude and impartiality in the observation of "the real." But if the realist novel is a genre, can we say that the *roman à thèse*, defined as a variety of realist fiction, is a genre as well? What is at stake here is not mere terminology, but the very concept of genre as a category or class of texts: how is one to define a class which can be called a genre? As we know, and as Gérard Genette recently reminded us, the traditional classification of genres, which was taken up and codified by the Romantics, was based on three archetypal genres or "archigenres" that the Romantics considered as "natural forms": the lyric, the epic, and the dramatic. But in fact, as Genette shows, these "archigenres" have no privileged status: every genre can contain several "species" that are *also* genres, and "no a priori limit can be ascribed to this series of inclusions."[27] By defining the *roman à thèse* as a subgenre of the realist novel, we can distinguish it from other genres, such as the religious or political allegory (*Pilgrim's Progress, Penguin Island, Animal Farm*) or the philosophical tale (*Rasselas, Candide*), which, although they share the didactic and persuasive vocation of the *roman à thèse*, are differentiated from it by their status as nonrealist narratives.

It must be emphasized, however, that the decision to include the *roman à thèse* in the broader category of the realist novel is just that: a decision, or choice, dictated by certain theoretical preoccupations. One of the problems that interest me is precisely the encounter between realism and didacticism. In a different theoretical perspective, one could study the *roman à thèse* as part of another category: that of didactic narrative, in prose or verse, which also includes allegory, the philosophical tale, and other genres like the fable or the parable. In my chapter on "exemplary" narratives, I emphasize the link between those genres and the *roman à thèse;* subsequently, however, I place the emphasis on the novelistic side of the *roman à thèse,* and this way of proceeding follows from the choice that founds my definition of the genre.[28]

The second problem posed by the inclusion of the *roman à thèse* within the category of the realist novel concerns the definition of the latter: in order to study the *roman à thèse,* wouldn't we have to have a generally accepted, rigorous definition of the realist novel? Despite a number of extremely interesting recent and not-so-recent works on this subject, our understanding of the realist novel remains partial and imperfect.[29] The theoretical—and practical—lacunae in this domain need not daunt us, however; on the contrary, it would be the existence of a general, universally recognized theory of the novel or of realism that would make all further research superfluous. For our purposes, a willfully approximate definition will do: the realist novel is the novel as it has been bequeathed to us by the nineteenth-century, which was the period of its full flowering. Founded on an aesthetic of verisimilitude and representation, the realist novel places in the foreground, and follows the destinies of, fictional characters who are presented as "real," and whose life unfolds in a context (a physical and historical setting) that corresponds, at least virtually, to the everyday experience of readers who are contemporaries of the author.[30] It is obvious that in seeking to describe the system of the *roman à thèse,* one is obliged at practically every step to encroach on the wider terrain of which it is a part. The challenge is to find specific criteria that will distinguish the *roman à thèse* from realist novels that are not "à thèse" (which does not mean that they are not concerned with ideas, or even with ideologies), such a distinction being useful for an understanding of the one as of the other.[31]

Finally, we can ask a more general question: what is, or should be, the relation between empirical observation and theoretical construction in the study of genres, and in particular in the study of the *roman à thèse?* In his book on the genre of the fantastic, Tzvetan Todorov proposed that we distinguish two kinds of genres: historical genres, which result "from an observation of literary facts," and theoretical genres, which are "deduced from a theory of literature."[32] According to this distinction, historical genres (Todorov cites French classical tragedy as an example) are recognized as such at the time of their appearance and "openly proclaim their belonging to [*a*] literary form," whereas theoretical genres are constructions made by the theorist on the basis of certain criteria considered adequate to found a classification. Historical genres are a subset of complex theoretical genres (based on more than one criterion of classification), their distinctive traits being their historical existence and the fact that their definition is based on the observation of facts, that is, on induction.

In a more recent article on genres, Todorov has abandoned this bipartite division. He now believes that one should "call 'genres' only those classes of texts that have been perceived as such in the course of history. The accounts of this perception are found most often in the discourse on genres (the metadiscursive discourse) and, in a sporadic and indirect fashion, in the texts themselves."[33]

In one respect, this modification of the theory strikes me as a positive one, for it recognizes that the study of genres cannot really do without empirical observation. Todorov's position is here close to Genette's, according to which "There is no generic level that one can decree to be more 'theoretical,' or that can be arrived at by a more 'deductive' method than others: every species, every subgenre, genre, or supergenre is an empirical class, established through observation of historical fact, or at the limit . . . by extrapolation from historical fact—in other words, by a deductive process superimposed on an initial process that is always inductive and analytic."[34]

In another respect, however, I find Todorov's new definition something of a setback, or at least a problem; it concerns the temporal relation of quasi-simultaneity that Todorov posits between the appearance of works that manifest the genre and the metadiscursive discourse that indicates the latter's perception. If we call "genres" only those classes of texts that have been perceived *as such* "in the course of history" (but that implies, in fact, at the moment of their appearance or very soon after, for otherwise the restriction would be superfluous—we are always within history), that means that no new generic constructions are allowed to operate on texts of the past. In order for a genre to exist, or to have existed, there must be (have been) a theoretical, metadiscursive discourse more or less contemporary to it to attest to its perception. (Pushed a little further, the definition seems even to imply that the perception of the genre must precede the appearance of individual works—in other words, that a writer always writes with a recognized generic model in mind. But in that case, how are we to explain the appearance of new genres?) What this new definition excludes is the possibility that a modern theorist might "invent" an eighteenth-century genre based on the empirical observation of a corpus and on analytic criteria not perceived, or at least not codified, at the time. Such an attempt may be unusual, but should it be excluded as a possibility? Should we refuse the name of "genre" to the new category that would be produced, and that would be both historical (since it was based on the observation of historically existing texts) and theoretical (since it was constructed on the basis of criteria formulated by the analyst), simply on the ground that the category was not "perceived as such" until our own day? In slightly different terms, must the set of traits—the system—that defines a genre be codified, or be at least sufficiently perceived to give rise to a metadiscursive discourse that *names* the genre at the time a work appears, in order for us to be able to say that a work manifests the genre or belongs to it?

If I ask the question (and a somewhat similar question could be asked as regards "genres of the future," which are in theory possible but are not, or not yet, manifested by any work),[35] it is not in order to suggest that the *roman à thèse* is a genre invented by me. The perception, and the historical existence, of the genre are attested to by a *name* (the clearest indication of metadiscursive discourse), even if the name has the particular characteristic of being pejorative.[36] If I ask the question, it is in order to affirm the constructive, and potentially innovative, character of the theory of genres, or of the analysis of a single genre. The construction of a generic model that allows us to read certain well-known works in a new perspective, or that allows us to "regroup" works differently than before, is a theoretical activity that operates on an already constituted, historical field. There is more than one way to divide the field of literature, however, and every new class that is proposed modifies the whole. The *roman à thèse* as a name designating a class of texts is not new, but since the class has never been studied until now as a valid genre, it must be constructed. Such a construction offers new possibilities both to the poetician or theorist of genres, and to the critic interested in the interpretation of individual works.

The distinction between "poetics" and "criticism" was one of the enabling notions of the formalist and structuralist approaches to literature, and is rather widely accepted today. The poetician is presumably interested in the resemblances between works and seeks to disengage their common traits (one of these being none other than "literariness"), while the critic is interested in what is specific or unique about each work. My own approach could be defined as an attempt to join the preoccupations of the poetician with those of the critic, for I wish not only to construct a generic model (or more than one), but also to *read* certain works in a detailed way in order to see to what extent they realize the models I propose and to what extent they constitute a difference—or even a problem—in relation to those models. If it is true, as Todorov has claimed, that one cannot study at the same time both the resemblance and the difference between works, and that one must "temporarily privilege one or the other direction,"[37] one can nevertheless attempt to elucidate the differences *within* shared properties, by emphasizing the variations, and, in some cases, the transformations effected by an individual work on the "rules of the genre."

The novels I shall discuss all belong to French literature of the first half of this century, spanning the period between the Dreyfus Affair and the beginning of the Second World War. Although my definition of the *roman à thèse* implies neither a national nor a historical limit (apart from the one implied by the "realist novel"), I have thought it preferable to limit my analyses to a single national literature and a single period. This limitation does not prevent the results obtained from being applicable to other national literatures and other periods (Russian literature in the second half of the nineteenth-century, for example, or American fiction in the 1930s). Claude Lévi-Strauss remarked, in his essay on "The Notion of Structure in Ethnology," that no structuralist study can escape this dilemma: "either to study many cases in a superficial and in the end ineffective way; or to limit oneself to a thorough study of a small number of cases, thus proving that in the last analysis one well done experiment is sufficient to make a demonstration."[38] The danger that the cases chosen may be too "special" to be generalizable always haunts the enterprise of the structural anthropologist. It also haunts the enterprise of the theorist of genres who works on a limited corpus. But, as long as one is aware of the risk involved, the experiment is worth undertaking.

Despite all of the above, however, it seems evident that national and historical variations do exist, and that certain literary and cultural traditions, as well as certain periods, are more apt to encourage the development of the *roman à thèse* than others. One may suppose, for example, that the *roman à thèse* flourishes in national contexts, and at historical moments, that produce sharp social and ideological conflicts—in other words, in a climate of crisis; furthermore, the genre is more likely to exist in a cultural tradition that fosters the involvement of writers in social and intellectual debates or problems. For all these reasons, France seems to have furnished an especially fertile ground for this genre. Nor is it completely by chance that the novels I shall discuss cluster around the Dreyfus Affair and the 1930s, since these two moments in French history (and, in the case of the 1930s, in world history) produced more acute ideological divisions than the decades immediately preceding and following them.

A detailed exploration of the local conditions that produce or foster the genre would be the subject of another book. However, the links between a specific historical situation and the *roman à thèse* become evident in my readings of works by Bourget, Barrès, Nizan, and Malraux in chapters 2 and 3.

Even within the limited French corpus, I can imagine being reproached for a certain arbitrariness in my choice of authors and works: if I speak about Barrès and Bourget, why not Henry Bordeaux? If about Mauriac, why not Bernanos? If about Nizan and Aragon, why not Louis Guilloux? If about Drieu, why not Brasillach? If about Malraux, why not Martin du Gard? If about Sartre, why not Camus? There is no lack of worthy candidates, even if one limits oneself to (relatively) well-known or highly lauded authors. The real question, however, is not whether the corpus is large enough, but whether it is representative enough to support the weight of my constructions. My readers will have to answer that question. As for me, I must take responsibility for my choices as the result of that combination of personal preference, professional intuition, and pure chance, which, despite all attempts at objective justifications, presides over any activity that has literature as its object—including the activity that Roland Barthes called, in one of his critical essays, "l'activité structuraliste."

Modernity and the *Roman à thèse*

Apart from questions of method, there is a more fundamental question that must be confronted: why devote time, today, to studying a genre as didactic, as doctrinaire, as "monological"—

in a word, as *antimodern*—as the *roman à thèse?* Would it not be wiser to forget about its very existence, and speak only about "real" literature—the literature which, according to Jean Ricardou's formulation, "borrows materials from the world only in order to designate itself"? [39] To ask this question is to enter a contemporary critical and theoretical debate that concerns not only the nature and function of literary texts, but also the way in which they should be read and *those* that should be read. Modern criticism has been tremendously wary of any literary work that "means to say something" (that has a "message"), and of any critic or reader who reads literature as an "attempt to say something"—who reads it for its "message." The Sartrian dream of transparent language ("there is prose . . . when the word passes through our gaze like glass traversed by sunlight") [40] has been replaced, in contemporary avant-garde criticism, by Mallarmé's dream of language as a mirror of itself ("le langage se réfléchissant"). This substitution (where the pertinent opposition is not between prose and poetry, but between "literary" language and "ordinary" language, or between literature and communication) has had as one of its consequences the devalorization of a whole vast field of literature—a field that includes not only a genre as unabashedly didactic as the *roman à thèse,* but all the realist genres founded on the aesthetic (or as some of its attackers say, on the ideology) of verisimilar representation.

Now it is precisely because it is founded on that aesthetic—as well as on the equally "outmoded" notion that literature is an act of communication between writer and reader—that the *roman à thèse* is interesting, and provocative. The *roman à thèse* is, in fact, but a particularly clear manifestation of the realist *and* didactic impulse that lies at the origin of the novel, and that persisted as a foundation for it until relatively recently. As Julia Kristeva has argued in her study of the fifteenth-century narrative *Petit Jehan de Saintré* (which she calls the "first French novel written in prose"), one of the "laws" of the novel is that "before being a story, the novel is an INSTRUCTION, a [form of] teaching, a knowledge [to be transmitted]."

Kristeva affirms, I believe rightly, that the novel as a genre emerged "from teaching as well as (and even more than) from the epic genre and from courtly poetry."[41] In other words, the novel at its beginnings was as much oriented toward the communicative function of language as toward the "poetic" one (to borrow Roman Jakobson's terminology). Georges May has shown that in the eighteenth-century, the novel sought to justify itself (with more or less sincerity depending on the author) by its utilitarian and moralizing aspect.[42] Even if later on—certainly by the time of Flaubert—the realist novel claimed the right to "tell all" and demanded total freedom of expression for the writer, it maintained its communicative and didactic role. One of the components of the realist impulse is the desire to *make others see,* to make the reader understand something about him or herself, or about the society and the world in which people live. This is one reason why a systematic study of the *roman à thèse* cannot fail to raise questions about nature and the functioning of any realist novel: the *roman à thèse* provides an extreme version of the didactic tendency at the origin of the novel—a tendency that theorists and practitioners of the modern "text" have sought to suppress.

I suggested just now that at its beginnings the novel was as much oriented toward the communicative function of language as toward the "poetic" one. But if we evoke Roman Jakobson's terminology, we must recall that according to Jakobson the hallmark of a "poetic" text (in the broad sense of a text characterized by "literariness") is that in it the communicative functions of language are subordinated to the poetic function—the latter not being limited to literature in verse, of course.[43] Whereas the communicative functions (the chief ones being the emotive, the referential, and the conative) place the emphasis either on the sender of the message, or on the context (the referent), or yet again on the receiver, the poetic function emphasizes the "message for its own sake"—by which Jakobson means not the semantic content of the message but the "palpability of [its] signs," independently of their semantic function. To say about a literary text or genre, then, that it is "as much" oriented toward communication as toward poetry seems to be to ignore the principle of the hierarchy of functions, for either a text is oriented chiefly toward communication (in which case it is not "literary"), or it is "literary," but in that case the communicative function must be subordinated to the poetic one. And yet, every reader feels—even if that feeling is no more than intuitive—that in certain literary texts, the domination of the poetic function is "stronger," or perhaps more exclusive, than in others: a sonnet by Mallarmé seems more exclusively oriented toward the palpability of signs than, say, Hugo's poem about the two Napoleons, "Le Châtiment"; and the same is true of a novel by Maurice Roche, or of William Burroughs' "cut-ups" in comparison to a novel by Balzac.

Jakobson himself noted, in the essay I have been referring to, that "the particularities of diverse poetic genres imply a differently ranked participation of the other verbal functions along with the dominant poetic function"; thus epic poetry "strongly involves the referential function of language" while lyric involves the emotive function, and so on.[44] What Jakobson did not envisage was the possibility of *tension*, or more exactly of competition, between the poetic function and the other functions. This possibility was, however, emphasized by Jan Mukařovsky, the principal theorist of the Prague Linguistic Circle (in which Jakobson also participated for a time). Mukařovsky, like Jakobson, distinguished artistic phenomena from extra-artistic ones by saying that in the former the aesthetic function dominates, whereas in the latter it plays only a secondary role.[45] But, going further than Jakobson, Mukařovsky saw a "fundamental antinomy" between "the subordination and the domination of the aesthetic function in the hierarchy of functions" *even in works of art*—whence he concluded that the field of art "resembles a whole influenced by opposing forces which simultaneously organize and disorganize it." Thus, in architecture the aesthetic function is "in competition with" a practical function (shelter), and in the domain of literature it is in competition with the communicative function: the genres of the essay and of the oratorical discourse, for example, "constantly oscillate between poetry and communication," and didactic poetry is a form based on "the struggle for domination between the aesthetic function and the communicative function."[46]

These remarks suggest the possibility of a classification of literary genres based on the more or less strong degree of domination of the poetic function (or, in Mukařovsky's terms, on the more or less strong degree of competition between poetry and communication) that they manifest. In such a classification, which might take the form of a graph or scale, oratorical discourse would occupy one extremity, while hermetic or glossolalic poetry would occupy the other. Between the two would be placed, at various levels, the genres of didactic and satiric poetry, allegory, fable, moralistic tale, essay, autobiography, as well as novels of all kinds, ranging from the *roman à thèse* to the "roman ludique" one sees idealized by some contemporary critics. Such a classification would, unfortunately, be totally approximative; furthermore, being static, it would not take account of a phenomenon analyzed by Gérard Genette, among others—namely, that the degree of "literariness" of a text varies with the circumstances of its reading. According to Genette, "every written text has the potential of being or not being literature, according to whether it is received (primarily) as spectacle or (primarily) as message."[47] This observation, which implies that literariness is not a quality inherent in certain texts but is a function that may "invest or divest in turn any object of writing,"[48] brings a corrective to Jakobson's theory, which implies that the domination of the poetic function is absolute and permanent in certain texts—those that deserve forever the name of literature.

Nevertheless, the relativism of a position that completely dissolves the notion of literariness as a stable notion seems to me too extreme to be wholly convincing. It may be more exact to say that there exists a category of written texts (a vast category with ill-defined limits), one of whose distinctive traits is that the poetic function is in a constant relation of tension with the communicative functions. Only the existence of this dialectical tension allows a text to be perceived sometimes as "message" and sometimes as "spectacle," and it is not at all certain that every written text manifests this tension. In certain texts, one of the functions may be *suppressed* (by the text, not only by the reader) in favor of the other, to such a degree that one cannot really speak of a dialectical tension, or an antinomy, between them. In a news article or in a chemistry textbook, the poetic function is almost totally suppressed in favor of the referential function; in a verse by Mallarmé ("aboli bibelot d'inanité sonore"), it is the contrary suppression that occurs.

The realist novel, founded on the aesthetic of verisimilitude and representation, is one of the most fully realized manifestations of the dialectic between "poetry" and communication, between spectacle and message. It is precisely against this kind of novel that the modern "textual" revolt has been directed—a revolt that has taken the form of an attempt to systematically suppress the referential element in writing, and corollarily to emphasize its self-referential element. It has been a revolt against (a single) *meaning*. To render impossible the emergence of an unambiguous meaning by the production of "plural" texts, to create works that will communicate "nothing but the dramatization of their own functioning"[49]—such has been the program of modernist writing.

The interest of the *roman à thèse* today resides in the fact that it incarnates the opposing tendency: where the modernist text seeks to multiply meaning or to "pulverize" it ("faire éclater le sens" was one of Roland Barthes' favorite expressions), the *roman à thèse* aims for a single meaning and for total closure. If the former proclaims itself to be the radical negation of the realist novel, the latter appears to be—by an intensification of its most characteristic traits—the realist novel's limiting case, or if one wishes, its folly.

But there is more to it than that, for the *roman à thèse* is also a genre divided against itself, split between "roman" and "thèse." The realist novel proclaims above all the vocation of rendering the complexity and the density of everyday life; the *roman à thèse,* on the other hand, finds itself before the necessity of simplifying and schematizing its representations for the sake of its demonstrative ends. Simplification and schematization are more suited to allegorical or mythic genres than to realist genres. The *roman à thèse* is perhaps condemned to missing its aim, either on one side or on the other.

An impure, unstable genre, rent by contradictory desires, inevitably inscribed in a position of lack, of guilty conscience—could we not say that the *roman à thèse* is one of the *emblems,* if not one of the manifestations, of our modernity?

Chapter 1
"Exemplary" Narratives

No tale ever happened in the way we tell it, said
Thomas, but the moral is always correct.
Donald Barthelme,
The Dead Father

MY AIM in this chapter is to lay a theoretical foundation for the *roman à thèse* as a didactic narrative genre. Our working definition already contained, implicitly, the question that must be answered if one is to arrive at a rigorous description of the genre: by what formal criteria can one identify a novel that "seeks to persuade its readers of the validity of a doctrine"? Instead of attacking this question head-on, let us look for a moment at the implications one can draw from the definition itself.

First, the definition implies that the principal distinguishing feature of a genre is the particular *relation* it establishes with the reader. The definition says nothing about the specific narrative or thematic content of the *roman à thèse*, nor about its style, nor about its discursive organization; it states merely that the *roman à thèse* is a type of novel that manifests the intention of being read in a particular way. This accords with what has already been suggested by some genre theorists: namely, that a literary genre is comparable to an illocutionary speech act.[1] An illocutionary speech act is defined first of all by the object or aim—in other words, by the manifested intention—of the speaker.[2] Promising, asking, praying, affirming, greeting, thanking, or commanding are illocutionary acts that are distinguished from one another by the intention they manifest: by asking a question, one manifests the intention of obtaining a reply, by thanking, the intention of showing one's gratitude, etc.

If illocutionary speech acts are defined in terms of the speaker's intention, *perlocutionary* speech acts are defined in terms of the effect they produce on a listener: persuading, convincing, frightening, making someone act in a certain way, are perlocutionary acts. Obviously, as John Searle points out, a great many illocutionary verbs can be defined in terms of the perlocutionary effect they are intended to produce; thus "commanding" can be defined as "attempting to make someone do something," "asking" as the attempt to elicit a reply, and so on.[3] Promising and thanking, on the other hand, are not necessarily linked to a perlocutionary effect, since neither of these acts implies a particular response as far as the listener is concerned. (The only necessary effect of a promise or a word of thanks is that they be understood as such by the listener; but understanding is not, according to Searle, a perlocutionary effect.)

Now the *roman à thèse* is founded on an illocutionary verb of the first type: demonstrating. A verbal demonstration (whose "weak" form is teaching and whose "strong" form is proving) can be defined by the perlocutionary effect it aims to produce: if I want to demonstrate (or teach, or prove) something to someone, I want to convince or persuade him or her of the validity of my proposition. And I can even go further: if my proposition is of a certain kind (religious or moral, for example), I can try to persuade my listeners to modify their actions accordingly. In that case, my demonstration is the prelude to another illocutionary act—exhorting or enjoining, which can be defined in perlocutionary terms as the attempt to make someone act in a certain way for his own good. (Example: I persuade you of the validity of the proposition that "God is just, he rewards those who observe His commandments and punishes those who don't"; this leads to the following exhortation: "Observe God's commandments!")

What this means is that the *roman à thèse* is a rhetorical

genre in the literal sense of the term: the reader of the *roman à thèse* occupies, in relation to the writer, a position analogous to that of the listening or reading public in relation to an orator, a teacher, or a preacher. But an oration, a pedagogical essay or a sermon are what Karlheinz Stierle has called systematic texts: they present, in a logically ordered way, a series of arguments.[4] The *roman à thèse,* on the other hand, is, like all novels, a narrative: it tells a story. But how can a story—and an "invented" story at that, which cannot be verified—demonstrate anything pertaining to the real life of its audience? This question, which is linked to a broader one: "How can a story become the bearer of an unambiguous meaning?" leads to a problematic that goes far beyond the specific case of the *roman à thèse;* but it is within this problematic that a study of the *roman à thèse* acquires its full significance.

For one answer to the question, we can turn to a venerable figure of classical rhetoric: the *exemplum.* The term *exemplum* (Greek *paradeigma*) designated persuasion by induction, or argument by analogy (in contrast to the *enthymeme,* or persuasion by deduction).[5] As its name implies, the *exemplum* was an example offered by the orator to his public; it took, most often, the form of a comparison or of a historical allusion from which the orator drew conclusions relative to the present.[6] Aristotle, however, already divided *exempla* into "real" and "fictional" ones—the former being drawn from history or mythology, the latter being the invention of the orator himself. In the category of fictional *exempla,* Aristotle distinguished parables, or brief comparisons, from fables, which constituted a series of actions, in other words, a story. According to Aristotle's definitions, many of the best-known parables of the New Testament are fables—invented stories whose function is to provide a concrete example from which a general conclusion (the "moral of the story") can be drawn. The didactic impulse behind primitive story-telling is nowhere more evident than in the case of such *exempla.* It is hardly surprising if, in the Middle Ages, *exempla* of all kinds—but especially fictional ones—were collected in volumes and were widely used by preachers who sought to inculcate Christian moral principles and the doctrines of the Church in their audience by telling them stories.[7] "Ad amorem Dei et proximi plerumque corda audientium plus exempla quam verba excitant": "The heart of the audience is moved to the love of God and of their neighbour more by examples than by words"[8]—this paradoxical assertion by Gregory the Great (paradoxical because *exempla* are also words) was echoed centuries later by Caesar of Heisterbach: "When I speak of God you sleep, but to listen to fables you rouse yourselves."[9]

As a starting hypothesis, we can posit that the *roman à thèse* and the *exemplum* have certain features in common, the principal one being that they are impelled by the same didactic motive. The *exemplum* is the earlier, and simpler, form; one can think of it as a distant ancestor of the *roman à thèse*. A detailed analysis of the way the religious or moral *exemplum* functions should also throw some light on the *roman à thèse*. I shall discuss, in what follows, the New Testament parables and their "wordly" homologues, the fables of La Fontaine.

The Parable As *Exemplum*

The first parable we find in the New Testament is the parable of the sower. Here is the text of the parable, as it appears in the Gospel according to St. Matthew (the numbering of the segments is my own):[10]

0] A sower went out to sow. 1] And as he sowed, some seed fell along the footpath; and the birds came and ate it up. 2] Some seed fell on rocky ground, where it had little soil, and it sprouted quickly because it had no depth of earth; but when the sun rose the young corn was scorched, and as it had no root it withered away. 3] Some seed fell among thistles; and the thistles shot up, and choked the corn. 4] And some of the seed fell into good soil, where it bore fruit, yielding a hundredfold or, it might be, sixtyfold or thirtyfold. 5] If you have ears, then hear.

The first thing we note is that this text tells a story; more exactly, it tells four "minimal" stories linked to each other by the initial gesture of the sower. Each of these stories consists of a single sequence, and they can be summarized as follows:

1) Sequence of the seed which fell along the footpath (segment 1)
2) Sequence of the seed which fell on rocky ground (segment 2)
3) Sequence of the seed which fell among thistles (segment 3)
4) Sequence of the seed which fell into good soil (segment 4).

Each sequence is reduced to a single sentence, containing a variable number of narrative units or "kernels."[11] Sequence 1, for example, contains two units: the seed falls along the footpath, and is then eaten by the birds; sequence 2 is more detailed, containing four units: the seed falls on rocky ground, sprouts quickly, is scorched by the sun, and then withers away. Regardless of the number of units, however, each sequence contains the essential elements of a complete story—namely, a *subject* or protagonist (the seeds) and a *transformation* that affects the subject over time.[12] Since the subjects of the four sequences are not the same (different seeds are involved each time), each sequence is virtually autonomous in relation to the others. As they all depend, however, on the initial gesture of the sower, they constitute, taken together, a single narrative that can be represented as follows:

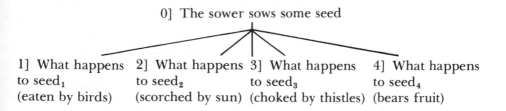

0] The sower sows some seed

1] What happens to seed₁ (eaten by birds)   2] What happens to seed₂ (scorched by sun)   3] What happens to seed₃ (choked by thistles)   4] What happens to seed₄ (bears fruit)

The second thing we note is that segment 5, which contains a sudden change in tense and mode ("If you have ears, then hear"), constitutes a radical break in relation to the preceding segments: whereas they were straightforward narrative, as indicated by the past tense and the chronological and causal links between events, in segment 5 we find a present conditional followed by an imperative. This places the emphasis on the "present" of the narrator and establishes a direct link between him and his audience—a link that exists outside the story he is telling.

To what action does that final imperative summon the listeners of the parable? To "hear" the story of the sower, "if they have ears." Since one can reasonably suppose that they all have ears, the kind of "hearing" to which they are summoned must be figurative: the narrator invites his public to understand his story, that is, to *interpret* it. This is the first indication in the text of the parable itself (independently of its context, which is a didactic one: Jesus surrounded by a crowd as in the Sermon on the Mount, but to whom he speaks this time "in parables") that the story which has just been told is not, or not only, what it seems to be, but that it harbors, beneath its straightforward recounting of events, a "lesson" that must be dug out—a meaning that must be unearthed.

This allows us to posit, as a first hypothesis, that every parable—and more generally, every story of an "exemplary" nature—is sooner or later designated, by the parabolic text itself, as needing interpretation, that is, as containing a meaning *other* (or *more*) than the immediate meaning of the events it recounts.[13] The interpretation makes explicit or "discovers" the meaning, which was "in" the story, but hidden. The relation between story and interpretation is thus hierarchical, both logically and in terms of value: the interpretation is "superior" to the story, as the general is to the particular, the universal to the singular, or truth to its manifestation. It is superior in another sense as well—strategically, as it were: the interpretation commands the story as the end commands the means, or a strategy commands a tactic. In sum, the story in a parable exists only in order to give rise to an interpretation.

This is made quite clear in the parable of the sower, where the last verse states explicitly that the story must be interpreted. But where are the listeners to find a model of interpretation? Since this is the first time that Jesus "speaks in parables," neither the disciples nor the crowd has the necessary interpretive competence. Jesus therefore obligingly interprets the story himself (admittedly, he does so only to the privileged group of his disciples), thus providing a model for interpreting the parables to follow. Jesus' authoritative interpretation (Matt. 13:18–23) informs the disciples—as well as any reader of the Gospel—that each of the elements in the story of the sower has a "second" meaning: the seed is the word that tells of the Kingdom, the places where it falls are different types of men; only the man who "hears the word and understands it" (i.e., the "good soil") will "bear fruit."[14] The interpretation ends there, without explicitly formulating the conclusion that is implied by it: "If you want to benefit from my word (i.e., be saved), hear it and understand it."

Although it is not *stated* in the parable of the sower, this kind of conclusion, which takes the form of an injunction addressed to those who have benefited from the interpretation of the story, is nevertheless an essential element of Jesus' parabolic discourse.[15] This is quite evident in another of the parables we find in Matthew (25:1–23), that of the wise and foolish virgins:

> When that day comes, the kingdom of Heaven will be like this. There were ten girls, who took their lamps and went out to meet the bridegroom. Five of them were foolish, and five prudent; when the foolish ones took their lamps, they took no oil with them, but the others took flasks of oil with their lamps. As the bridegroom was late in coming they all dozed off to sleep. But at midnight a cry was heard: "Here is the bridegroom! Come out to meet him." With that the girls all got up and trimmed their lamps. The foolish said to the prudent, "Our lamps are going out; give us some

of your oil." "No," they said; "there will never be enough for all of us. You had better go to the shop and buy some for yourselves." While they were away the bridegroom arrived; those who were ready went in with him to the wedding; and the door was shut. And then the other five came back. "Sir, sir," they cried, "open the door for us." But he answered, "I declare, I do not know you." Keep awake then; for you never know the day or the hour.

Here, as in the parable of the sower, the narrative text ends with a sentence in the imperative, which signals the presence of the speaker and of his listeners; (in fact, this presence, as well as the need to interpret, is already signaled at the beginning, with the phrase "the kingdom of Heaven will be like this"). Unlike what happens in the parable of the sower, however, the listeners here are not summoned to interpret the story, but rather, *having already interpreted it,* to bring their actions into line with the underlying meaning of the story. Why, after all, should they "keep awake"? So that they will not be turned away from the door of the wedding, like the foolish virgins. But in order to understand the meaning, and the importance, of that injunction, one must already have understood that the "bridegroom" is not a bridegroom but Christ triumphant, the "wedding" not a wedding but the Kingdom of Heaven, and the "virgins" not young girls but human types.

This interpretation—which can be stated in the form of a generalization: "Only those who prepare for the coming of Christ will be saved"—is not explicitly stated in the parable, but is suggested by the opening sentence which precedes the narrative proper; above all, it is implied by the final injunction, which is explicit: the injunction makes sense only if it is addressed to listeners who have already correctly interpreted the story of the ten virgins.

The relation between story, interpretation, and concluding injunction can be defined as a chain of implications: the story implies ("calls for") the interpretation, which in turn implies—but is also implied by—the concluding injunction. This conforms to the inductive process characteristic of the *exem-*

plum: from a particular fact (story) one accedes to a generalization (interpretation), which allows one to accede to another particular fact, expressed this time in the imperative mode (injunction).

Let us suppose that the "real" message conveyed by the storyteller to his listeners resides in the concluding injunction—thus, in the parable of the sower: "Hear my word and understand it." The story and its interpretation then become the indirect means by which this imperative is communicated. Direct communication, which can be represented schematically as follows:

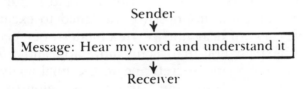

is replaced by an indirect communication:

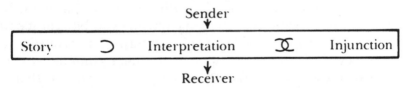

One could raise, here, a question similar to the one that the disciples pose to Jesus: why speak in parables? In slightly more explicit terms: if one wants to convince one's listeners of an important truth, why choose such a roundabout way to do it? On the one hand, we may suppose that the speaker considers indirection a more effective means of persuasion than direct statement. This is no doubt what Lucretius had in mind when he spoke of coating the bitter pill of truth with his honeyed verses. In the case of Jesus' parables, however, the opposite explanation is also possible, and has been proposed: if Jesus speaks in parables, it may be not in order to facilitate the communication of his message, but in order to prevent its communication to those who are not worthy of receiving it.

Thus Jean Starobinski has remarked about the parable of the sower: "[Jesus'] teaching seems to take on here a restrictive and defensive aspect: it is closed to those who do not have ears, and at the same time closes off to them the road to salvation. Far from being motivated by the pedagogical impulse toward a figural approach to truth, the recourse to parable deliberately restricts the number of the elect: it excludes those who lack intelligence."[16]

Starobinski touches here on a very old problem concerning Jesus' intentions in his parables. Are the parables veritable *exempla*, designed to facilitate the communication of a message to those who otherwise would not understand it? Or are they, on the contrary, willfully obscure, designed to exclude those who "have ears but hear not"?[17] In a modern perspective, it is the second explanation that seems more appealing, for it emphasizes the enigmatic, secret, and in the final analysis, cruel aspect of the New Testament parables—bringing them closer to those of Kafka, for example. Frank Kermode, in *The Genesis of Secrecy*, proposes just such a reading of Jesus' parables, his main argument being that *every* narrative, even biblical narrative, has the property of "banishing interpreters from its secret places."[18] Despite the appeal of this argument for our skeptical sensibility, nourished on suspicion, I believe that as far as the New Testament parables are concerned one cannot entirely exclude the "pedagogical impulse" behind them. Even if one admits that Jesus may want to maintain the crowd in its ignorance, we must suppose that he wants to enlighten his disciples. Yet, he often speaks to them in parables even when he is alone with them. Furthermore, it happens more than once that he explains his parables even to others, who are not his disciples: the parable of the servants who kill the landowner's son, for example (Matt. 21:33–43), is addressed and explained to the Pharisees, while the parables of mercy (Luke 15:1–31) are similarly addressed to the Pharisees and the Scribes (as well as, perhaps, to the publicans and sinners, depending on how one reconstructs the scene).

At the same time, one must admit that the "figural approach to truth," even when it is motivated by a pedagogical impulse, is always, in the last analysis, problematic: indirect communication always runs the risk of not being understood, or of being misunderstood. It is precisely in order to palliate this danger that didactic narratives usually propose, in more or less evident fashion, their own interpretation, which *fixes* the meaning of the story and eliminates (or tries to) the possibility of multiple interpretations and meanings. Another problem (and here things become more complicated) is that there always exists the possibility that the "correct" interpretation proposed by the narrator does not exactly "fit" the story; the space left open by the slippage between the story and its authoritative (authorial) interpretation allows for the entry of other, divergent meanings—and the longer the narrative becomes, the more such openings become possible. This is one place where the difference in length between the *roman à thèse* and the *exemplum* (which is by definition a short genre) may become qualitatively significant.

Let us return, however, to our model: what does it tell us as far as our parables are concerned? First, it tells us that a parabolic text, whether written or spoken, implies the presence (either real or virtual) of a sender and a receiver—the former being the agent responsible for the story, its interpretation, and the injunction that results from it, while the latter occupies the position of a patient: the one who receives the text, on whom the text "operates." Second, the model summarizes our previous discussion by showing that the parabolic text is organized along three hierarchically related levels: the narrative, the interpretive, and the pragmatic. To each level there corresponds a specific type of discourse: the narrative discourse tells a story; the interpretive discourse comments on the story in order to expose its meaning, which takes the form of a generalization; the pragmatic discourse derives from that meaning a rule of action, which takes the form of an imperative addressed to the receiver (reader or listener) of the text. A parable that would conform perfectly to the model would therefore include three types of utterances, succeeding each other in an invariable order: first the narrative, then the interpretive, then the pragmatic. All of these utterances would have as their source the teller of the parable, while the prescribed role of the receiver would be purely passive.

But, of course, it is quite evident that not a single one of the New Testament parables fully realizes this model. Each one "omits" at least one of these types of utterances, even while implying its possibility. Thus, in the case of our two examples, the parable of the sower (in its version for the disciples) states the interpretation but omits the pragmatic injunction, while the parable of the ten virgins states the injunction but omits the interpretation (it merely suggests it by the opening sentence). In both cases, it is the receiver of the parable who must provide the missing utterances. The model is thus realized after all (the "omitted" utterance is virtually present, waiting to be actualized by the audience), but not in as simple a fashion as our schema suggests. In fact, the audience becomes here an agent participating in the elaboration of the text, which depends on their competence in order to be fully realized. Admittedly, it is a somewhat limited participation, since the role of the audience is but to fill in the spaces left blank by the text, and the spaces are such that they cannot be filled in arbitrarily. Even this limited participation is enough, however, to oblige us to modify our model. It would appear, in effect, that the presence of interpretive and pragmatic utterances is not indispensable in order for a text to function as a parable. It is sufficient if the interpretive generalization and the injunction can be deduced from the narrative discourse—in other words, if the story is constructed in such a way that the interpretation and the injunction "follow from it" without being stated.

This leads to a somewhat paradoxical conclusion as far as the status of the *story* is concerned. Even though the story occupies, in the hierarchy of levels, the lowest position (since it exists only in order to give rise to an interpretation), it is the only element that a parable cannot "omit" without becoming, by that very fact, something else. This is due not only to the

fact that the story provides the narrative element essential to
the parable, but also to the fact that it is the only element in a
parable that can in no case be deduced from the two others.
Starting from the injunction: "Keep awake, for you never know
the day or the hour," and from the generalization: "Only those
who prepare for the coming of Christ shall be saved," it is
impossible to deduce the ten virgins and their lamps. On the
contrary, a theoretically limitless number of stories can be
imagined—all of them having the same "deep" structure but
all of them different on the surface—which could serve as the
basis for the same generalization and the same injunction.

All of this can be summarized by the following schema,
which is a modified version of the first one:

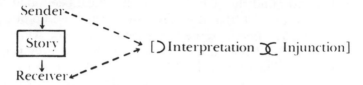

According to this new model, the parabolic text tells a story,
such that the story gives rise to a univocal interpretation[19] and
to an injunction or rule of action. The brackets around interpretation and injunction, and the dotted lines linking sender,
bracketed elements, and receiver, indicate that the interpretation and the injunction can be—but are not necessarily—present in the form of explicit statements made by the sender
(teller or writer) of the story. Whenever such statements are
absent, it is the receiver (reader or listener) who supplies the
interpretation and the injunction, according to directives inscribed, perhaps implicitly, in the story itself. The story in a
parable is thus a kind of story which, if necessary, "speaks for
itself"—or, as Roland Barthes put it in his discussion of the
exemplum, which "expressly entails a meaning."[20]

The question is: How does one recognize a story that "expressly entails a meaning"? Putting it slightly differently, by
what formal indices does a story signal its own interpretation?
This is a variant of the question with which this chapter be-

gan. A look at yet another parable will allow us to suggest some answers.

Here is the parable of prodigal son, as told in the Gospel according to St. Luke (15:11–31; the numbers refer to my own division of the text):

0] There was once a man who had two sons; 1] and the younger said to his father, "Father, give me my share of the property." 2] So he divided his estate between them. 3] A few days later the younger son turned the whole of his share into cash and left home for a distant country, where he squandered it in reckless living. 4] He had spent it all, when a severe famine fell upon that country and he began to feel the pinch. 5] So he went and attached himself to one of the local landowners, who sent him on to his farm to mind the pigs. 6] He would have been glad to fill his belly with the pods that the pigs were eating; and no one gave him anything. 7] Then he came to his senses and said, "How many of my father's paid servants have more food than they can eat, and here am I, starving to death! I will set off and go to my father, and say to him, 'Father, I have sinned, against God and against you; I am no longer fit to be called your son; treat me as one of your paid servants.' " 8] So he set out for his father's house. 9] But while he was still a long way off his father saw him, and his heart went out to him. He ran to meet him, flung his arms round him, and kissed him. 10] The son said, "Father, I have sinned, against God and against you; I am no longer fit to be called your son." 11] But the father said to his servants, "Quick! fetch a robe, my best one, and put it on him; put a ring on his finger and shoes on his feet. Bring the fatted calf and kill it, and let us have a feast to celebrate the day. For this son of mine was dead and has come back to life; he was lost and is found." 12] And the festivities began. 13] Now the elder son was out on the farm; 14] and on his way back, as he approached the house, he heard music and dancing. 15] He called one of the servants and asked what it meant. 16] The servant told him, "Your brother has come home, and your father has killed the fatted calf because he has him back safe and sound." 17] But he was angry and refused to go in. 18] His father came out and pleaded with him; 19] but he retorted, "You know how I have slaved for you all these years; I never once disobeyed your orders; and you never gave me so much as a kid, for a feast with my friends. But now that this son of your turns up, after running through your money with his women, you kill the fatted calf for him." 20] "My boy," said the father, "you are always with me, and everything I have is yours. How could we help celebrating this happy day? Your brother here was dead and has come back to life, was lost and is found."

We note that this text is entirely narrative, in the special sense in which I am using the term here:[21] it does not contain any interpretive or pragmatic utterances made by the narrator, Jesus.[22] The meaning of the story is thus not made explicit by the teller. And yet, any reader who has read a certain number of Jesus' other parables, and who reads this parable in its specific context (that is, immediately after the parables of the lost sheep and of the lost coin, each of which ends with an explicit interpretation made by Jesus)[23] is capable of providing the "right" interpretation—namely, "God rejoices over the repentant sinner." This interpretation gives rise to two complementary injunctions, which the reader can also derive without difficulty: one is addressed to sinners ("Repent!"), the other to the righteous ("Rejoice over the repentant sinner!").

How does this occur? By means of what internal indices does the story impose its own interpretation? I have already alluded to the general competence of the reader who is familiar with Jesus' parables, and to the specific competence created by this parable's context. Those, however, are factors external to the parable itself: they increase its readability without being internal indices. What is internal, however, is the presence, *within the fictional world,* of utterances that function as interpretations of the events that take place in that world. To put it more concretely: it is the characters themselves who interpret their story, thus rendering the narrator's interpretation superfluous.

Let us take a closer look. The story involves three principal characters: the father and the two sons. It is divided, however, into two distinct episodes, each of which has only two main characters: the younger son and the father in the first (segments 1–12), the elder son and the father in the second (segments 13–20). The subject (protagonist) of the first episode is the prodigal son. The narrative structure realized here is the following: *alienation from the father's world* (travel to a distant country and squandering of father's wealth)—*change of heart* (repentance)—*return*—*reintegration into father's world.* The crucial event, which changes the direction of the story and provokes the return, is the change of heart, when the son himself realizes his alienation from the father and "comes to his senses." This change of heart, which is provoked (or, to use the Russian Formalists' term, motivated) by the event of the famine, is expressed by a statement that functions as an interpretation of the son's previous actions: "Father, I have sinned, against God and against you." By seeing his past actions in this light, the prodigal son becomes, in a sense, the reader of his own story even while remaining within that story. The son's interpretation of his own past thus fulfills a double function: it constitutes a narrative unit that motivates the next event (the son's return); at the same time, it constitutes a commentary that defines the meaning of the preceding events and is addressed indirectly to the "real" audience of the parable.

The same thing can be said about the next interpretation, which is made by the father: "For this son of mine was dead and has come back to life; he was lost and is found." This statement functions both as a narrative unit (it motivates the festivities) and as a commentary on the son's story; as commentary it is situated on a more general level than the son's interpretation, for it accounts for the whole story, from the son's initial alienation to his final reintegration into the paternal world (dead→ come back to life; lost→ found).[24]

Correlatively to the double function of these internal commentaries, one can speak of a double function of the characters themselves: they are both actors in, and interpreters of, their own story. As interpreters, they function as representatives—or as fictional doubles—of the primary interpreter who is the teller of the story; as actors, on the other hand, they are comparable more to the audience of the parable, since they accomplish the actions (repenting, rejoicing over the repentant sinner, *and* interpreting) which the parable invites the audience to make their own.

It is in this context that the episode of the elder son takes on its full significance. The narrative structure here is the following, with the elder son as subject: *integration to the father's world—threat of alienation* ("he was angry and refused to go in")—*threat eliminated* (by the father's explanation). The transformation undergone by the elder son takes place entirely on the level of consciousness: his material situation does not change. What "happens" to him is, simply, that he acquires a "correct" understanding of his brother's story—and in particular of the father's action toward his brother—after his initial misunderstanding, which was manifested by his anger and his refusal to join the festivities. By correcting the elder son's initial error, which was an error in interpretation ("How could we help celebrating this happy day?"—i.e., "you were wrong to think that we shouldn't"), the father occupies, in relation to the elder son, the position of the story's teller in relation to a recalcitrant listener. The elder son, in turn, "imitates," as actor, the reaction of a self-righteous listener, who needs to be enlightened about the proper way to act toward repentant sinners. This is precisely the attitude of the Pharisees and the Scribes who provoked the parable in the first place, by reproaching Jesus for "welcoming sinners and eating with them."

The episode of the elder son ends with a practically word-for-word repetition of the interpretation already formulated by the father at the end of the previous one: "Your brother here was dead and has come back to life, was lost and is found." One could even suppose that the episode of the elder son exists only in order to allow for this repetition—as if the parable wished to underscore its own meaning by introducing a sequence whose principal function is to produce a supplementary (and redundant) gloss on the story of the prodigal son. This redundancy seems all the more necessary since the parable contains no interpretive statements on the part of the narrator. In the two short parables immediately preceding, which do include an interpretation by Jesus, there is no episode corresponding to the one of the elder son. It would seem that the more a story "speaks for itself," without interpretation by its teller, the more it must rely on redundancies to make its point.

In fact, we should distinguish between two kinds of redundancies: those that occur only on the level of the story, as is the case here, and those that occur between different levels. For example, if the parable of the prodigal son ended with an interpretation by Jesus, which "repeated" the father's, his interpretation could be considered redundant in relation to the first, even while occurring on a different level: it would be a form of authorial commentary addressed directly to Jesus' listeners, whereas the others are internal commentaries addressed by one character to another. The effect would be to reinforce even more the "meaning" of the parable, to the exclusion of other meanings. The fact that Jesus does not add his own interpretation is perhaps due to the internal redundancies of the story, which make its point sufficiently clear.

Without stretching the parallel too far, one could say about a story like this one what Roland Barthes has said about the image in advertising: "in advertising, the meaning of the image is certainly intentional . . . if the image contains signs, we can be sure that in advertising these signs are full, designed to be easily read: the advertising image is *frank,* or at the very least *emphatic.*" [25] It is precisely because of its emphatic character that Barthes chose advertising when he wished to study the "rhetoric of the image," or the relation between image and meaning. Furthermore, in advertising as in the parable, the image (or the story) always leads to a pragmatic statement: the ultimate aim in both instances is to provoke an action or a change of attitude on the part of the receiver.

To come back to the parable of the prodigal son: we must admit that, despite the redundancies and despite the internal interpretations which must be considered authoritative, one could not really arrive at a *doctrinal* interpretation (that is, in terms of the doctrine of mercy, which is nowhere formulated in this text: "There will be greater joy in heaven over one sinner who repents than over ninety-nine righteous people who do not need to repent"—Luke 15:7) without previous knowledge that one is dealing with a parable—that is, with a story that "means something other" (or something more) than what it says. The father does not enunciate the doctrine, and his own interpretation must be interpreted in order to arrive at it. Nor does the doctrinal interpretation depend only on the reader's previous recognition of the genre to which the story belongs; it also depends on the reader's previous knowledge of the doctrine, which he will then see "illustrated" in the story at hand.

But that being the case, it follows that there is no such thing as a story that "expressly entails *a* meaning." If a story is to be read as having a single specific meaning, it must either be interpreted in a consistent and unambiguous way by the teller, *or* it must exist within a context that invests it with intentionality. Now this context is none other than another text (or a set of other texts), in relation to which the story presents itself as a variant or an illustration—or, more generally, which can be "read into" the story. What we have here, then, is a particular kind of intertextuality.

Intertextuality has been defined as the coexistence of "several discourses" in a single (inter) textual space.[26] What has not been sufficiently emphasized, however, is that the relation of these discourses to each other can be conflictual, negative, or affirmative. In the first case, a number of heterogeneous discourses confront each other without canceling each other out and without being integrated into a single unified discourse: this is what happens in the novels of Dostoevsky, according to Bakhtin. In the second case, one discourse "repeats" another but in such a way as to negate it: this occurs in parody, where the parodied text is evoked only to be ridiculed, or in certain "misquotations" where the original text is modified so as to say the opposite of what it said.[27] Finally, in the third case, one discourse "repeats" another without negating it—on the contrary, the other discourse functions as an authority or guarantor: in the *Confessions* of St. Augustine, for example, the epistles of Saint Paul—and in general all the biblical writings—function as an intertext, but as an "affirmed" one. Using Bakhtin's terminology we would have to say that the intertextual space is here not dialogical but monological, *despite* the presence of "several discourses."

In the case of the New Testament parables, what one finds are "affirmed" intertexts, or more precisely an *intertextual context* that endows a given parable with a single well-defined meaning. The intertextual context can be of the same kind (for example, one parable functioning as intertextual context for another parable that "says the same thing"), or it can be of a different kind (example: a non-narrative, doctrinal text functioning as intertextual context for a parable). In the case of the prodigal son, the immediate intertextual context is of the same kind: it consists of the other two parables of mercy. But one may also consider as the intertextual context of this parable (and probably of all the New Testament parables) any of the doctrinal statements made by Jesus, and in particular the central doctrinal text of the New Testament: the Sermon on the Mount. Without this intertextual context, the story of the prodigal son would not have *a* meaning, but would be susceptible of multiple, no doubt contradictory, interpretations. A striking example of this can be found in Gide's *Le Retour de l'enfant prodigue,* which reproduces the story, and even the words of the characters, but surrounds them with a different context (which in the narrow sense is what Gide adds to the parable in his version, but in the broad sense is the whole set of Gide's works) and thus completely reverses the "meaning" of the parable.[28]

The determining role of the intertextual context is equally evident in the case of advertising. If, as Barthes puts it, the viewer immediately recognizes the intentionality and the "meaning" of the image in advertising, it is not only because such images are emphatic, redundant; nor is it only because they are generally accompanied by written texts which do the necessary interpreting. The viewer's recognition is also (perhaps chiefly?) due to the fact that the image is found in an intertextual context that *defines* it as advertising: it is in a magazine that contains other, similar images, or else plastered on the wall in the subway. If the same image, painted on canvas, were hung in a museum, the way Andy Warhol's Campbell's soup cans are, its intentionality, as well as its "meaning," would be transformed. The intertextual context of the image would then no longer be other pieces of visual advertising, but the other works of a given artist, or the whole set of works we designate as paintings.

Now, where does all this leave us as far as our model is concerned? If there is no such thing as a story that implies a single interpretation, how can one claim that a parable will signal its own meaning even in the absence of any interpretive or pragmatic statements on the part of its teller? In fact this is a minor objection, for most of the New Testament parables *do* contain interpretive or pragmatic statements by Jesus. However, in order to account for the rare cases where, as in the prodigal son, the story is presented with no authorized interpretation, we can introduce a final qualification regarding the context: in the absence of interpretive or pragmatic statements by the teller, the interpretation of a parable—and by extension, of any story derived from the *exemplum*—is inscribed in the internal redundancies of the story *and* in the intertextual context that surrounds it.

A Test of the Model: The Fable

Before exploring the implications of the "exemplary" model for the *roman à thèse,* I propose to test the model on a corpus other than the New Testament parables. The corpus this time is strictly literary: the *Fables* of La Fontaine. I need hardly add that my aim is not to offer an exhaustive reading of the *Fables*. It will be sufficient to examine them in the perspective of the "exemplary" model, to see whether—or how—they realize it.

First observation (as if we did not know): all of the fables tell a story. Second, most of the stories are accompanied by

interpretive or pragmatic statements on the part of the "omniscient" (in Gérard Genette's terminology, which will be useful later: "extra-heterodiegetic") narrator; third, these statements are always addressed to the extra-diegetic narratee, that
is, the encoded reader of the fable; finally, in cases where the
story is presented with no accompanying gloss, the reader can
fairly easily provide one by relying on internal indices and on
the intertextual context, which is the *Fables* as a whole.

Despite this structural uniformity, however, one soon discovers that there are two large categories of fables in the collection, only one of which fully realizes the "exemplary" model.
According to the model, the story must give rise not only to a
"meaning" (a lesson), but also to a rule of action: its aim, in
other words, is not only to teach something, but also to influence the receiver's actions or attitudes in a particular way. Inversely, the role of the receiver, according to the model, is to
interpret the story correctly (or, if it is already interpreted by
the narrator, to accept the latter's interpretation) and to act in
accordance with the truth he has just learned. The fact is,
however, that many of La Fontaine's fables do not propose a
rule of action, whether implicitly or explicitly. Certainly, they
"teach" the reader some general truths (on the inconstancy of
the human heart, the injustices and inequalities of life, etc.)
that he may find useful by and by, since everything one knows
can come in handy at some point. But to claim that they propose rules of action comparable to the ones in the New Testament parables would be rather difficult, and would enlarge
beyond usefulness the fairly precise meaning of the term "rule
of action."

Let us, for the sake of convenience, call the fables without
a rule of action (which include some of the best-known ones,
like "The Ant and the Grasshopper," "The Wolf and the
Lamb," or "The Young Widow") "non exemplary." What distinguishes them from the "exemplary" fables is that, even while
they tell a story "rich in lessons about life" (whence a certain
degree of didacticism), they do not imply a value system or an
ethic. If the wolf eats the lamb, if the grasshopper sings all

summer, and if the ant is ungenerous, that is because such is their nature—and, as everyone knows, nature is immutable. If the young widow remarries after having vowed eternal mourning, that too is to be expected: Time is irreversible, the human heart inconstant. The function of these fables is thus not at all to communicate values that might serve to construct an ethics (or even a pragmatics), but simply to depict, without illusions, the world as it goes. Their "realistic" and "cynical" aspect brings them closer to La Rochefoucauld's *Maximes* (several of them are in fact dedicated to La Rochefoucauld) than to the *exemplum*.

The "exemplary" fables, on the other hand, all contain a moral (even if only of a fairly elementary kind): they all claim to instruct us on what we should or should not do in order to live well: "One should, as much as possible, be obliging to everybody" (book II, 11); "We should help each other" (book VIII, 17); and so on. Most of the time, these rules of action are formulated directly by the ominiscient narrator, but they can also be derived from certain fables that lack such explicit statements: the lesson taught by the fox to the crow implies a rule of action, as does the sad end of the oak laid low by the wind.

There is, of course, at least one essential difference between these "exemplary" fables and the New Testament parables: the teachings of the parables are founded on an absolute doctrine—one might even call it "totalitarian," in the sense that it seeks to regulate the whole of life; the fables, on the other hand, are founded on what can at best be called popular wisdom. Although this difference is important as concerns the content or the ultimate significance of a particular parable or fable, it does not alter their formal similarity. This becomes evident if one looks in detail at one of the "exemplary" fables. Here is fable 18 of book VIII, "Le Bassa et le Marchand":

1 Un marchand grec en certaine contrée
2 Faisait trafic. Un bassa l'appuyait;
3 De quoi le Grec en bassa le payait,
4 Non en marchand: tant c'est chère denrée
5 Qu'un protecteur! Celui-ci coûtait tant,

6 Que notre Grec s'allait partout plaignant.
7 Trois autres Turcs, d'un rang moindre en puissance,
8 Lui vont offrir leur support en commun.
9 Eux trois voulaient moins de reconnaissance
10 Qu'à ce marchand il n'en coûtait pour un.
11 Le Grec écoute; avec eux il s'engage;
12 Et le bassa du tout est averti:
13 Même on lui dit qu'il joûra, s'il est sage,
14 A ces gens-là quelque méchant parti,
15 Les prévenant, les chargeant d'un message
16 Pour Mahomet, droit en son paradis,
17 Et sans tarder; sinon ces gens unis
18 Le préviendront, bien certains qu'à la ronde
19 Il a des gens tout prêts pour le venger:
20 Quelque poison l'enverra protéger
21 Les trafiquants qui sont en l'autre monde.
22 Sur cet avis le Turc se comporta
23 Comme Alexandre; et, plein de confiance,
24 Chez le marchand tout droit il s'en alla,
25 Se mit à table. On vit tant d'assurance
26 En ses discours et dans tout son maintien,
27 Qu'on ne crut point qu'il se doutât de rien.
28 Ami, dit-il, je sais que tu me quittes;
29 Même l'on veut que j'en craigne les suites;
30 Mais je te crois un trop homme de bien;
31 Tu n'as point l'air d'un donneur de breuvage.
32 Je n'en dis pas là-dessus davantage.
33 Quant à ces gens qui pensent t'appuyer,
34 Ecoute-moi; sans tant de dialogue
35 Et de raisons qui pourraient t'ennuyer,
36 Je ne te veux conter qu'un apologue.

37 Il était un berger, son chien et son troupeau.
38 Quelqu'un lui demanda ce qu'il prétendait faire
39   D'un dogue de qui l'ordinaire
40 Etait un pain entier. Il fallait bien et beau
41 Donner cet animal au seigneur du village.
42   Lui, berger, pour plus de ménage,
43   Aurait deux ou trois mâtineaux,

44 Qui, lui dépensant moins, veilleraient aux troupeaux
45   Bien mieux que cette bête seule.
46 Il mangeait plus que trois; mais on ne disait pas
47   Qu'il avait aussi triple gueule
48   Quand les loups livraient des combats.
49 Le berger s'en défait; il prend trois chiens de taille
50 A lui dépenser moins, mais à fuir la bataille.
51 Le troupeau s'en sentit; et tu te sentiras
52   Du choix de semblable canaille.
53 Si tu fais bien, tu reviendras à moi.
54a Le Grec le crut.
54b   Ceci montre aux provinces
55 Que, tout compté, mieux vaut en bonne foi
56 S'abandonner à quelque puissant roi,
57 Que s'appuyer de plusieurs petits princes.

THE PASHAW AND THE MERCHANT
    A TRADING Greek, for want of law,
    Protection bought of a pashaw;
    And like a nobleman he paid,
    Much rather than a man of trade—
    Protection being, Turkish-wise,
    A costly sort of merchandise.
    So costly was it, in this case,
The Greek complained, with tongue and face.
    Three other Turks, of lower rank,
Would guard his substance as their own,
    And all draw less upon his bank,
    Than did the great pashaw alone.
    The Greek their offer gladly heard,
    And closed the bargain with a word.
    The said pashaw was made aware,
    And counseled, with a prudent care,
    These rivals to anticipate,
    By sending them to heaven's gate,
    As messengers to Mahomet—
    Which measure should he much delay,
    Himself might go the self-same way,
    By poison offered secretly,

Sent on, before his time, to be
Protector to such arts and trades
As flourish in the world of shades.
On this advice, the Turk—no gander—
Behaved himself like Alexander.
Straight to the merchant's, firm and stable,
He went, and took a seat at table.
Such calm assurance there was seen,
Both in his words and in his mien,
That e'en that weasel-sighted Grecian
Could not suspect him of suspicion.
My friend, said he, I know you've quit me,
And some think caution would befit me,
Lest to despatch me be your plan:
But, deeming you too good a man
        To injure either friends or foes,
        With poisoned cups or secret blows,
I drown the thought, and say no more.
        But, as regards the three or four
            Who take my place,
            I crave your grace
        To listen to an apologue.

        A shepherd, with a single dog,
            Was asked the reason why
        He kept a dog, whose least supply
        Amounted to a loaf of bread
        For every day. The people said
        He'd better give the animal
        To guard the village seignior's hall:
        For him, a shepherd, it would be
        A thriftier economy
            To keep small curs, say two or three,
That would not cost him half the food,
        And yet for watching be as good.
        The fools, perhaps, forgot to tell
        If they would fight the wolf as well.
        The silly shepherd, giving heed,
        Cast off his dog of mastiff breed,

And took three dogs to watch his cattle,
Which ate far less, but fled in battle.
His flock such counsel lived to rue,
As, doubtlessly, my friend, will you.
If wise, my aid again you'll seek—
And so, persuaded, did the Greek.

Not vain our tale, if it convinces,
    Small states that 'tis a wiser thing
    To trust a single powerful king,
Than half a dozen petty princes.

(Elizor Wright, Jr., tr.,
Grandville edition of
Fables, Boston, 1841)

Why I chose this particular fable should be fairly evident: its very subject matter is none other than the functioning of "exemplary" narratives. By a process of internal reduplication or *mise en abyme,* which one frequently finds in modern fiction but which is by no means restricted to it, the fable of the bassa and the merchant points a finger at its own genre.

The fable consists of two stories related to each other hierarchically: the story of the shepherd and the watchdog (let us call it H_2) is embedded in the story of the bassa and the merchant (H_1), whose narrative content it partially repeats. The telling of H_2 by the bassa, who is an intradiegetic narrator (i.e., who exists within the fiction) constitutes a narrative unit within H_1 and in fact determines the outcome of that story. The intradiegetic narratee (the merchant) plays, in relation to the bassa's tale, a role analogous to that of the reader of the fable as a whole.

The story of the bassa and the merchant (H_1) is told by the extradiegetic narrator of the *Fables.* His narratee, to whom the "moral" of verses 54b–57 is addressed, is, in the strict sense, "the provinces" ("Ceci montre aux provinces . . ."); in the broad sense, it is any reader of the fable. Whichever of these senses one chooses makes no difference as far as the functioning of the narrative is concerned. The broader definition simply allows for a more "universal" interpretation, as we shall see.

There are three principal actors in H_1, one of them being plural: the merchant (M), the bassa (B), and the "trois autres Turcs" (T). If we consider the merchant as the subject of the story, we obtain the following narrative structure:

0) M benefits from the protection of B (at a price) (vv. 1–6)
1) M abandons B in favor of T (vv. 7–12)
2) M realizes that he made an error (vv. 28–54a)
3) M abandons T in favor of B (implied by 54a)[29]

The story thus consists of two reversals: the first narrative unit reverses the initial situation (0), while the last unit reverses the situation created by the first, bringing things back to what they were. What interests us is why this second reversal takes place. We must therefore look more closely at the second narrative unit, which includes the embedded story of the shepherd and the watchdog.

If we subdivide the second unit into its constituent parts, we obtain the following:

2-1) B addresses conciliatory words to M (vv. 28–36)
2-2) B tells H_2 to M (vv. 37–51a)
2-3) B draws a lesson from H_2, pertinent to M (51b–53)
2-4) B succeeds in convincing M of his error $\equiv$ M realizes that he made an error (v. 54a)

The relation between the bassa and the merchant is, on one important point, analogous to the relation that links, on the level of the fable as a whole, the extradiegetic narrator and his narratee. In both cases, what is at stake is an enterprise of persuasion (convincing someone of the truth of a proposition that will have practical consequences), and in both cases this is accomplished by the telling of a story. If the merchant reverses his initial action and returns to the bassa, it is because he perceives the similarity between his own story and the story of the unfortunate shepherd; more exactly, he understands that the two stories are structurally identical, *up to a certain point*. It is in order to avoid an identical ending that he changes his mind.

And what about the reader of the fable? His role—at least as it is encoded in the fable, for we are not dealing here with the reactions that an actual reader might have—is similar to that of the merchant. It consists in an act of recognition—of identifying oneself with another—and of reasoning. If the merchant acts as he does, it is because he identifies himself momentarily with the shepherd, and reasons that what happened to the shepherd could happen to him as well. The reader is presumed to do likewise: identify with the merchant and act as he does. There is, however, an important difference: the merchant identifies with the shepherd because he recognizes the structural identity of the two situations—his and that of the other. In the case of the reader, such an identity of situations is possible, but not necessary: the reader need not actually recognize himself in the subject of the fable; it is sufficient if he merely imagines the possibility of such recognition. "If ever I were in a situation similar to that of the merchant (*or* the shepherd), here is what I ought to remember: 'tis a wiser thing / to trust a powerful king / Than half a dozen petty princes!" So the reader might tell himself—and of course, if he is not a "province" but merely an ordinary mortal, he will replace the "powerful king" and the "little princes" by their equivalents in his own world.

The function of the fable, then, is to allow us to live vicariously—to provide us with experiences lived by others, but whose "lessons" will affect us as if we had lived them ourselves. In the fable of the bassa and the merchant, only the shepherd learns his lesson by living his experience to its end; the merchant lives part of the experience, but does not allow it to run its course, having "seen" what happened to the shepherd. As for the reader, he needn't even make the first step into error—the experience of the merchant is there to warn him against it.

That, at least, is how things "ought" to happen according to the ideal of the fable. As for reality, where action is not, in Baudelaire's phrase, the "sister of dreams" and words are not always efficient, we need not worry about it for the present. Let us merely recognize that the project of the fable, as of all "exemplary" narratives, is utopian: to modify the actions of men (and women) by telling them stories. In the universe of the *exemplum*, rebellious readers, or merely indifferent ones, do not exist.[30]

"Exemplary" Narratives and the *Roman à thèse*

It is time to conclude—or rather, to begin. How pertinent is the "exemplary" model for an understanding of the *roman à thèse?* This question is all the more important since at first glance it seems difficult to assimilate a narrative genre as long and as complex as the novel to a genre whose most characteristic traits are brevity and (relative) simplicity.[31] The assimilation between the *roman à thèse* and the *exemplum* can be made only on an abstract level. It is, however, useful, for it allows us to formulate a number of hypotheses about the functioning and about the elementary devices of the *roman à thèse*.

As a start, then, we may suppose the following: the story told by a *roman à thèse* is essentially teleological—it is determined by a specific end, which exists "before" and "above" the story. The story calls for an unambiguous interpretation, which in turn implies a rule of action applicable (at least virtually) to the real life of the reader. The interpretation and the rule of action may be stated explicitly by a narrator who "speaks with the voice of Truth" and can therefore lay claim to absolute authority, or they may be supplied, on the basis of textual and contextual indices, by the reader. The only necessary condition is that the interpretation and the rule of action be unambiguous—in other words, that the story lend itself as little as possible to a "plural" reading.

We shall have to study in detail the rhetorical means by

which a work seeks to impose a "single" reading. On the basis of the foregoing analyses, however, we may already suppose that the rhetoric of the *roman à thèse* is founded on redundancy. A redundant discourse is a discourse where "meaning is excessively named," to use Roland Barthes' expression.[32] In linguistics and information theory, redundancy is defined as a "surplus of communication," which comes down to the same thing: the redundancies of a communicative system reduce the quantity of information that is transmitted, but augment the probability of a correct reception of the message.[33] Redundancy functions, in other words, as a means of disambiguation: if the meaning is "excessively named," it is in order that it should be understood without ambiguity. In the parable of the prodigal son, we saw how the redundancies on the level of narrative structure assured the communication of the father's message; in a subsequent chapter (chapter 4), we shall see how redundancies function in the *roman à thèse*. In the meantime, we may suppose that the rhetoric of the *roman à thèse* consists in multiplying redundancies on every level, in order to reduce the "openings" that might make a plural reading possible.

Admittedly, redundancy and the reduction of ambiguity are not unique to the *roman à thèse*. They can be found, to varying degrees, in every kind of "readable text" (what Roland Barthes has called "le texte lisible"), and in particular in the realist novel.[34] But in realist novels that are not "à thèse"—*Le Père Goriot,* for example—the reduction of ambiguities occurs chiefly on the syntagmatic level, comprising what Barthes calls the proairetic code (which determines the sequence of actions) and the hermeneutic code (which regulates the resolution of narrative enigmas). The semantic or thematic level (which includes Barthes' semic, cultural, and symbolic codes) is a great deal less constrained, more susceptible of being broken up, multiplied, reversed; on this level there exists the possibility of a "flickering of meaning."[35] In the *roman à thèse*, on the other hand, meaning does not "flicker": it emerges gradually, but once it is there it does not fade away or lend itself to "pulverization." On the contrary, the more one advances, the more the redundancies constrain meaning, reducing it and making it *one*.

But there is more: the assimilation to the *exemplum* allows us to see that the *roman à thèse* seeks not only to impose a single meaning, but to propose a system of values. Only the presence of an unambiguous, dualistic system of values allows the *exemplum*—and the *roman thèse*—to produce rules of action. It is only in a universe where the difference is always clear between truth and falsehood, or between right and wrong, that one can categorically affirm the necessity of doing one thing, or going one way, and not another.

We may therefore formulate two specific criteria that set the *roman à thèse* apart within the larger category of the realist novel: the presence of an unambiguous, dualistic system of values, and the presence (even if it is only implied, not stated) of a rule of action addressed to the reader.

Finally, there is a third criterion that we can draw from our analysis of the parables: the presence of a doctrinal intertext. Unlike the fables, whose lessons are founded on popular wisdom, the New Testament parables can be fully understood only in function of a specific system of thought, which exists outside them in explicitly doctrinal texts: the parables all refer, in one way or another, to the doctrine stated in the Sermon on the Mount.[36] A similar phenomenon exists in the *roman à thèse*. The determination of values, and of the rules of action to which they give rise, is made in reference to a doctrine that exists outside the novel and functions as its intertextual context. It makes no difference whether the doctrine is Marxism, fascism, nationalism, Catholicism, or any other "ism" (or variation thereon). Nor does it matter whether the doctrine is explicitly stated in the novel—by an omniscient narrator or by a character who acts as an authoritative interpreter— or whether it is only presupposed. In one way or another it is always "there," and its presence is what finally determines the thesis of the novel.

Naturally, these are very broad criteria that will have to

be tested (and if necessary refined) by specific analyses. They define, furthermore, a *theoretical* model that may be fully realized by very few, if any, actual works. But every generic model is in the final analysis an "ideal type" to which individual works conform only approximately. In order for a number of individual works to be included in a single generic category, it is sufficient if they have "family resemblances" in common, which set them apart from other works belonging to different families. If a set of generic criteria allows us to distinguish one "family" of texts from another, they are workable criteria.[37]

To demonstrate the workability of the criteria I have proposed for the *roman à thèse*, I shall end this chapter with a brief comparison between Aragon's *Les Beaux Quartiers* (1936), which I classify as a *roman à thèse*, and Balzac's *Le Père Goriot*, which is a realist novel, but not, I maintain, a *roman à thèse*.

Les Beaux Quartiers tells two intertwined stories, of two brothers whose paths follow opposite directions. Edmond Barbentane, the elder son of a provincial doctor and local politician (hence, an inhabitant of "les beaux quartiers" in the provinces) leaves his hometown and enters the world of the Parisian "beaux quartiers"—the world of financiers, arms manufacturers (the action of the novel takes place on the eve of the First World War) and international wheeler-dealers. Armand Barbentane, in contrast, discovers and makes his own the "other Paris," the Paris of the poor—a world of wretchedness, but in which he finally finds working-class solidarity. Each of these stories realizes, in its own way, the thematic and narrative structure of apprenticeship, which I shall analyze in detail in the next chapter. This structure is, to be sure, not restricted to the *roman à thèse*. It is realized in a very large category of novels. It is the structure of the *Bildungsroman*, a category that also includes *Le Père Goriot*. What makes *Les Beaux Quartiers* a *roman à thèse* is not the structure of apprenticeship *per se*, but the way this structure is adapted to the purposes of a particular system of signification.

The distinctive trait of this system is the dualism of values.

The whole novel can be thought of as the result of an initial disjunction, with the "beaux quartiers" of the title representing the *negative* pole: the title, in other words, is ironic. All of the fictional elements (characters, events, places) that are associated with this pole are endowed with a negative value, whereas all the elements associated with the opposite pole (the working-class neighborhoods) are positive in value. This clearcut division makes Armand and Edmond exemplary figures, signifying opposite values—one showing the "right road," the other the wrong one. Naturally, an actual reader may contest the value system of the novel—saying, for example, that Edmond is "right" and Armand is stupid, or else declaring that *Les Beaux Quartiers* is a piece of communist propaganda typical of the Aragon of the thirties and forties. But since such a judgment necessarily implies the reader's previous recognition of the values propounded by the novel, it confirms their lack of ambiguity even while denying their validity.

Les Beaux Quartiers thus "fits" our first two criteria: it has an unambiguous, dualistic value system and contains an implicit rule of action addressed to the reader (clearly, one should "follow" Armand, not Edmond). The novel also fits the third criterion, for the positive values are all explicitly identified as *socialist* (the action takes place in 1913, before the founding of the French Communist Party) and the negative values as *capitalist*. The socialist values are embodied, within the fiction, by the historical figure of Jean Jaurès, who functions as a paternal "purveyor of truth" in relation to Armand: it is while listening to Jaurès speak at a mass demonstration, and later by reading one of his speeches before Parliament, that Armand realizes what he must do. The negative values are embodied in a series of fictional characters, including the industrialist Wisner and the banker Joseph Quesnel, who plays a "fatherly" role in relation to Edmond. Now the name of Jaurès necessarily evokes a doctrinal intertext. Even if one has not read a single line of Jaurès, his name alone is sufficient to evoke, metonymically, a set of ideas—and of texts—summarized by the label of "socialism." The names of Wisner and Quesnel do not immediately connote a meaning—their meaning as "capitalists" emerges gradually, through their words, their actions, where they live, and so on. Quesnel, however, alludes admiringly, the very first time we see him, to J. P. Morgan, whose name he cites as "an example to follow." The name of J. P. Morgan plays a role analogous to that of Jaurès, since it immediately evokes the label: "capitalist."

At first glance, *Le Père Goriot* has many features in common with Aragon's novel. It too tells the story of a young provincial in Paris, it too is a *Bildungsroman,* it too explores both the underside and the glittering surface of Parisian society. Most importantly, it too invites the reader to make ethical and moral judgments about the characters and their actions: we are surely asked to judge Goriot more favorably than his daughters, or than Mme Vauquer; Mme de Beauséant is a more admirable character than the other aristocratic women— or men—in her world; even the ex-convict Vautrin elicits a favorable judgment, especially in comparison to the treacherous little couple who betray him to the police. But the necessity of moral judgment, which is one of the hallmarks of the realist novel, does not make *Le Père Goriot* into a *roman à thèse.* First of all, this novel does not set up a dualistic value system according to which all of the principal characters fall unambiguously into a positive or negative category: if Goriot is admirable in his self-sacrificing love for his daughters, we know that he was at one time a ruthless speculator and businessman; if Vautrin's ideas and personality command a certain respect, we know that he is not right in urging Rastignac to participate as a silent accomplice in the murder of a man in order to make a wealthy marriage; if Mme de Beauséant is a figure of true nobility, we know that her final rejection of Parisian society is based on personal disappointment more than on some general principle. None of these characters can be said to offer a model for the reader to follow (or to avoid). They offer partial solutions to complex problems, not definitive answers to fairly simple questions.

Second, even if we are able to reconstruct a world view or

an ideology that informs the novel as a whole—and with suf-
fucient effort one can always reconstruct such a view in a given
novel, as the work of Lucien Goldmann and other Marxist
critics has shown[38]—that still does not allow us to say that the
story told in *Le Père Goriot* represents the advocacy of a particular doctrine. Balzac was a Catholic and a legitimist monarchist, as everyone knows—and as everyone also knows, his novels
invariably show, if not the bankruptcy, at least the inadequacy
of Catholicism and legitimism as "solutions" in the new economic and social world created by the French Revolution and
Napoleon.

Finally, and correlative to all this, there is the matter of
the hero and what he discovers in the process of his "education." Rastignac learns a lot, that is certain: he learns that society is an elaborate game in which only those who know the
rules and how to manipulate them can win; he learns that this
game can be murderous, and that only those who have no
illusions about the virtues of the human heart can be among
the victors; he learns the value of money, of dissimulation and
calculation; finally, he learns how to use people to obtain his
own ends. Is this good or bad? Nothing in the novel allows us
to make a definitive judgment on that subject. The famous
challenge Rastignac flings at Paris from the heights of Mont-
martre at the end of the novel ("A nous deux maintenant!")
remains profoundly ambiguous, as does our view of Rastignac
himself. He has completed his education, and will now de-
scend into the battlefield of the Parisian *salons*, disenchanted
and determined to win. Who is to say whether he is right or
wrong?

There would of course be a lot more to say about both
Les Beaux Quartiers and *Le Père Goriot;* I shall certainly return
to Aragon's novel elsewhere in this book. Even our brief comparison has, however, accomplished what it was designed to
do: it has shown that *Les Beaux Quartiers* manifests, *as dominant
traits,* the distinguishing features of the *roman à thèse,* whereas
Le Père Goriot does not. Despite all that the two novels have in
common—realism, the structure of the *Bildungsroman,* related

themes such as "the provincial in Paris," "Paris the capital of pleasure and of poverty"—they belong to different "families." There remains now but to explore in detail the dynamics of the "family" that forms the subject of this book.

2 The Structure of Apprenticeship

THEORETICALLY, THE narrative content of a *roman à thèse*, as of any exemplary narrative, can be infinitely varied. As I suggested in the preceding chapter, it is not a particular story that makes a given novel a *roman à thèse*; it is, rather, the way a story is integrated into a specific system of signification—or, if one prefers, into a specific mode of discourse. The three distinctive traits I proposed in order to characterize the *roman à thèse* are modal traits, in the sense that they allow us to define the "essence of the genre" independently of the narrative or thematic structures that might be realized by an individual work that belongs to the genre. The modal approach is, however, only one possible approach to the analysis of genres—the other main approach being, as Fredric Jameson has remarked, a syntactic one. Whereas the modal approach aims for a definition in terms of a global meaning, or "essence," the syntactic approach seeks to construct a structural model of the genre as a "fixed form."[1] The complete description of a genre might therefore include, according to Jameson, both a modal definition and an attempt to construct the fixed form or structural model that somehow corresponds to that particular mode.

A structural model is always, in the last instance, an abstraction drawn from a specific content; in works of fiction, this is a narrative content—a story. Constructing the structural model of a novelistic genre would therefore consist in defining a "type" of story that characterizes the genre and *only* that genre. If one considers, however, that at a certain level of abstraction there exist only a limited number of "types" of stories, one is led to conclude that the number of narrative genres *exceeds* the number of structural models—in other words, that a given narrative or thematic structure can be realized by more than one genre. This means that the question one must try to answer in describing a genre is not, as Jameson suggests: "What is *the* structural model that corresponds to a given mode in order to constitute the genre?" but rather: "How does a given mode 'appropriate' a given structural model in order to produce a work that we call tragedy, epic, melodrama, fantastic tale?" or whatever genre happens to interest us. The genre, in other words, is not the product of a one to one correspondence between a single structural model and a mode; it is, rather, the result of an intersection between a general model (or more than one) and a set of specific modal traits.

In this chapter and the following, I shall analyze two narrative models—two "types" of stories—as they are appropriated by the mode of discourse specific to the *roman à thèse*. The first, together with its variants, is what I call the structure of apprenticeship: it links the *roman à thèse* to the *Bildungsroman*. The second, which I call the structure of confrontation, links the *roman à thèse* to certain popular genres like the western or the war novel, as well as to their common ancestor, the epic.

Bildungsroman and *roman à thèse:* Bourget's *L'Etape*

"The way towards a man's recognition of himself"—this broad definition of the "normative content" of the novel as a genre, proposed by Lukács,[2] applies above all, and perhaps only, to the *Bildungsroman*.[3] If Lukács' blindspot (at least in *The Theory of the Novel*, which concerns us here) was that he considered all novels as variants of the *Bildungsroman*, his analysis still provides the most solid basis for a structural definition of that particular genre. According to Lukács, the form of the novel, that "epic of a world without gods," is that of a biography of the "problematic individual"—problematic because the world where the individual's action takes place has become contingent, deprived of transcendental meaning. In such a world, human individuality has ceased being "organic": being neither the possession of the individual nor the immediate basis of his existence, individuality becomes the *object of a quest*—whence Lukács' definition of the novel as "the story of the soul that goes to find itself, that seeks adventures in order to be proved and tested by them, and by proving itself, to find its own essence." [4] This definition—formulated in the Hegelian vocabulary characteristic of Lukács' early works—contains just about all the necessary elements for a structural model of the *Bildungsroman*.

Syntagmatically, we may define a story of apprenticeship (of *Bildung*) as two parallel transformations undergone by the protagonist: first, a transformation from *ignorance* (of self) to *knowledge* (of self); second, a transformation from *passivity* to *action*. The hero goes forth into the world to find (knowledge of) himself, and attains such knowledge through a series of "adventures" (actions) that function both as "proofs" and as tests. The adventures in which the hero triumphs are the means whereby he "discovers his own essence"—they thus fulfill the traditional function of a test; but they constitute, at the same time, a "proof" of his new-found knowledge of self, which is the necessary precondition for authentic action in the future. In effect, the hero's "adventures" are but the prelude to genuine action: a story of apprenticeship ends on the threshold of a "new life" for the hero—which explains why, in the traditional *Bildungsroman*, the hero is always a young man, often an adolescent. [5]

Paradigmatically, or in terms of its system of characters (what A. J. Greimas calls its actantial system), [6] the *Bildungsroman* may be defined by the following minimal configuration: the categories of subject, object, and receiver of the object (*destinataire*) are syncretized in a single actor, who is the hero of the novel. The hero goes forth in order to find knowledge of *himself* (object), and it is he who will benefit from that knowledge (receiver). He can, of course, and usually does, receive the help of a donor (*destinateur*) or a helper (*adjuvant*), just as he will also probably have to confront a number of adversaries who play the actantial role of opponent (*opposant*). Since these are not absolutely necessary figures, however—the minimal configuration requires only the first three actants—we may leave them aside for the moment.

To return to *The Theory of the Novel*, it is somewhat surprising to note that after having defined the novel in terms that apply only to the *Bildungsroman*, Lukács constructs a typology of novelistic forms which leads to the conclusion that the veritable *Bildungsroman* has almost never existed. According to his typology, the entire category of the *Bildungsroman* is occupied by a single novel: Goethe's *Wilhelm Meister*. Only Goethe's hero fully realizes, according to Lukács, the ideal of *Bildung:* an authentic knowledge of self and authentic action in the world. Other novelistic heroes all fall into one or the other of two categories of failed heroes, thus defining two types of novels: the novel of abstract idealism, and the novel of romantic disillusionment. In the first type, whose fully realized model is *Don Quixote,* the successful quest of the hero is prevented by his "demonic blindness": the hero acts and goes from adventure to adventure, but since his subjectivism allows for only a "distorted image" of the world (and of himself in the world), his action never comes to grips with reality. In the novel of romantic disillusionment, on the other hand (Lukács' example here is *L'Education sentimentale*), the hero does not act at all: he refuses to confront the world, judging all confrontation to be "hopeless and merely humiliating." In both instances, the hero's quest ends in failure and powerlessness. Wilhelm Meister thus appears to be the only example of a hero who succeeds in his *Bildung:* he represents a precarious synthesis between action and contemplation, resigned lucidity and optimism, individuality and solidarity.[7]

One can certainly criticize Lukács' categories. They are too few to account for the immense variety of the novel as a genre, leaving no place, for example, for the novels of Balzac, Austen, Sterne, Diderot, and many others. Furthermore, there is a contradiction between the implicit affirmation that the *Bil-*

dungsroman is the archetype of the novel, and the explicit assertion that this type of novel has been fully realized by only a single work. Despite all this, however, *The Theory of the Novel* is an excellent starting point for our own discussion—not only because it offers (when read in a contemporary perspective) a structural definition of the novel of apprenticeship, but also because it proposes a classification of three types of apprenticeship, which can in fact be reduced to a simple opposition: "positive" or authentic apprenticeship vs. "negative" or inauthentic ones.

Now the "positive" vs. "negative" opposition is precisely what characterizes the "exemplary" apprenticeships realized in the *roman à thèse:* a "positive exemplary" apprenticeship leads the hero to the values propounded by the doctrine that founds the novel; a "negative exemplary" apprenticeship leads him to opposite values, or simply to a space where the positive values are not recognized as such. Lukács' categories of success and failure, authenticity and inauthenticity are thus pertinent for the analysis of the *roman à thèse*—with the difference, however (which makes all the difference!), that the *roman à thèse* invests these categories with nonproblematic meanings. For Lukács, nonproblematic authenticity, defined as an immediate and total adhesion between the individual and the world, is precisely what is *lacking* in the modern (post-epic) world, and the novel as a literary form resulted from the awareness of this lack: the novel's mission is to reveal the modern, degraded, irremediably problematic character of any quest for authenticity. This may explain, in fact, why Lukács' categories of failure are much more heavily populated than his category of success. Even the success of Wilhelm Meister consists merely in a precarious synthesis between two positions of failure.

In the *roman à thèse,* things are very different. By defining authenticity as the "truth" of a doctrine and inauthenticity as whatever does not conform to that truth, the *roman à thèse* simplifies and deproblematizes Lukács' notion of authenticity; it appropriates the structural model of apprenticeship to its own ends.

The analysis of a few specific works will allow us to see how this appropriation takes place. Paul Bourget's *L'Etape* (1902) will serve as my principal reference. I have chosen this novel, which very few people read today but which was, after *Le Disciple* (1889), the most widely read (and perhaps the most characteristic) work of its once highly considered author, for two reasons: first, it will allow us to study both the positive and the negative variants of the structure of apprenticeship; second, it is without a doubt a "novel with a thesis," and was recognized as such by its first readers. Bourget's admiring biographer, Albert Feuillerat, presents *L'Etape* as a work of transition, marking its author's passage from "le roman de l'analyse expérimentale" to "le roman social" (a label that Bourget preferred, for reasons already discussed, to that of *roman à thèse*). According to Feuillerat, *L'Etape* served as the "vehicle" for a doctrine, allowing Bourget to "express, by means of fictional beings, the principles he considered essential for normal and healthy political life."[8]

We shall see in a while the link between the novel's fictional beings and the political principles they allowed Bourget to "express." What we must first note is that, historically, *L'Etape* appeared in an intellectual and political climate that was still seething from the ideological battles of the Dreyfus Affair. This fact is important not only because the Affair is specifically referred to in the novel (it is part of the hero's "prehistory"), but also, and above all, because the Dreyfus Affair could figure as an emblem for the whole period that concerns us. Historians generally agree that in the France of the last years of the nineteenth century, the Dreyfus Affair created a definitive division between what François Goguel has called two "spiritual families": "the party of order" and "the party of movement."[9] Certainly, this division was not new—it went back at least as far as the French Revolution; but as Goguel shows, its presence has rarely been felt as strongly, its consequences rarely been as grave and prolonged, as in the period between 1898 and 1940. Between the *dreyfusards* and the supporters of the Popular Front there is a definite continuity, just as there is one be-

tween the admirers of the virulently anti-Semitic Drumont and
the supporters of the fascist Doriot or of the Vichy minister
Laval. But between these two groups, there was no common
ground. It should not surprise us if this ideologically polarized
period constitutes one of the "strong" moments of the *roman
à thèse* in France. The *roman à thèse* is a genre that thrives on
ideological polarization, which becomes both a fundamental
theme and an organizing principle.

L'Etape is the story of a young man who, having started
out as an anticlerical socialist, becomes a Catholic monarchist.
The story takes place in 1900. Jean Monneron, the hero, raised
according to the "fanatical,"[10] pro-republican, violently anticlerical principles of his father, Joseph Monneron, ends up
repudiating those principles and espousing the ideals (as well
as marrying the daughter) of his onetime professor, the "traditionalist" Victor Ferrand. Ferrand, an "enemy of the false
dogmas of 1789" and "one of the leading Catholic philosophers in the University," is in every way the opposite of Jean's
father, a "professor with his head in the clouds," an "absolute
exemplar of the Jacobin." Victor Ferrand and Jean Monneron
thus define, at the very outset of the novel, two separate semantic fields (in reality, two ideological fields), the first of which
is marked as euphoric (positively valorized by the omniscient
narrator), the second as dysphoric (absolute negative valorization). It is this initial disjunction that generates—and allows us
to foresee the broad outlines of—Jean's story. There are only
two possibilities: either Jean will choose to remain with the ideas
of his father, in which case he will accomplish a negative exemplary apprenticeship; or he will choose those of Ferrand,
and accomplish a positive exemplary apprenticeship. As it
happens, it is the second option that is realized in the novel;
but we should note that either one would have served its demonstrative and didactic purpose. It is not the specific outcome of the story, but the presence of two separate and op-
posingly valorized ideological fields that is crucial to the
demonstration.

How are such unambiguous valorizations effected, and by

what means are they imposed (or sought to be imposed) on the reader? As far as *L'Etape* is concerned, the answer to the first question is quite simple: the valorizations are effected through the omniscient narrator, who speaks with the "voice of Truth" and who *judges* the ideas represented by the principal characters. If we consider Victor Ferrand and Joseph Monneron as representatives of two opposed ideological systems (roughly speaking, the system of "traditionalist" values and the system of "progressive" values), then the role of the narrator is to privilege one system at the expense of the other. The narrator functions thus as the representative of yet another system: an ideological "supersystem" that *puts in their proper place* the systems represented by the characters. These relations can be conveniently summarized by means of the semiotic square elaborated by Greimas and Rastier.[11] In the narrator's supersystem the system represented by Ferrand occupies, exclusively and in its entirety, the positive side or *deixis*, while Monneron's system occupies, in symmetrical fashion, the negative side.

Figure 2.1

The Narrator's Supersystem in *L'Etape*

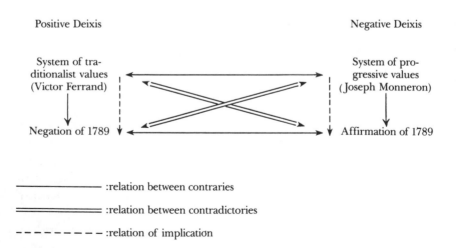

Positive Deixis   Negative Deixis

System of tra-   System of pro-
ditionalist values   gressive values
(Victor Ferrand)   (Joseph Monneron)

Negation of 1789   Affirmation of 1789

———————————— :relation between contraries

════════════════ :relation between contradictories

– – – – – – – – – :relation of implication

The schema also allows us to see exactly what makes a novel, or any other literary work, monological. Bakhtin, who coined the term in distinction to his well-known notion of the dialogical, defined a monological work as one in which ideas are either affirmed or refuted, with no middle ground possible; the affirmed idea is what gives the monological work both its narrative shape and its "unity of ideological tone."[12] Our bipolar schema makes clear what Bakhtin meant by "no middle ground possible," as well as showing how a unity of ideological tone is achieved. Any ideological conflict is resolved by a narrative supersystem that is itself ideological and that evaluates the competing ideologies: only one of them is "right," while the others are discredited. In a dialogical work, on the other hand, the "voices" of both (or several) ideologies retain a certain authority. As F. Rastier has shown in his detailed analysis of Molière's *Dom Juan*, a dialogical work requires a "double" or "plural" reading (Rastier somewhat misleadingly calls it a "totalizing" reading), since a reading in terms of only one system of values is unable to account for all the elements in the work.[13] In the case of *Dom Juan*, a reading that privileges the system of individual values (represented by Dom Juan) must be complemented by a reading that privileges the system of social values (represented by the other characters)— whence Rastier's conclusion that the work is ambiguous, since "one reading necessarily evokes the other, and . . . both are necessary."[14] In *L'Etape*, as in the *roman à thèse* generally, a single (minded) reading *can* account for all the elements in the work; indeed, it is precisely toward such a reading that the work's ideological supersystem orients the reader.

If this supersystem is represented by an omniscient narrator who "speaks with the voice of Truth" and makes explicit judgments, as is the case in *L'Etape*, we have the clearest, least ambiguous manifestation of monologism. It is for that very reason that I chose *L'Etape* as a first reference, a model *roman à thèse*, as it were. Omniscient narration, although it is the surest way to insure a "single" reading, is, however, not an absolutely necessary condition for monologism. As we shall see in a subsequent chapter, even a first-person narrative like Mauriac's *Le Noeud de vipères* can be monological.

There remains the second question: how are the unambiguous valorizations effected by the *roman à thèse* imposed on the reader? In slightly different terms, how does the rhetorical mechanism, the mechanism of persuasion, function? First, we may again invoke the role of the omniscient narrator: to the extent that the narrator figures as the source of the story he is telling, he functions not only as "author" but also as *authority*. Since it is his voice that informs us of the characters' actions and of the circumstances in which they occur, and since we must consider—by virtue of the pact which, in the realist novel, links the teller of the story to his audience—that what the narrator recounts is "true," there occurs a blurring of boundaries that makes us accept as "true" not only what the narrator tells us about the events and circumstances of the fictional world, but also what he tells us in the way of judgment and interpretation. The narrator thus becomes not only the source of his story, but the authoritative interpreter of its *meaning* as well—and this meaning is, in realist fiction, invariably linked to our non-fictional world. To refuse the narrator's judgments (to say, for example, that *L'Etape* is the work of an arch-reactionary, and therefore to be distrusted) is equivalent to breaking a contract. This kind of break is always possible, and indeed becomes inevitable if the reader's own system of values is in strong conflict with that of the narrator.[15] At that point, the reader (to whom I refer here as a "she" but who can obviously also be a "he") no longer reads the work *as fiction*, for she perceives the fictional world as an obvious attempt on the part of the novelist to manipulate her responses. The realist novel requires, on the part of the reader, a certain willingness to "play the game," to act as if she did not perceive the devices of the novelist: she must accept, or pretend to accept, the novel as a "natural," innocent representation of the real. This "naturalness" is what constitutes the verisimilitude of the work. By suddenly affirming her own values *against* the values propounded by the work, the reader stops playing the game and accuses the novelist of having broken the rules: the representation no longer appears "natural," but distorted and manipulative—implausible, unfaithful to the real. Paradoxically, it is at the moment when her own convictions break into her reading that the reader of novels becomes fully conscious of the artifices of the novelist.

But there exists another means of persuasion no less powerful than the voice of the omniscient narrator. It is the story itself, the lived *experience* (or transformation) of a subject over time. Here is where we encounter the structure of apprenticeship, which is a structure on the level of the story: the fictive subject who "lives" the story has his counterpart in the real subject who *reads* it. The persuasive effect of a story of apprenticeship "with a thesis" results from the virtual identification of the reader with the protagonist. If the protagonist evolves toward a euphoric position, the reader is incited to follow him in the right direction: the protagonists's happiness is both a proof and a guarantee of the values he affirms. If the protagonist's story "ends badly," his failure also serves as a lesson or proof, but this time *a contrario:* the protagonist's fate allows the reader to perceive the wrong road without following it.

These formulations may appear a bit simplistic, but we must remember that they do not claim to describe a concrete work; they are structures whose relation to actual works is like that of the bone structure to a living body. The structure underlies the work and gives it its shape, but can in no instance be considered a substitute for it. There are few novels, no matter how didactic, that do not complicate and flesh out in unexpected ways the elementary schemas derived by analysis. On the other hand, it is undeniable that the rhetoric of the *roman à thèse* is simple—that is, without ironic self-awareness or self-reflection—just as the rhetoric of the *exemplum* and of any pragmatic discourse is ultimately simple. As I have already suggested, however, it is the very simplicity—or, to put it in more brutal terms, the simplistic character—of its rhetoric that makes the *roman à thèse* theoretically interesting. If it is easy to condemn such simple rhetoric in the name of "the modern," it is less easy to uncover and name its devices. And unless they are named, they continue to exert their power.

Apprenticeship: The Positive Exemplary Version

I shall analyze the positive and negative versions of exemplary apprenticeship first in terms of the linear unfolding of the story (i.e., in terms of its large-scale syntagmatic structure), then in terms of its actantial configuration. This will allow at the same time for a more detailed reading of *L'Etape*.

At the end of the novel, Jean Monneron defines his own transformation as follows: ". . . I thought I was a socialist, and . . . I am one no longer; I was a partisan of 1789 and of the Revolution, now I am no longer; all of the ideas in which I was raised, and which I accepted as indisputable for so long, appear to me today to be radically wrong."[16] If we add to this what we know from our reading of the novel: namely, that Jean has not only become a "nonsocialist," a "nonpartisan of the Revolution" and "non anticlerical," but a monarchist, an "enemy of 1789" and a practicing Catholic, and that, furthermore, monarchism and Catholicism occupy in this novel the positive pole of Truth while socialism and anticlericalism are at the negative pole of Error, then we can summarize Jean's evolution by the following broad sequence:

(1) affirming Error→ negating Error→ affirming Truth

This sequence is the "strong" or extended version of the following one:

(2) not knowing the Truth———→ knowing the Truth

since it takes longer to arrive at knowledge if one starts from Error rather than from mere ignorance; similarly, it takes an additional step to affirm or proclaim the truth after knowing it.

If the hero himself explicitly proclaims the "truth" at the

end of his story—if he becomes, like Jean Monneron, the spokesman and possibly a theorist of the doctrine whose validity the novel seeks to demonstrate—then we are dealing with the simplest and most direct way of inserting a real doctrine into a fictional world. In addition to direct statement, however, the *roman à thèse* has a predilection for indirect or embedded statements like "He finally understood that *p*" or "He now knew that *p*," where the proposition *p* is the truth discovered by the hero. Oswald Ducrot has shown that in sentences of this type, *p* is logically presupposed as true. The characteristic trait of a presupposition is that it is implicit: its truth is supposedly taken for granted. As Ducrot remarks, in presupposition the proof of truth "presents itself as something experienced, which makes it all the harder to contest . . . What the speaker tends to suppose is that his interlocutor will immediately accept the presuppositions even when he was unaware of them before, that he will not question them, that he will accept them without protest."[17] One can see why presuppositions are useful to the *roman à thèse:* they are a way of "slipping in" the doctrine without its being contested by the reader, and this is especially true in sentences where the presupposition follows the verbs "knowing" or "understanding" (in the sense of "realizing"). As Ducrot points out, "when one places the expression *X knows that* in front of a proposition *p*, it is often simply in order to reinforce the truth of *p*. *X knows that* . . . can, in such cases, almost be considered as a modal phrase, analogous to *It is true that* . . . One has the impression, in these instances, that where knowledge is concerned it is impossible to separate the subjective mode of belief from its objective value . . . knowledge is a belief that functions as proof, a belief that is self-demonstrative."[18] This impression is of course reinforced when it is the hero who "knows" or "understands," since the reader is already, both by convention and by the formal pressure of the fiction, predisposed in his favor.

If the hero does not explicitly state the doctrine that guarantees the authenticity of his personal evolution, there remains a certain margin of indeterminacy that the reader will be called upon to fill in. That is the case, for example, in Nizan's *La Conspiration,* where the hero (if we can pin that label on Laforgue, the only one of the novel's young protagonists whose story has a "positive" ending) does not actually *say* that he will become a Communist, but where all that precedes allows one to infer that conclusion. The point is that, whether he actually *says so* or not, the hero must end up with knowledge that is judged "correct" (authentic) within the ideological supersystem of the work. We shall therefore retain sequence (2) as the primary sequence in a positive exemplary apprenticeship, with sequence (1) as a variant.

This primary sequence allows us to see more clearly the relationship between the *Bildungsroman* as it is defined by Lukács and the *roman à thèse* with a positive exemplary pattern. In the *Bildungsroman,* the protagonist's story is defined by two parallel transformations: ignorance (of self)→ knowledge (of self), passivity→ action. In the *roman à thèse,* these same transformations occur, but they are subordinated to another one, which radically modifies their meaning. The hero's self-knowledge is no longer an end in itself, but a simple consequence: it is *because* he acquires knowledge of an objective, totalizing "truth" that the hero discovers, at the same time, "his own essence." The adhesion to a doctrine guarantees the authenticity of the self, and the self is defined essentially in terms of adhesion to a doctrine. "What is outside you right now is your true self," Ferrand tells Jean at the beginning of *L'Etape* (1:42). At the end, having rediscovered "the faith of his ancestors," Jean has found at the same time his "true self."

Similarly, it is the adhesion to a doctrine that makes possible the hero's transition to action and the beginning of a "new life," which is here defined as a "life in accordance with truth." Strictly speaking, the hero's apprenticeship ends when he acquires authentic knowledge; but the evocation, at least, of his future "life in accordance with truth" is a necessary part of his story. In *L'Etape,* what is evoked at the end is the conjugal, bourgeois, Catholic happiness that Jean will enjoy with Ferrand's daughter; the causal link between doctrinal convictions and the authenticity of the new life is explicitly marked by Ferrand's explanation to Jean: "You will found a genuine family [*foyer*] *because* you have acquired . . . the certitudes that . . . [your father] lacked" (2:244, my emphasis).

The successful quest for certitudes—this is perhaps the formula that most succinctly defines the evolution of the hero of a positive exemplary apprenticeship—provided, of course, that the certitudes he discovers be the "right" ones! How is this quest realized? By what means does the hero pass from ignorance to knowledge? One can reply to this question by looking at what anthropologists call the "scenario of initiation."[19] This scenario consists in an individual's progress from a state of ignorance to a state of knowledge by means of a series of trials; the object of knowledge is always linked to the sacred, and the end in view is an essential transformation of the individual—a "new birth"—which will make him worthy of becoming a member of the group constituted by other initiates.[20] The *roman à thèse* offers a desacralized version of this scenario: the hero attains a knowledge that transforms him, and his transformation is the prelude to action undertaken by a group: those who share the knowledge—in reality, the values—of the hero. As in the scenario of initiation, the progress toward knowledge is achieved through experience, and in particular through one or more trials. It goes without saying that in a positive apprenticeship the hero always emerges from such trials victorious.

The following schema summarizes the complete large-scale sequence of a positive exemplary apprenticeship:

Ignorance———Trial(s)———>Knowledge————————>"New life" in
of truth   surmounted of truth   accordance with truth

Passivity -->Action based
                                                                        on knowledge

The dotted line between knowledge and the "new life" indicates that the latter may be merely evoked, not represented. Although the representation of the hero's "new life" is not necessary in a story of apprenticeship, its evocation is, because it is in his "new life" that the hero will undertake the action for which his apprenticeship has prepared him. The evocation of this future life and action may be very brief, as in *L'Etape,* or it may take up considerable space. In Nizan's *Aden Arbie,* for example (which may for our purposes be considered a *roman à thèse* in autobiographical form), all of the last chapter, which is the longest in the book, consists in a program for future action based on a Marxist interpretation of European society: the hero, having emerged victorious from his experience of initiation, which here takes the classical form of the voyage, returns to France determined to fight against his enemy, "Homo Economicus." Since the new life he foresees for himself is that of a militant, *Aden Arabie* evokes, projected into the future, the principal elements of what I call the structure of confrontation.

The trial in a story of apprenticeship has a rather special status. The notion of a trial, or test, implies a confrontation or struggle: in order to surmount the trial, the hero must conquer an opponent. But the hero of an apprenticeship story is basically passive: it is the acquisition of "true" knowledge that inaugurates his life of action. That leaves us with the somewhat anomalous notion of a "passive trial," or more exactly a trial in which the hero does not (yet) act. This kind of trial has a name: it is the trial of interpretation, where the candidate is placed before a situation—or a text—that he must understand and explain. Surmounting the trial consists in nothing more— but nothing less—than discovering the right meaning, giving the correct interpretation. But in order to interpret correctly, doesn't one already have to possess the necessary knowledge? It would appear, then, that rather than *leading* to the knowledge of truth (which is what our schema suggests), the trial of interpretation, if it is passed by the hero, simply *manifests* a knowledge he has already acquired. This paradoxical status is perhaps that of any act of interpretation; by interpreting correctly, one discovers what one already knows. But if that is so, it merely confirms the circularity of any interpretive act: a "correct" interpretation is finally but the consequence of the presuppositions on which it is founded—and these presuppositions are always open to question.

The rhetoric of the *roman à thèse* requires the suppression—or more exactly, the repression in the psychoanalytic sense—of this circularity. The theory of interpretation that underlies the *roman à thèse* is of necessity blind to the vulnerability of interpretation. The hero's trials lead, not merely to the affirmation of what is at best a personal conviction, but to the discovery of an absolute truth. In the *roman à thèse*, trial by interpretation functions as yet another strategy of persuasion: it is one of the means by which the reader is led to a "correct" understanding, both of the story and of what it is designed to demonstrate. In *L'Etape*, the hero's apprenticeship consists in rejecting certain ideas as false and affirming their contraries as true. This apprenticeship is accomplished through a series of trials by interpretation: Jean Monneron discovers the truth of traditionalist doctrine by interpreting the misfortunes of others as the consequences of the false ideas that regulate their lives. Jean "reads" the stories of his brother (who becomes an embezzler) and of his sister (who ends up "seduced and abandoned") as *negative exemplary* tales that demonstrate the falsehood of his father's progressive ideas. In relation to the stories of his brother and sister, Jean thus occupies a position analogous to that of the reader of these stories and of the novel as a whole. His act of interpretation is a mimesis of the general activity of the reader—and the consequence of his interpretation, which is a change in his whole way of being and acting, is also presumably supposed to function as a model, or as a mirror image, for the reader. We already saw this kind of inner reduplication in La Fontaine's fable of the bassa and the merchant. The positive exemplary hero, like the "good" reader, knows how to interpret correctly the stories of others, and puts his interpretation to use in his own life.

We shall return in a while to the question of trial by interpretation. First, however, we must look at the actantial configuration of a positive exemplary apprenticeship. As in the *Bil-*

dungsroman, the subject, object, and receiver are syncretized in a single character, who is the hero. The object, however, is a complex category, for besides finding his "authentic self" the hero also finds the "right" doctrine. The category of object is therefore occupied by two actors, one animate and one abstract; other actors may also be present in the category of object, but their presence is not necessary. In *L'Etape,* Victor Ferrand's daughter, Brigitte, also functions as an object: a traditional triadic love story (boy, girl, and girl's parents—Brigitte "gives herself" to Jean but is also given by her father) is thus grafted onto the apprenticeship story even while being subordinated to it. Brigitte is the reward of the victorious hero, but she is actually a secondary object—the primary object is Jean himself, and the truths he discovers. This is made clear by the fact that at the moment of his conversion, Jean gives up all hope of marrying Brigitte (2:163). It is as if the narrative wished to emphasize that the discovery of the right doctrine has as its necessary corollary not the possession of an external object, but the hero's *self*-possession—the possession of his true self. Love, or the quest for possession of another, is rarely, if ever, an important preoccupation of the hero in the *roman à thèse.*

There remain the categories of donor, helper, and opponent. The donor, according to Greimas, is situated on the axis of communication (he communicates or gives the object), whereas the helper and the opponent are situated on the axis of aid—the helper acts to facilitate the acquisition of the object, the opponent to prevent it. The categories of donor and helper can in fact be syncretized in a single actor; there can be no such fusion, or confusion, however, between either of these two categories and that of the opponent. In a positive apprenticeship, the donor and the helper define the euphoric space where the hero ends up; the opponent defines the dysphoric space against which the hero affirms himself.

The archetypal donor is a paternal figure. Possessing a knowledge similar, if not identical, to the one sought by the hero, the paternal figure functions as donor and/or as helper:

he communicates what he knows, helps the hero surmount his trials. His beneficial presence guarantees, in a sense, the hero's success. What is striking is that the father-donor, if he is present, is rarely the hero's biological father. He is, rather, a spiritual, elective father, whom the hero chooses as his own. In *L'Etape,* the opposition between the biological father and the elective father is the very stuff of the story, since Jean's apprenticeship involves negating the values of the former and affirming those of the latter. The biological father is thus, in this instance, not only a non-donor, a neutral element; he is an anti-donor, an opponent. More exactly, he is an actor who, even while occupying the structural position of a donor, plays, according to the work's ideological supersystem, the role of an opponent. He therefore defines a complex actantial category, that of the "malevolent" or pseudo-donor. We shall look at this category in greater detail in studying the negative exemplary version of apprenticeship. For now it is enough to note that the donor and the pseudo-donor are opposed to each other along the semantic axis of *truth* vs. *falsehood,* or *being* vs. *seeming.* One of the elements of a positive apprenticeship is the recognition of this opposition by the hero himself, and his choice of the "true" donor over the "false" one.

Naturally, the categories of donor and of opponent (or of pseudo-donor) can, like any actantial category, be occupied by several actors. That is one of the surest way in which the novel can create redundancies. In *L'Etape,* for example, the category of donor includes, besides Ferrand, two other Catholic and paternal figures: a physician, Dr. Graux, and a priest, Abbé Chanut. Both of them appear at crucial moments to give Jean a "lesson on the power of deep faith" (2:134). Curiously, neither of them has anything to teach Jean about politics: Dr. Graux's political ideas are not mentioned, while those of Abbé Chanut are presented as downright dangerous—he is a socialist sympathizer, which makes him politically an "anti-Ferrand." The ambiguity that might result from this (since the *abbé* would be both a true donor and a socialist, an impossible combination in the supersystem of the novel) is eliminated by the omniscient narrator, who makes a point of stating that the priest is "admirable" only in his "deep faith," not in his political ideas, which are those of a "dupe" and a *naïf* (2:110, 134). Jean's political education is reserved for Ferrand, who combines in himself the "right" political doctrine and the "right" religious convictions. Since Ferrand in any case plays a more important role in the novel than the other two characters (he appears more frequently, is more explicit in his affirmations, and combines the role of donor in the apprenticeship story with that of donor in the love story), he functions as the principal, necessary, and sufficient donor, as it were. The other two characters simply reinforce one of Ferrand's traits (Catholicism), and are thus semantically redundant. I say semantically, because syntagmatically their presence is highly motivated: Dr. Graux appears when the narrative calls for a doctor (he takes care of Jean's sister after she tries to commit suicide), while Abbé Chanut plays a functional role in the subplot concerning *l'Union Tolstoi* (about which more later).[21]

The category of opponent (more exactly, of pseudo-donor) in *L'Etape* is also divided, but somewhat differently. The role of principal opponent belongs, as we have seen, to Joseph Monneron: in his political as in his religious convictions, Monneron is the antithesis of Ferrand. There is, however, another character who plays a similar role: the Jewish socialist Crémieu-Dax, a friend of Jean's who is the same age but who for a long time exerted a great influence over Jean's ideas. Crémieu-Dax and Joseph Monneron both possess, but to different degrees, the two negatively valorized traits—republicanism and anticlericalism—that characterize Jean himself at the beginning of his story. In Crémieu-Dax, it is the political side that is emphasized: he is a militant socialist, but even though he is not a Catholic, he does not have strong anticlerical convictions; he is willing, for example, to engage in a dialogue with Abbé Chanut. In Joseph Monneron, on the other hand, the dominant trait is the religious one: he is "fanatically" anticlerical and refuses categorically to have anything to do with priests, whoever they may be; but his radical republican politics don't go as far as socialism—he believes in private property, for example. Semantically, then, Crémieu-Dax and Joseph Monneron are not so much redundant as complementary figures. Both are "negative" when compared to Ferrand, but Crémieu-Dax's negativity is more strongly emphasized along political lines (at least so it appears at first glance), whereas Monneron's is more strongly emphasized in terms of religion. Jean's apprenticeship requires his "liberation" not only from the influence of his father, but also from the complementary influence of his brother-in-arms.

Finally, there is the actantial category of helper. In general, any actor, whether animate or inanimate, who facilitates the hero's progress toward the "right" doctrine belongs to this category. What is less obvious at first glance is that the hero himself can belong to it. All the good qualities of the hero—his intelligence, his powers of observation and interpretation, his desire for the quest, etc.—can be considered as helping elements. It may even happen, in the rare cases of positive apprenticeship where the "true" donor is absent (this is a configuration one finds in Nizan's novels), that the hero succeeds entirely on his own, merely by knowing how to take advantage of exceptional circumstances. Thus the hero of *Aden Arabie* puts his voyage to Aden to good use, since it helps him to understand the "essence" of European capitalism: in Aden he discovers "the significance of European existence, so often hidden by the multitude of actors and the criss-crossing of their destinies" in Europe.[22] This discovery, which transforms him into a Marxist revolutionary, is entirely the result of his own investigations and observations; there is no true donor in *Aden Arabie,* only malevolent fathers who offer the hero images of man that he finds horrifying.[23] Generally, however, the absence of a donor carries with it a serious risk of failure for the hero, as is apparent in Nizan's novels *Antoine Bloyé* and *La Conspiration.* In such cases the hero will need exceptional circumstances and personal qualities (fulfilling the role of helper) in order to end up on the right side.

If we now return to the question of trial by interpretation, we can see that the result of the hero's trials in a given work will be determined by its particular actantial distribution: a hero backed up by a strong donor and/or helper will overcome the trials and accomplish a positive exemplary apprenticeship; a hero lacking in such support will fail to pass the test of interpretation and will accomplish an exemplary negative apprenticeship. The doctrine that founds the novel has, in the positive case, a paradoxical actantial status: it is the object (of knowledge) discovered as a result of the trial, but it is also, and at the same time, a helper, since it is thanks to the doctrine that the hero interprets his situation (or someone else's) correctly. This paradoxical status, which is in fact a logical contradiction, emphasizes the circular aspect of the demonstration: in the *roman à thèse,* one always and only discovers what was already known (even if it was not stated) before one started.

In any case, what we should retain for now is the overdetermined character (redundancy, presence of several actors, including the subject himself, in the positive actantial categories) of the donor and of the helper; this overdetermination is the distinctive actantial trait of a positive exemplary apprenticeship.

Negative Apprenticeships

Since positive and negative apprenticeships are variants of a single structure, we can use one to elucidate the other. This possibility is often exploited by the *roman à thèse* itself, on the level of the story: by juxtaposing two or more apprenticeship stories, each of which realizes one of these variants, the narrative emphasizes the contrast between them and reinforces the positive or negative value of each. The novel then consists in a cluster of apprenticeships, the meaning of each one emerging partly through contrast with the others. There exists an archetypal "folk" version of this kind of construction, in the story of the three brothers who set out to seek their fortune:

one is eaten by wild animals, the second becomes prisoner of an evil magician, while the third kills the dragon that was ravaging the kingdom and obtains as his reward the hand of the king's daughter. The hero's success is defined partly through its contrast with his brothers' failure, and vice versa: the "meaning" of the tale emerges from the antithetical juxtaposition of their stories.

In *romans à thèse* with an apprenticeship structure, this elementary schema of the "antithetical brothers" appears when the novel tells at least two stories with similar characters (not necessarily brothers) as protagonists: starting out from the same situation, the protagonists evolve in contrasting directions. Aragon's *Les Beaux Quartiers,* as we saw in the preceding chapter, realizes the minimal version of this double structure: two stories, two protagonists, two diametrically opposed itineraries. A maximal version can be found in Barrès' trilogy, *Le Roman de l'énergie nationale,* which tells not two apprenticeship stories, but seven: seven young graduates of the *lycée* in Nancy go to make their fortune in Paris, and the trilogy follows the vicissitudes of their individual and collective apprenticeships over a number of years. The multiplication of stories does not affect the fundamental opposition between positive and negative apprenticeships; on the contrary, the opposition is reinforced by the fact that each version is realized by more than one "example." The "positive" stories are related to each other synonymically—in that sense they can be called redundant with each other—and so are the "negative" stories; taken as a whole, however, each group is in a contrary relation to the other group.

L'Etape too can be read as a cluster of apprenticeship stories. Besides Jean Monneron's story, the novel recounts, in more or less detailed fashion, four others, each of which realizes, in its own way, the negative variant of exemplary apprenticeship; the protagonists of these stories are Joseph Monneron, Crémieu-Dax, Julie Monneron (Jean's sister) and Antoine Monneron (Jean's brother). We shall look at all four of them, for they differ in interesting ways; like unhappy families according to Tolstoy, negative exemplary protagonists are more varied than their positive counterparts.

One can derive the syntagmatic and actantial models of such stories deductively, by taking the preceding models and introducing negative signs in the appropriate places. Thus, for the large-scale syntagmatic structure, we obtain the following:

Ignorance ———— Trial(s) ————→ *Non*-knowledge ----------→ *No* "new life"
of truth   *not* surmounted   of truth   in accordance
                                                         with truth

Passivity ---→ *Non*-action
                                                         (inauthentic action)

The subject of a negative exemplary apprenticeship evolves in a morphologically similar, but semantically opposite, direction from the subject of a positive apprenticeship. In both cases, the subject undergoes a transformation over time (without such transformation there would be no story), but whereas the hero[24] succeeds, the negative exemplary subject fails: the former ends up in the euphoric space of the "right" doctrine, the latter does not; the former will live a new life "in accordance with truth," the latter will not. The antithetical relation between these types of subjects is comparable to the relation that A. Jolles has analyzed between the legend and the "anti-legend," the saint and the "anti-saint."[25] The hero, like the saint in the legend according to Jolles, functions essentially as an *imago:* his evolution is to be followed, or imitated, by the reader. The negative subject, by contrast, functions as a cautionary figure: his story shows the reader what one must not do, or be.

As for the actantial configuration, we obtain the following negative transformations: the object—whether it be the protagonist himself in his final incarnation, or an abstract object like a doctrine that the protagonist espouses—is designated as inauthentic, degraded; the benevolent donor is absent or ineffectual, as is the helper; the opponent is present, and over-determined.

Let us see how these models are realized in *L'Etape,* starting with Joseph Monneron and Crémieu-Dax. The son of a poor but ambitious peasant, Joseph Monneron was separated from his family from childhood on. A brilliant scholarship student, he obtained the necessary diplomas for becoming a bourgeois civil servant—a *lycée* professor like the *haut-bourgeois* Ferrand. Being himself the product of the democratic system, "whose spirit is to do away with class differences, give everyone an equal chance at the start, facilitate the individual's rapid rise" (1:26), Joseph Monneron has become an ardent defender of the Republic, which in his eyes represents progress, equality, and justice. At the same time, he has developed a veritable horror for religion, especially the Catholic religion, which for him is synonymous with "the past, with prejudice, with Superstition" (1:90). Crémieu-Dax was also a brilliant student, and he too is a "partisan of 1789." The son of a rich Jewish banker, he has been deeply influenced by the Jewish philosophers Salvador and Darmesteter,[26] especially by their thesis that the history of Israel and the history of post-Revolutionary France are linked by two identical ideas: the belief in "united power and the belief in progress" (1:121–122). The Dreyfus Affair made Crémieu-Dax into a "disciple of Karl Marx" (1:124); he founded a workers' university, *l'Union Tolstoi,* whose aim was to disseminate Marxist ideas and to create an alliance between intellectual and manual workers.

Interestingly enough, both of these stories (which actually take place before the beginning of the novel's main action, and are reported retrospectively by the narrator) contain all the necessary elements of a *positive* exemplary apprenticeship, the only difference being that the ideological supersystem of the novel condemns the ideas and the "selves" of the two protagonists. What Joseph Monneron and Crémieu-Dax consider to be the knowledge of truth is, according to the novel's supersystem, an error (hence, the ultimate form of non-knowledge), and what they consider to be a life in accordance with truth is here designated as its opposite. Monneron and Crémieu-Dax thus realize one of the possible versions of the negative exemplary subject: a protagonist who affirms as true a doctrine that the *given context* rejects as false, but that in a different context (a different novel) might well have a positive value, with a corresponding value attached to both the protagonist and his story. One need but imagine the story of Crémieu-Dax, for example, transplanted to one of Aragon's novels of the 1930s, to see it immediately take on a positive exemplary status.

This type of protagonist corresponds point by point, but in reverse, to the type of positive exemplary protagonist represented by Jean Monneron: like Jean, he lives his life according to explicitly affirmed political or ideological principles; he ends up possessing the "right" doctrine (or what he believes to be so), and he defines his inner being in terms of that doctrine. It is the context alone that endows him with a negative value. The most fully realized version of this type is doubtless to be found in Sartre's *L'Enfance d'un chef,* a totally ironic work whose protagonist, in terms of the context, becomes more and more negative, even as in his own mind he becomes more and more positive. For a number of reasons, including its irony, *L'Enfance d'un chef* poses special problems if one reads it in the perspective of the *roman à thèse.* I shall return to it in detail in my concluding chapter.

There exists another, less frequently encountered but equally interesting type of negative exemplary subject: the protagonist who never attains political or ideological consciousness, and whose life consequently unfolds without his being aware of where it is going. Whereas the first type ends up with false knowledge or error (according to the work's supersystem), this second type—whom we meet in Nizan's *Antoine Bloyé,* for example—ends up merely with an absence of knowledge, a kind of somnolence. Antoine Bloyé lives his life without ever understanding the system ("the social machine," as the omniscient narrator puts it) that regulates it. His apprenticeship is a failure, because he does not learn what he should have learned, but what the reader presumably learns in his stead: the horror of the capitalist system and the necessity for class struggle.

Antoine differs sufficiently from Joseph Monneron and Crémieu-Dax to constitute a separate type. In both cases, however, it is theoretically possible to envisage a "conversion," or the protagonist's sudden discovery of the "right" doctrine. Any negative apprenticeship has the potential for being converted into a positive one, even if only at the eleventh hour. However, the "last-minute conversion" is fully realizable only in the Catholic *roman à thèse*. One understands why if one compares *Antoine Bloyé* to Mauriac's *Le Noeud de vipères*, for example. Nizan's protagonist recognizes, before he dies, the nullity of his existence ("This life which was not life"),[27] and realizes at the same time that he had always "obscurely known" that "genuine union, a union that was already a challenge to solitude, that already swept away the dust of bourgeois life, was the union of workers."[28] One could interpret this final recognition as a last-minute conversion to Marxism—but if conversion there is, the main point about it is that it comes too late. Antoine's belated knowledge—which in any case remains "obscure" and is always filtered through the narrator's commentary—serves at best to *confirm*, not to change, the negative exemplary value of his story; it makes the character of Antoine more appealing, it surrounds him with a pathetic, perhaps even a tragic aura—but it changes nothing. According to Nizan's Marxist and existentialist perspective, the "lesson"—as well as the tragedy—of Antoine's story lies precisely in the fact that no man can start his life over at the end: if self-knowledge comes too late, it merely seals the verdict of an unlived life. In the Catholic perspective of Mauriac, on the other hand, a last-minute conversion can totally transform the meaning of a life—and of a story—as well as the exemplary value of its protagonist, since the recognition of truth, no matter how belated, opens the way to a new life after death. The negative protagonist of *le Noeud de vipères* discovers God at the very moment of his death, but this discovery is enough to transform him into a positive exemplary figure, and to transform his story, despite its somber cast, into an edifying tale.

Returning to *L'Etape,* we note that Jean's story involves a similar reversal, with the difference that it does not take place at the last minute. Since Jean's positive apprenticeship begins precisely at the point where Joseph Monneron's and Crémieu-Dax's end, we could summarize his "prehistory" (i.e., before the action of the novel begins) in exactly the same terms as the two others. That is why Jean's story realizes the "strong" version of a positive exemplary apprenticeship, where the hero starts out from a position of error, not from one of mere ignorance. But as a matter of fact *L'Etape* cheats a bit on that point, for even though we are repeatedly *told* that Jean shared for a long time the ideas of his father and his friend, by the time the novel begins he is already extremely critical of those ideas. What we *see* of his evolution—in contrast to what the narrator and Jean himself *say* about it—is not a movement from error to truth, but rather a movement from the awareness of truth to its explicit affirmation. This weakens somewhat the demonstrative force of the novel, since the transformation that is *shown* is not as spectacular as the transformation that is *told.* It may perhaps have been too difficult to motivate, with sufficient plausibility, such a radical transformation in a short period of time (the action of the novel takes place in less than two weeks); or perhaps Bourget did not want to take the risk of having his hero affirm any "wrong" ideas, even as a start and even if he was to reject them later. This is an interesting technical problem, which concerns the novelist's choice of devices for presenting the story. As concerns the "stuff" of the story itself, however, we can maintain our observation that Jean's positive apprenticeship follows upon an earlier negative one, and that this kind of succession is always possible. One can even imagine a novel that would consist in a whole series of negative apprenticeships for a single protagonist, followed at last by a positive one.

What seems less likely is that a positive apprenticeship will be followed by its opposite. Once the truth has been found, it is inadmissible, in the "exemplary" world of the *roman à thèse*, that it be abandoned in favor of error. We find a subtle confirmation of this in Nizan's *La Conspiration*, in the character of Pluvinage. Pluvinage, the only one of the novel's adolescent protagonists who becomes a member of the Communist Party—the only one, consequently, who fully possesses the truth in terms of the novel's ideological supersystem—ends up betraying his comrades and joining the Parisian police as an informer. His story thus seems to contradict the above rule of succession. However, *despite his betrayal*—which is motivated in the novel on psychological grounds—Pluvinage does not succeed in rejecting the revolutionary ideas he formerly espoused. In the "confession" he writes to one of his former friends (who is not a Communist) shortly after becoming a police informer, he asks himself: "Will I have to believe from now on, in order not to lose hope in myself, that capitalism is an eternal order, capable of sanctifying like a God all the betrayals men commit in its name?" To which he immediately replies: "It is painful to think that the Communists *were right*, that I have betrayed not only men I detested, but *truth* and *hope* as well."[29] Even though he has definitely abandoned the "right" doctrine, Pluvinage cannot help proclaiming its truth. Here, as elsewhere in Nizan's novels, we find an unusual but nevertheless consistent realization of the "rules of the genre."

Naturally, there is a third possibility: that in which a negative exemplary apprenticeship is not followed by any conversion, despite the opportunities that present themselves. The story will then be one of persistence in error, or refusal to recognize the truth. This schema is precisely the one that is realized by the diegetic (i.e., unfolding *during* the fictional time, not reported retrospectively) stories of Joseph Monneron and Crémieu-Dax. It is by their stubborn adherence to the "wrong" doctrine that these two characters are most clearly distinguished from the positive exemplary character, Jean.

Crémieu-Dax's diegetic story, which fits into the overall action of the novel as a subplot, takes place chiefly in the setting of *L'Union Tolstoi,* the workers' university that is Crémieu-Dax's brainchild. (The link with Jean's story is that until the very end of the novel Jean is on the governing board of this organization). After an internal crisis precipitated by one of the working-class members of the board—who leads a demonstration to stop the socialist priest Abbé Chanut from speaking at a lecture organized by Crémieu-Dax—*l'Union Tolstoi* falls apart, thus revealing, according to the narrator, "the madness of the whole idea" (2:141). The pandemonium created at the lecture shows, again according to the narrator, "the savage state that awaits our unhappy country, if ever the infantile doctrines of socialism triumph here—that of an insane asylum without any guards." The lesson to be drawn from this spectacle confirms what the narrator had already stated earlier: *l'Union Tolstoi* was a "criminally antisocial" enterprise (2:110), which must not be resumed. This is precisely the lesson that Jean draws from it: on the morning after the break-up, which is also the morning after his religious conversion, he resigns from the board and advises Crémieu-Dax to abandon the project (2:235). Crémieu-Dax, however, does not see things the same way: "the lamentable collapse of his workers' university had not discouraged that idealist. He was already busily at work reconstituting his board" (2:234). If we consider the episode of the collapse of *l'Union Tolstoi* as a trial by interpretation, we can see that the positive protagonist differs from the negative one as the right interpretation differs from the wrong one.

This opposition appears even more clearly in Joseph Monneron's diegetic story, which consists essentially in this: Monneron discovers, after having been totally unaware of what was going on, the disgrace of his daughter Julie (seduced by a young unprincipled aristocrat—who just happens to be another member of the governing board of *l'Union Tolstoi!*—Julie is pregnant and will give birth to an illegitimate child) and the criminal activities of his elder son Antoine (to satisfy his *demi-mondaine* mistress and his own love of luxury, Antoine has embezzled funds from the bank in which he was employed). Jean too has discovered these calamities, and he draws the following conclusion from them: if Julie and Antoine have turned out so badly, it was not only because of their own weakness of character, but above all because they lacked the religious principles and the family traditions that would have checked them in their course. Through his too rapid rise in society, itself the product of democracy, Joseph Monneron made of these two children, as of his whole family, "transplanted and uprooted individuals"—*des transplantés, des déracinés* (2:180).[30] By depriving them at the same time of religion—by replacing God with the abstract notions of Reason and Justice—Monneron had made them incapable of resisting the least temptation. In a word, Antoine and Julie have been victims of the ideology of their father. This interpretation—which, in the economy of the novel, is the "right" one—is founded on an axiom formulated by Ferrand at the very beginning of the novel and developed at the end by the narrator: "Le malheur démontre l'idée fausse, comme la maladie la mauvaise hygiène" (1:55; 2:199–201). Julie's and Antoine's misfortunes, like illnesses that "prove" the lack of hygiene, are so many proofs that their father's republican and anticlerical ideas are wrong—and above all harmful.[31]

To this interpretation, Joseph Monneron opposes his own. According to him, Antoine and Julie are ungrateful and depraved children, who despite an irreproachable upbringing have ended up dishonoring their father (2:181). Monneron rejects the theory of *déracinement* as "good for casuists and Jesuits" (2:182), reaffirms his belief in democracy and reason, and categorically refuses the axiom on which Jean's interpretation is founded. The father, in other words, fails the test of interpretation that the son passes with flying colors. He persists in his "errors," whereas Jean renounces his.

Now it is quite evident that logically, Joseph Monneron is not wrong. The axiom that founds Jean's interpretation—"misfortune is the proof of false ideas"—is not proven. On the contrary, it is based on reasoning by analogy, a purely rhetorical kind of reasoning characteristic of the *exemplum*. In *L'Etape,* however, this axiom functions as a founding proposition, stated not only by the benevolent donor Ferrand, but also by the "voice of Truth" belonging to the omniscient narrator.[32] Against these two dominant voices, which Jean himself echoes, Joseph Monneron's voice does not stand a chance. Despite a situation that appears ostensibly dialogical (father and son confront each other and exchange arguments), genuine dialogism is repressed in favor of a monologism that assigns, *in the dialogue itself*, a positive or negative value to each of the participants. Joseph Monneron, like Crémieu-Dax, is the spokesman of a false doctrine. On the axis of *being* vs. *seeming*, Monneron and Crémieu-Dax always find themselves, by definition as it were, on the side of *seeming*.

This is evident if one analyzes their stories in terms of their actantial configurations. A negative exemplary apprenticeship, as I have suggested, involves the presence of an inauthentic or degraded object and a strong opponent, with the roles of donor and helper reduced or absent. But this definition is already formulated in terms of the "right" perspective (*being*); in terms of the wrong perspective, or of *seeming*, which is the perspective of the negative protagonists themselves, the actantial configuration can appear very different. Joseph Monneron's story, for example, has an actantial configuration which, as seen by Monneron himself, is positive: the subject-receiver (Monneron) comes into possession of an authentic object (the "right" doctrine on the one hand; the definition of himself as a republican and anticlerical on the other), thanks to his own intelligence (helper), thanks to his ambitious father (benevolent donor) and above all thanks to "the State, as it was created for us by the Revolution" (1:26—benevolent donor). As seen by the narrator and his fictional representatives, however, this same configuration is negative: by abdicating the religion of his ancestors, Joseph Monneron turned his intelligence and his will "against his race" (1:26), adopting a position of radical alienation in relation to it. Since according to the ideological supersystem of *L'Etape* the only way to acquire an authentic being is by "prolonging one's race," it follows that those who made Joseph Monneron's evolution possible acted not as genuine donors but as pseudo-donors. In the complex actant of this pseudo-donor, we find the same role that Joseph Monneron himself plays in Jean's story. But the father's story differs in two important ways from the son's: first, it lacks the presence of a genuine donor to offset the influence of the pseudo-donor—there is no figure analogous to Ferrand; second, in Jean's story the pseudo-donor is recognized as such and repudiated by the subject, whereas in Joseph Monneron's he is not—Monneron considers the "State created by the Revolution" as his permanent benefactor.

A negative exemplary apprenticeship consists above all in a failure of the interpretive faculty—in a word, in a failure of intelligence. Rather than being contradicted, this conclusion is reinforced by the fact that Joseph Monneron is presented throughout the novel as an intelligent man; in his case, the failure of intelligence consists in a voluntary blindness—or more exactly, in the perversion of genuine intelligence by opposing forces that come both from external circumstances and from his own will. According to the wise Ferrand, Monneron "not only does not see life, but does not want to see it, because reality would appear too harsh to him" (1:48). This suggests that the opponent in a negative exemplary apprenticeship cannot be reduced to something exterior to the subject; it is also internal, a part of the subject himself. This overdetermined opponent is the counterpart to the overdetermined helper that characterizes a positive exemplary apprenticeship.

Crémieu-Dax's story brings an interesting variation to the actantial structure and to the difference between *being* and *seeming*. We may recall that the role of donor in his story is fulfilled, according to Crémieu-Dax himself, by the Jewish philosophers Salvador and Darmesteter, who sustained the thesis that there existed a continuity of thought between biblical Israel and post-Revolutionary France. Now in contrast to Monneron's case, this donor is *not* a pseudo-donor in the perspective of *being*. On the contrary, the narrator affirms that by following this theory Crémieu-Dax is "entirely consistent with his Jewish origins" (1:132). Being a *dreyfusard* and a Marxist as

well (reactionary writers, even today, rarely neglect to mention
or to insinuate that Marx too was a "Jewish philosopher"),
Crémieu-Dax is triply marked as belonging to the "Jewish
race," which he "consistently" prolongs. According to the criterion of authenticity proposed by the novel's own supersystem (authenticity equals continuity with one's race), Crémieu-
Dax's self as object is altogether authentic; in that respect the
actantial configuration of his story seems to conform to a positive exemplary model. To say this, however, is to overlook a
crucial fact—namely, that all of Crémieu-Dax's story is marked
by the sign of "non-Frenchness." The very fact of being an
authentic Jew makes him, according to the work's supersystem, an inauthentic Frenchman, a *foreigner*.[33] This means that,
for a French reader, Crémieu-Dax's exemplarity can only be
negative. Bourget, to his credit (and unlike some of his contemporaries and fellow reactionaries, from Barrès all the way
down to Drumont, the author of the infamous *La France Juive*)
does not insist on this too much: he even treats Crémieu-Dax
with a certain sympathy, and endows him with qualities of intelligence and sincerity. This merely puts into sharper focus,
however, the fundamental opposition, the unbridgeable difference, between Crémieu-Dax's "race" and that of a "real
Frenchman" like Jean. The final break between the two friends
(provoked in fact by Crémieu-Dax, after he learns of Jean's
conversion) makes this difference explicit and relegates Crè-
mieu-Dax forever on the side of "those who are not saved."

I have hardly spoken until now about the other two negative exemplary subjects in *L'Etape:* Antoine and Julie. At first
glance it would appear that their stories do not lend themselves
to a reading in terms of the structure of apprenticeship,
whether in its positive or negative version. Syntagmatically, Julie's story realizes the narrative cliché of "seduction and betrayal," whereas Antoine's realizes the narrative cliché of "the
ungrateful son, dishonoring his father." Indeed, the principal
function of their stories (which are developed at some length—
Julie's takes up more than one third of the novel) seems to be
to furnish one of the necessary elements for Jean's apprentice-

ship. It is significant that Jean's actual moment of conversion, indicated by the fact that he falls on his knees and prays for the first time, takes place at Julie's bedside after she has tried to commit suicide (2:160–165).

Still, we can bring the apprenticeship model into play by considering Antoine's and Julie's experiences as failures of interpretation. Julie succumbs to her seducer Rumesnil when he promises to marry her because she does not possess the moral convictions that would prevent her, but also because she does not understand her own situation well enough to realize that Rumesnil is lying; furthermore, even after Rumesnil abandons her and she faces total disgrace, she does not give up "the prideful nihilism of her father's upbringing" (2:165)—which means that she does not follow Jean's example and convert. As for Antoine, his actions are founded on a consistent interpretation of his situation, but a perverse one: having understood that the only equality offered by the democracy so highly prized by his father is that of universal (male) suffrage, he decides to take by means of theft and blackmail the share of riches he considers as his due; thus he tells Jean, defiantly: "I'm a pleasure-seeker and an *arriviste,* that's all, and I'll succeed, any way I can, but I'll succeed . . ." (1:219). Antoine even interprets Jean's love for Brigitte Ferrand in perverse terms: he insinuates that what interests Jean about her is her "petit magot"—her inheritance (1:220).

The actantial configurations of Julie's and Antoine's stories also conform to the model of a negative exemplary apprenticeship: absence of a benevolent donor (neither Julie nor Antoine is influenced by a character homologous to Ferrand); presence of the pseudo-donor (Joseph Monneron and the seducer Rumesnil in Julie's story; Joseph Monneron and "Monsieur de Montboron," the *nom de guerre* adopted by Antoine himself, in Antoine's story); overdetermination of the opponent (Julie and Antoine are intellectually and emotionally their own worst enemies); and finally, the presence of a degraded object. The degraded nature of the object (their own selves) attained by Antoine and Julie is indicated by the culturally negative labels that the narrator attaches to them: Julie is designated as a "seduced girl" (*fille séduite*) and an "unwed mother" (*fille-mère*), Antoine as a "thief," "forgerer," and "blackmailer" (*voleur, faussaire, maître-chanteur*).

Indeed, the negative exemplary significance of these two characters is wholly summed up by these designations; simply by naming them, the text elicits a negative reaction, a refusal to imitate on the part of the reader. Of course, the negative force of such labels depends on the cultural taboos of a given period; and, on the other hand, one can imagine a novel in which culturally negative designations such as "unwed mother" might be neutralized, or even endowed with a positive value. In such a case, however, the value system of the novel would have to affirm itself in explicit opposition to the dominant cultural values of the period, which is not at all the case here. On the contrary, *L'Etape* exploits the culturally negative connotations of the labels attached to Julie and Antoine, just as *Les Beaux Quartiers* exploits the negative connotations of the label attached to Edmond Barbentane: "a gigolo."

Culturally negative designations are among the clearest ways of defining the value of a fictional character (provided, of course, that the negative connotations be understood as such by the reader), which doubtless explains the frequency of such designations in the *roman à thèse*. A negative exemplary protagonist who ends up in a culturally reproved position functions as an elementary symbol whose meaning is immediately apparent: to become a gigolo, a blackmailer, an unwed mother, or a murderer (like Racadot and Mouchefrin in *Les Déracinés*) is *in any case* a negative destiny. The strategy of the *roman thèse* is to link such destinies to an ideological subtext, by postulating—either explicitly or implicitly—a relation of cause and effect between certain beliefs, or the absence of certain beliefs, and the character's negative destiny. In *L'Etape*, Antoine and Julie "prove" by their misfortunes the nefariousness of their father's progressist doctrines; similarly in *Les Déracinés*, the brutal murder committed by Racadot and Mouchefrin supposedly demonstrates the destructive ("uprooting") influence of the pseudo-donor Bouteiller, their one-time teacher who functions in the novel as a representative of the new parliamentary State. In such stories, the reader is called on to judge by its results, as it were, the doctrine whose falseness the novel seeks to demonstrate. Characters like Bouteiller or Joseph Monneron *proclaim* the false doctrine, which in their mouths may actually appear attractive: it is only the ideological (and monological) context of the novel that endows them with negative value. Antoine and Julie, or Racadot and Mouchefrin, on the other hand, do not (or do not only) proclaim the false doctrine—they *incarnate* it. That is what makes them into elementary symbols, as if the text had merely to name them, merely to point to them, to make the reader see how dangerous "wrong" ideas can be.

If we attempt to systematize the various types of negative exemplary protagonists we have been discussing, we can define them in terms of three pairs of variables:

1. negative valorization of the object attained (the protagonist's self at the end of the story): solely contextual vs. contextual *and* cultural. *Example:* Joseph Monneron vs. Antoine Monneron.
2. conscious espousal of a "wrong" doctrine by the protagonist vs. indifference or lack of doctrinal awareness. *Example:* Joseph Monneron or Crémieu-Dax vs. Antoine Bloyé.
3. recognition of his own "negativity" on the part of the protagonist (extreme case: conversion) vs. non-recognition. *Example:* Antoine Bloyé vs. Julie Monneron.

According to the distribution of these variables in a given character, we obtain negative protagonists who are more or less likable, more or less pathetic or tragic or despicable. Antoine Monneron and Edmond Barbentane, for example, realize what might be called the "scoundrelly" type: they are contextually *and* culturally negative (gigolo, blackmailer), indifferent to doctrinal or ideological questions (Antoine and Edmond make no attempt to reflect on the world, they merely exploit it for their own advancement), and they at no point recognize their own negativity. Antoine Bloyé realizes the pathetic type: he is negatively valorized only by the context, has no ideological awareness, recognizes his own negativity, but too late to make any difference; Joseph Monneron, the tragic type: negatively valorized only by the context, espouses the "wrong" doctrine, willfully blinds himself to his own negativity; finally, the protagonist of *Le Noeud de vipères* manifests the extreme case of a negative exemplary subject who is transformed at the last minute into a positive one.[34]

With the exception of this last type, we can say that all of the negative exemplary subjects, whatever their exact profile, bear witness to what a theological discourse would call the power of evil. Whether they end up as victims or criminals, dupes, charlatans, or false prophets, whether they elicit pity or scorn, negative exemplary subjects are opposed to positive exemplary ones as falsehood is opposed to truth. One thinks of Dante's hell, inhabited by so many attractive sinners who nevertheless bear witness, like the others, to the action of Lucifer. Where judgment of right or wrong is concerned, the law of the *roman à thèse* is hardly less categorical than the law that reigns over the nether and the upper worlds in an allegorical universe.

Chapter 3 The Structure of Confrontation

They were living in a torn, divided world that
consisted, like the backgrounds of medieval paintings,
of celestial divisions and infernal partitions, of a
struggle between heaven and hell.

Nizan, *Le Cheval de Troie*

Political animals? Yes, indeed, certainly, political
animals above all. But we must look fearlessly and
without too much disgust at what that means. It means:
animals determined to liquidate their adversaries.

Michel Serres[1]

THE ABOVE epigraphs define quite precisely, albeit from different perspectives, the type of story I call "confrontational" or "antagonistic." Nizan speaks about it from the inside: his commentary functions as an authorial gloss, a kind of metacommentary, on the story told in *Le Cheval de Troie*. A story of this type is always, in the last resort, that of a "struggle between heaven and hell." The *roman à thèse* assumes this Manichean view and prides itself on it, like the revolutionary character in Malraux's *L'Espoir* who affirms that "Every revolutionary is a born Manichean—as is every political man."

Michel Serres, on the other hand, is speaking from the outside. His statement can be read as a critique of confrontational behavior, and hence of Manicheanism of any kind.

Why did I choose to juxtapose these opposing perspectives? In order to warn the reader that despite my avowed desire for "neutrality"—since my aim here is not to pronounce value judgments but to attempt a description, which must precede any evaluation—despite my desire for neutrality, my descriptive discourse will no doubt alternate between a blind inside and a hostile outside, between apology and indictment. Such, at any rate, is the permanent risk it faces. If ideologically neutral description is always a (critical) fiction, it is doubly so when the object described is itself as ideologically polarized as the *roman à thèse*.

This need not stop us, however. Forewarned and armed with suspicion, let us forge ahead and . . . describe.

History as Myth: Nizan's *Le Cheval de Troie*

The *roman à thèse* is not the only narrative genre that realizes the structure of confrontation. Any narrative having as its hero a "man of the law" or a righter of wrongs, whether his name is the Lone Ranger or Prince Rodolphe,[2] as well as any story of a "holy war" or a war of national defense (and here one thinks of a Christian epic like the *Song of Roland*, but also of a novel like *War and Peace*) realizes this structure at least in part. Here again, the specificity of the *roman à thèse* resides not in a particular narrative structure, but in the contents with which the structure is invested and in the mode of discourse that appropriates it.

Before studying this specificity, let us consider for a moment a story of confrontation in its most general form. It is the story of a struggle, or of a series of struggles, between two adversaries who are not on the same ethical or moral plane—whose conflict, for that reason, cannot be considered as simply a question of prestige or glory. The antagonistic hero fights, in the name of certain values, against an enemy who is defined as such by the fact that his values are diametrically opposed to those of the hero. In a very general way, then, we may define a story of confrontation or of "holy war" as a conflict between two forces, one of which (the hero's) is identified as the force of good, and the other as the force of evil. Such a conflict can take the form of physical battle, and that is its most common version; but it can also take the form of a legal or judicial battle (as in Zola's *Vérité*, which is a fictional "retelling" of the Dreyfus Affair), of a parliamentary confrontation (as in Barrès' *Leurs Figures*, which I shall discuss later), of a struggle between striking workers and their bosses (as in *Germinal*, or in Aragon's *Les Cloches de Bâle*), or of any confrontation in which values other than that of mere personal advancement or glory are at stake.

It is worth noting that the antagonistic model thus defined is altogether different from the model of "agonistic" conflict described by Huizinga in *Homo Ludens*. According to Huizinga, war can be considered as a playful or ludic activity, even if it leads to the death of the combatants, as long as it "takes place in a circle whose members regard each other as equals, or antagonists with equal rights."[3] In an antagonistic struggle as I am using the term, this equality in right is precisely what is *not* recognized: the antagonistic hero does not fight in order to achieve "glory," either for himself or for the group to which he belongs; he fights for truth, justice, freedom, or his fatherland—in a word, for transcendental and absolute values. In such a case, war has a moral purport, and as Huizinga remarks: "It is the *moral* content of an action that makes it serious. When the combat has an ethical value, it ceases to be play."[4] In an antagonistic conflict, the pleasure of play—which, *pace* Huizinga, does not exclude seriousness, but in which it is the game itself that is "taken seriously," rather than what is at stake in the game—has no place.

In what follows I shall use Nizan's *Le Cheval de Troie* (1935) as my principal work of reference, not only because it presents a particularly "pure" version of the structure of confrontation in the *roman à thèse*, but also for historical reasons. If the traumatic event that lies behind, and in a sense explains, *L'Etape* is the Dreyfus Affair, the event that fulfills a similar role in *Le Cheval de Troie* is February 6, 1934, when it looked for a brief moment as if the parliamentary regime of the Third Republic might be toppled by its right-wing enemies. Today, historians generally agree that February 6 was less an attempt to seize power by the Right than a spontaneous "demonstration of anger against parliamentary corruption and ineffectiveness."[5] Following closely upon the Stavisky scandal, itself the latest in a long series, the riots of February 6 were a momentary outburst with no real chance of being converted into a *coup d'état*. Nevertheless, they were not without lasting effect on the political life of the country. The Left saw in the riots "the face of fascism as it knew it in Italy and Germany."[6] The Right saw in them the beginning of "social nationalism in our country."[7] The birth of the Popular Front as the union of antifascist forces can be traced to February 6; so can the general exacerbation of the ideological divisions between Left and Right, divisions which at times manifested themselves in physical encounters and street-fighting. If one adds to this the fact that France was in the middle of a grave economic crisis with an alarming number of unemployed and no foreseeable upturn (as well as the fact that some of the right-wing organizations were receiving regular subsidies from private banks and even from the government),[8] then one begins to see the possibilities offered by the structure of confrontation to a Communist novelist in 1935.

Le Cheval de Troie—The Trojan Horse: that title is somewhat paradoxical, since the war it evokes is known to us through a poem whose spirit is altogether different from that of Nizan's novel. The *Iliad* is a consummate realization of an "agonistic" war story in Huizinga's terms: Homer's noble warriors, whether Trojan or Greek, worship the same gods, share the same values—and all of them recognize this fact. Hector's corpse is no less worthy of a solemn funeral than that of Patroclus. The world of the *Iliad* is not the Manichean world that Nizan speaks of; it is a world without villains.

In *Le Cheval de Troie,* on the other hand, there are villains—and heroes as well. If we wanted to find an epic intertext for Nizan's title, we should have to look in Virgil rather than Homer—specifically in Book Two of the *Aeneid,* where Aeneas tells the story of the last days of Troy. The Trojan war, as seen by Aeneas, is a war of national defense—in other words, a holy war. But there too there is a slight contradiction, for in Virgil it is the "villains" who employ the stratagem of the horse whereas in Nizan's novel the horse serves as a symbol for the clandestine war that the revolutionary workers wage against the repressive bourgeois society in which they live. Nizan's title, then, evokes not so much an earlier *text* relative to the Trojan war, but rather the principal aspect of that war as a historical (?) event: the annihilation of a city and a culture by an enemy striking from within.[9]

Le Cheval de Troie tells a story set in a small city in the center of France in the summer of 1934. The central event is a street battle between the working-class population led by the Communists, and a group of fascist demonstrators who "invade" the city for a mass meeting. The fascists disband rather quickly and are replaced by the police and the armed and helmeted national guard. A Communist is killed; the workers are driven back to their own neighborhood and dispersed. But the Communists, who organized and led the battle, regroup in private and vow to continue the fight for human freedom and dignity. The war they are waging is a long one, but worth fighting and dying in: they are helping a new world to be born.

Of course this summary, like all summaries, is reductive and designed to make a point. But anyone who has read the novel will, I think, agree that I have not distorted its "message." The elements I have left out (notably the episodes involving Lange, and the death of Catherine) can be shown to reinforce the message rather than contradict it. If one may invoke the old comparison between a novel and a symphony, then this one has a very clear melodic line and virtually no discords in its harmonies.

A fuller reading will emerge in the process of constructing our model. I shall discuss the status of the hero, the large-scale syntagmatic structure, and the actantial configuration.

The Antagonistic Hero

The pertinent characteristics of the hero in a *roman à thèse* that realizes the structure of confrontation in its "pure" form are the following: he espouses, from the beginning, the values defined as good, and is ready to expound on them; he represents, or is part of, a group that fights for the triumph of those values; and as far as his adherence to those values is concerned—that is, in terms of his most fundamental outlook on life—he does not change in the course of the battle. The antagonistic hero—and I use the term "hero" in its strong sense, since the protagonist in a story of confrontation is always positively valorized—is barely an individual, if by an individual one means a character whose destiny is important because it is the destiny of that *particular character* and not of someone else. In the case of the antagonistic hero, individual destiny tends to merge with a collective one: it is as the representative and spokesman of a group that the hero elicits our interest.

I should note that the hero thus defined (as the representative of a group) is not identical to the "typical" hero envisaged by Lukács and some other Marxist critics. According to Lukács, the "typical" hero found in Balzac or Tolstoy, for example (and generally in great realistic fiction), is an individual who sums up, most often without knowing it, the aspirations and the contradictions of a social group (or more exactly of a social class) at a given historical moment. The antagonistic hero is not "typical" in this sense; rather, he is the conscious representative of a group whose values he expresses and with which he identifies himself. It is his identification with the group that allows the hero to be only minimally individualized. Even if he bears a proper name that sets him apart, the antagonistic hero tends to merge into the anonymity (and unanimity) of the heroic group.

This becomes quite clear if one looks at the Communist characters of *Le Cheval de Troie*. Although they are named and are endowed with different physical traits and different personal histories, the overall effect when one watches their actions or hears them speak or "overhears" their thoughts through the narrator's commentaries is that they are interchangeable. Toward the beginning of the novel, for example, when the group begins to discuss the possibility of organizing a confrontation with the fascists, one of the characters says: "If we organize a counter-demonstration, they'll call in the National Guard, and with those creeps . . ." to which another replies: "It would really be too bad to die before the revolution." Then the narrator comments: "Everything seemed to them to be just beginning . . . France, where workers were not often killed in the streets, was becoming a country like the others, where it was possible to die other than through illness, or an accident or a crime—to be simply killed. That was the thought they had."[10] Not only do the characters merge into a single "thought," but the narrator himself espouses that thought in reporting it. Individual differences in interpretation and judgment, whether among the characters or between the characters and the narrator, are eliminated in favor of unanimity. The members of the group merge into a single collective hero. And since the omniscient narrator shows himself from the beginning to be someone who shares their fears and their aspirations, his commentaries underline the unanimous (in a hostile perspective one would say totalitarian) character of the group whose story he is telling.

The intellectual in the group, Pierre Bloyé, might appear to constitute an exception, since we see more of him and know more about his inner world than about the others. Bloyé is a *lycée* professor, a graduate of the Ecole Normale Supérieure, who has renounced his bourgeois background (he is in fact the son of Antoine Bloyé)—in other words, he has gone through a positive exemplary apprenticeship. But by the time the story begins, Bloyé's apprenticeship is far behind him; it is part of his past history, and is merely evoked retrospectively by the narrator: "It had taken him years to rid himself of the manners and customs of that world of screens and dodges from which he had started out; he had had to reverse the direction of his thought, but now it was done; his comrades thought of him as one of them" (p. 135). Bloyé's "reversal of thought" (a notion that, from a post-Stalinist perspective, appears somewhat sinister—but Nizan was writing in less disenchanted days) has made him into a "comrade" like the others. The whole point of this retrospective evocation is to reinforce Bloyé's nonindividuality, his merger with the heroic group. By the time the action of the novel begins Bloyé *is* a Communist militant, and neither his vision of the world nor his way of acting in the world will change in the course of the narrative.

If Bloyé's personal evolution shows that the antagonistic hero is the logical and chronological successor to the hero of a positive exemplary apprenticeship, it also points to the principal trait that distinguishes the former from the latter: the antagonistic hero does not *become*, he *is*. This does not mean, of course, that nothing "happens" to him—if that were the case, he would have no story and there would be no story to tell. It does mean that this type of character does not undergo a transformation in his way of seeing or acting in the world. If he asks himself questions, they concern the means of his action, not its essential nature or its ends.

One might wish to argue that the tendency to merge the individual with the group is specific to the Communist novel. In *Le Cheval de Troie,* the opposition between individualism and collective action is thematized as the opposition between bourgeois solitude and working-class solidarity. Opposed to Bloyé is the nihilist intellectual Lange, who is always alone and in despair, obsessed by death. Lange, who was Bloyé's classmate at the Ecole Normale, functions as an "antithetical brother" in relation to Bloyé. On the day of the battle, he finally joins a straggling group of fascist demonstrators, but is not the less solitary for all that. His nihilism and his solitude are presented as the negative counterpart to Communist solidarity.

One finds the same opposition in Aragon's *Les Beaux Quartiers,* published a year after *Le Cheval de Troie.* One of the fundamental differences between Edmond and Armand Barbentane is that the former chooses "la maison individuelle," the private villa that stands as a metonym for bourgeois individualism, whereas Armand chooses the "Maison des Syndicats," the meeting hall of the striking workers which stands for solidarity and class struggle. Indeed, Armand's next appearance will be in the multi-volume novel *Les Communistes* (whose title already indicates a collective protagonist), where he appears from the beginning as an antagonistic hero.

If the Communist novel seems especially predisposed to merging the individual with the heroic group, this tendency is nevertheless not limited to it. Although it may be more or less emphasized in a given work, it is part of the structure of confrontation, and as such is not linked to a specific doctrine. Thus, even a writer as narcissistic—and right-wing—as Drieu La Rochelle conforms to the model as soon as he begins to tell a story of confrontation.[11] In the Epilogue to *Gilles* (1939), which up to that point is a story of apprenticeship, we find the hero, Gilles, in Spain at the beginning of the Spanish Civil War, transformed into a man of action; his transformation is so radical that he now even has a new name, Walter. This solitary, weak-willed, misunderstood young man, whose apparently aimless itinerary we have followed for hundreds of pages,[12] is suddenly presented as a militant ideologue ("Il vivait une idée"—"He was living an idea") and as the member not of one but of two heroic groups. On the one hand, he considers as "his own" all those fighting on the side of Franco; on the other hand, he claims to belong to "a new military and religious order founded somewhere in the world and working, in the face of all odds, for the reconciliation of the Church and of fascism, and their double triumph in Europe."[13] The existence of this mythical "order" may seem unlikely, just as Gilles' metamorphosis into Walter may appear less than convincing. But that is beside the point. Indeed, the very unlikeliness of the story shows how strong are the constraints imposed by the structure of confrontation (or by any structure for that matter). The choice of turning Gilles into an antagonistic hero necessarily entails another: he must belong to an "order," no matter how mythical—an order that he represents, that transcends him as an individual, and for whose values he fights.

As for the fact that the hero does not fundamentally change in the course of the conflict, that too is part of the logic of confrontation. A major change would involve a change in beliefs or values, but it is precisely in order to affirm certain absolute values, defined *a priori* as good, that the hero fights. Were he to question them, or to stop fighting for them, that would threaten their unproblematic status as right or good. As far as the struggle and the reasons for the struggle are concerned, the hero must therefore not change. There exists, of course, the possibility of a false hero, or traitor: a character who, like Ganelon in the *Song of Roland*, pretends to represent the heroic group but seizes the first opportunity to betray it. In that case, however, we are dealing precisely with a *false* hero, whose very betrayal emphasizes the fidelity—the unchanging and unconditional loyalty—of the true hero (or heroes).

It should be noted, however, that the criterion of non-transformation, or steadfastness, applies only to the structure of confrontation. In a novel like *Gilles,* where the story of confrontation is preceded by an apprenticeship story having the same protagonist, the latter evidently changes over time—but his personal evolution ends where his activity as a militant begins. A more interesting, because more complicated, case occurs in novels where the apprenticeship story and the confrontation story unfold not consecutively, but simultaneously. That is what happens in Malraux's *L'Espoir* (1937), where one of the main characters, Manuel, functions as the protagonist of two stories that are analytically distinct even though they unfold at the same time and are hierarchically linked to each other: on the one hand, a story of confrontation—the war between the Republicans and Franco's forces in Spain; on the other hand, a story of positive apprenticeship focusing on Manuel's personal evolution in the course of the war.

Now, *as a protagonist of the confrontation story,* Manuel does not change: at the beginning as at the end, he is one combatant among others fighting for the triumph of the Republican cause, and for the values of dignity and social justice the latter represents. In terms of his espousal of these values and of his reasons for fighting, Manuel is consistent from beginning to end; in this he resembles the other characters who form part of the heroic group: Garcia, Magnin and the aviators, Hein-

rich and the International Brigades, "le Négus" and the anarchists, and so on.

At the same time, it is true that Manuel changes a great
deal: he is transformed from a happy-go-lucky young man into
a hardened military chief. But it is not being unduly paradoxical to say that his transformation is "another story." Manuel's
positive apprenticeship supports the specifically Communist
thesis of the novel, as distinct from the more general Republican thesis (I shall develop this distinction later in this chapter). In becoming a "chief," Manuel discovers the necessity for
organization and discipline, as well as the burdens that come
with responsibility and leadership. Within the Republican
forces, it is the Communists who argue for the priority of discipline over "enthusiasm" and for the necessity of transform-
ing "the Apocalypse into an army." Manuel's apprenticeship
"proves" them right. But in the overall design of the novel,
and despite the weight accorded to the Communist thesis,
Manuel's apprenticeship is subordinated to the story of confrontation. There is a complex narrative structure here, in
which the story of apprenticeship is "grafted" onto the story
of confrontation; and it is only in the former that Manuel's
evolution functions as a necessary—that is to say as a structural—element.[14]

Syntagmatic and Actantial Structures

The basic sequence that characterizes a story of confrontation is extremely simple, but the simpleness is perhaps compensated for by the "stuff" of the story. As everyone knows, a
conflict between good guys and bad guys has its undeniable
charm.

The sequence can be schematically represented as follows:

As the schema makes clear, what matters in such a sequence is not the psychology or the personal development of the hero, but the outcome of the conflict in which he is engaged. In an exemplary *apprenticeship* story, the underlying question that accounts for narrative suspense is: will the protagonist end up espousing the "right" values, discovering and following the way (and the voice) of truth? The stakes here are essentially cognitive, and the protagonist's principal test is a test of interpretation. The stakes in a *confrontation* story, on the other hand, are essentially performative; the question underlying it concerns not the internal evolution of the protagonist, but the external evolution of the conflict.

The suspense of the story consists in the uncertainty of the outcome. What is interesting, however, is that despite the apparent uncertainty, the outcome can never be the definitive triumph of the enemy. If the hero is defeated, he can nevertheless claim a spiritual or moral victory, *since he is right.* His defeat can mean only a *delayed* triumph (as is indicated by the broken arrow in the schema). This explains why, in *Le Cheval de Troie,* the Communist group that functions as hero sees their day of battle as only a beginning; there will be other battles, and the day will come when they will kill all their enemies (pp. 238–239).

A story of confrontation in which the hero is defeated is thus necessarily open-ended, allowing for future battles that will reverse the initial defeat. Even if the hero dies, he will be relayed by others fighting for the same cause—whence the possibility of a cycle of confrontation stories, all of them having the same general group as hero; whence also the possibility that a single work will consist of a series of smaller sequences, each of which realizes the basic sequence. This is especially the case in war novels (*L'Espoir, Les Communistes*), where every battle unfolds as an individual confrontation and at the same time forms part of a larger sequence, within which it functions as a progression or a reversal depending on who wins. The only necessary condition is that at the end of the work (the end of the larger sequence) the hero not be definitively defeated.

And what if the hero wins? In that case we might speak of a definitive triumph of the good; but in reality, or rather logically, even the victory of the hero is provisional. The passage of time will bring new enemies, who again will have to be fought and conquered. This possibility is not always recognized or evoked in a given work (whence the question mark in the schema), but it forms part of the narrative logic of confrontation. Whether he wins or loses, the antagonistic hero is never really done with his labors; the cycle of conflicts can be prolonged indefinitely.[15] This is quite clear in the Soviet socialist-realist novel, where even after the Revolution the "positive hero" has plenty of enemies to fight.[16] In our own corpus, it is *L'Espoir* that indicates the open-endedness of this type of story most strikingly, for the novel ends with a major victory for the Republican side. Since *L'Espoir* was written and published during the war, at a moment when its end was not yet certain, the concluding victory functions *on the level of the fiction* as the forerunner of a definitive victory. But in light of what we know to have actually happened, this ending emphasizes the provisional status of any closure in a story of confrontation, which is always potentially "to be continued."

The actantial structure of stories of confrontation is somewhat more complex than that of apprenticeship stories. That is because the subject is not syncretized with other actants, allowing for greater diversity. As we have seen, the subject is collective—either a group, or one or more individuals who represent a group. The group's object is the triumph of certain values or the realization of an ideal, defined from the start as "good." The receiver of the object is the community at large, and by extension humanity in general. The category of helper is occupied by those who provide material or moral support to the hero and share the latter's values; the category of opponent, by those who affirm values contrary to the hero's. But the opponent should in fact be split into two separate categories: that of anti-subject, who leads the fight against the hero (in the name of the "wrong" values); and that of anti-helper, who aids the enemy materially and/or morally. This division has the advantage of making the actantial categories more symmetrical; it also shows that the enemy is a negative "double" of the hero—having similar characteristics, but in reverse (endowed with negative value in the context of the work). As for the donor, he might at first glance be assimilated with the subject, but in fact must be kept separate. Since the hero's values are defined as unproblematically good, and since the donor is their ultimate source and guarantor, he must not be a merely human creature. This need not (and usually is not) stated explicitly; however, it is only the transcendent nature of the donor—whether he is God, historical necessity, national destiny, or the law of justice—that makes the values unproblematically good.

This observation allows us to see, furthermore, that even in an exemplary apprenticeship story, the ultimate donor is an absolute, mythical being. The character who plays the role of donor is merely his representative; the real source of any Truth with a capital T must be a god. But since, in fact, we know that the real source of any truth enunciated in a novel is the novelist, our observation leads us to recognize the vulnerability, the irremediable lack of authority, of any *roman à thèse*.

If we look at the way *Le Cheval de Troie* "fills in" the actantial configuration, we can see most clearly how the confrontation model both simplifies and mythically aggrandizes contemporary history. The subject-hero, as we have seen, is the small nucleus of Communists who lead the confrontation with the fascists. The helper is the whole working-class population of the city, including the socialists and those who are usually apolitical. This distribution corresponds to the political line of the Communist Party at the beginning of the Popular Front: the antifascist forces can and must unite in a broad grouping, and they must be led by the Communists. Obviously, this line does not take account of the very real ideological divergences within the Left, divergences which eventually dissolved the Popular Front (just as they dissolved the *programme commun* of the late seventies). It creates a more simple and monolithic division between fascists and antifascists. And it suggests that those who are not one must be the other.

The heroes' object is a double one. In the short term, it is simply the triumph of antifascist values, the latter being defined indirectly in the course of a long scene that shows a dinner party at the home of the *Préfet* a few days before the demonstration (chapter 5). The discussion between Lange and the other guests suggests that fascism is in its essence a philosophy of solitude and death. The struggle against fascism is thus a struggle for solidarity and life. This struggle is overshadowed, however, by yet another one: the long-term struggle for the coming into being of a new world, which "we [the Communists] must help to be born" (p. 242). In this new world, "there will no longer be any deaths for which men alone are responsible . . . death in an accident because the machines were faulty, or because the contractor had saved money on his scaffoldings; death because one has lost all hope of getting work, death because of tuberculosis, death because of torture" (p. 242). The long-term object of the hero is thus a world of equality and justice for all, defined as a world from which the *avoidable* death of men—and women—will have been eliminated.[17]

We can see here how one of the major themes of the interwar and the immediate postwar period in French literature, the existential theme of death, is orchestrated by a Communist writer. Nizan, a graduate of the Ecole Normale and an *agrégé de philosophie* like his friend Sartre, had found in Communism the solution to the question posed by so many works of the 1930s and 1940s, and that was posed, perhaps most urgently, in Sartre's short story "Le Mur": how can one find life meaningful, knowing that death exists and that after death there is nothing? In *Le Cheval de Troie*, Pierre Bloyé, the Communist intellectual who resembles Nizan like a brother, formulates the answer: "We can begin by destroying all the unjust ways of dying, and then, when we'll be left only with the kind of death for which no one is responsible, we'll have to try and make it meaningful (*lui donner un sens*) as well. It's not dying in battle that's difficult, but dying alone, under torture, or in your bed. We must die uncompromising deaths; confront illness like an enemy, so that dying should be a final honor, a final victory of consciousness" (pp. 242–243). This is "Marxist humanism" with a vengeance—or, some might say, the Marxism of a philosopher immersed up to his ears in bourgeois culture. Those are not necessarily negative traits, however; if one had to choose among Marxisms, one could do worse than choose the humanistic kind.

Let us return to our actants, however. The disjunction of the opponent into an anti-subject and an anti-helper allows us to see how Nizan brought about an important assimilation (important for his thesis) in *Le Cheval de Troie:* the assimilation between the fascist Leagues and bourgeois society as a whole. Just as, in the context of the novel, the Communists constitute the avant-garde of the working class, so the fascist Leagues constitute the tip of the capitalist iceberg or, to use a metaphor closer to Nizan's own, they are but the noisiest part of an immense machine, which crushes human beings and must itself be crushed (pp. 86, 207).

The assimilation between the fascists and the bourgeoisie as a whole operates both on the level of the characters and on the level of events. On the level of the characters, the scene of the dinner party shows that the fascists could not hold their meeting without the tacic approval of the town's leading citizens: the *Préfet* himself, the head of the local factory, an army officer, a prosperous *notaire.* Although they are not themselves members of the Leagues, they belong to the same world and are ultimately on their side. As if to underline this fact, Lange, who in the beginning (and at the dinner party) is presented as a nihilistic but apolitical philosopher, ends up joining the retreating fascists on the day of the demonstration; he gets particular pleasure out of shooting (however ineffectually) at the workers with a small revolver he finds on the ground. Lange thus passes from the category of anti-helper to that of anti-subject—a move that goes entirely in the direction of the assimilation the novel is effecting.

This assimilation is further reinforced by a crucial event in the story: soon after the start of the confrontation between the workers and the fascists, the latter (a fairly disorganized bunch—they retreat right away) are replaced by the National Guard, armed and wearing helmets. These representatives of order, who kill one of the Communists and force the workers to retreat and disperse, are there to demonstrate that the true enemy of the Communists—but also of all the antifascists—is bourgeois society as a whole. The fascists, who were the *apparent* anti-subject, are revealed to be merely a screen (or a synecdochic substitute) for the real one. At that point, all the bourgeois characters in the novel pass from the category of anti-helper to that of anti-subject.[18]

The foregoing analysis suggests a more general conclusion about the relationship between historical reality and the structure of confrontation. The latter polarizes reality, reducing its complexities to simple dichotomies. In *Le Cheval de Troie*, the first dichotomy is between fascists and antifascists; but it is soon subsumed by another dichotomy, between bourgeoisie and proletariat. Through its particular investment of the confrontation model, *Le Cheval de Troie* "proved" three things: that a union of the Left against fascism was necessary and possible; that fascism and capitalism were essentially the same (the one being but an extreme form of the other); and that the struggle against fascism was the first step toward the coming revolution. It is significant that in the last chapters of the novel, when Bloyé and his comrades discuss the meaning of their day, they never mention the fascists. The future they foresee is not the antifascist struggle, but the revolution:

> Devant eux s'étendait un avenir chargé de combats, de coups de feu, de cadavres, soumis aux signes du sang. [. . .] Pendant des années, cette explosion de l'histoire avait paru un songe et une légende qui ne concernaient pas plus les provinces françaises distraites et dormantes dans une terre de catastrophes que les typhons des mers de Chine. Elle prenait enfin cette réalité, cette lourdeur des engagements qui comportent la mort. Ils avaient sauté le pas de la mort. La lutte presque invisible que les communistes avaient menée dans l'ombre de cette ville et de centaines de villes arrivait au seuil des bouleversements. Un monde naissait.

La France entrait dans le jeu des nations, pour elle aussi la violence qui refait l'histoire commençait. (pp. 237–238)

[Stretching before them was a future full of battles, gunshots, corpses, subject to the signs of blood. [. . .] For years, that explosion of history had appeared to be a dream and a legend, as far removed from the sleepy and distracted French provinces as the typhoons of the China seas. Finally it was assuming the reality, the weight of commitments that involve death. They had crossed over the threshold of death. The barely visible struggle that the Communists had led in that town and in hundreds of towns was approaching the point of upheaval. A world was being born. France was entering into the game of nations; for her, too, the violence that remakes history was beginning.]

The structure of confrontation masks contradictions ("There are no divergences on the Left—witness the fight against fascism") and prevents certain questions from being asked ("Is the current government profascist? Does a revolutionary situation exist in France?"). Its dichotomies are those of myth, not history. As Lévi-Strauss once remarked, "nothing resembles mythic thought more than political ideology."[19]

The Constraints of the Real:
Barrès' *Le Roman de l'ènergie nationale*

The interest of a narrative model—which corresponds to what Weberian sociologists call an "ideal type"—is that it allows one to see similarities between works that may at first glance appear widely divergent. But having constructed the model, one would find it extremely boring to "apply" it to work after work. What becomes interesting at that point is another question: to what extent does a work that realizes the model (in fact, the genre) *in a general way* nevertheless diverge from it in particular ways, and for what reasons?

Barrès' *Le Roman de l'énergie nationale* offers, from this perspective, a fertile field for analysis. In discussing this trilogy I shall focus on the following question: how did historical circumstances, or what might be called the constraints of the real, perturb the mythic structure of the fiction? This question reformulates, in more precise terms, the larger question concerning the relation between individual works and generic models; at the same time, it will allow us to look more closely at the relation between the *roman à thèse* and contemporary history, since it asks how an individual work modifies the genre not for aesthetic, but for circumstantial—historical and political—reasons.

Le Roman de l'énergie nationale—consisting of *Les Déracinés* (1897), *L'Appel au soldat* (1900), and *Leurs Figures* (1902)—was written in large part during the years of the great battle around Dreyfus. Although the action of the trilogy takes place before the Affair (the fictional time goes from autumn 1879 to December 1893), and although the Affair is mentioned only once by the omniscient narrator—who does not hesitate to interrupt his narrative with generalizations and references to the present—it hovers over the trilogy and ultimately shapes it. Zeev Sternhell has noted in his study of Barrès' political ideas: "For Barrès, the confrontation between *dreyfusards* and nationalists is that of Good and Evil."[20] This Manichean vision dominates the trilogy and makes it realize, in a general way, the confrontation model. The broad dichotomies that organize the trilogy—nationalism vs. "cosmopolitanism" (read "the Jewish menace"), traditionalism vs. *déracinement,* patriotism vs. egotism, collective energy vs. individualistic waste—are political themes that became fully elaborated at the time of the Affair and in the years immediately following it. As Sternhell again notes: "On the whole *Le Roman de l'énergie nationale* . . . is a reconstruction of one period of French history according to the political norms of the next period."[21]

According to Philippe Barrès, Barrès' intention in the trilogy (which he conceived "en un seul bloc")[22] was to "paint a fresco of the France of his time," placing in the foreground a group of young men, "imaginary characters set in real life among characters who actually existed; the former allowing him to expose his ideas, the latter furnishing the historical framework."[23] This clear division of functions between the fictional and the historical characters is not found in the trilogy, however. All the major characters, whether "real" or "imaginary," serve to expose ideas (the principal one being that France could only regain health and vigor if it expelled from its midst all "foreign" influences—a cherished and long-lived theme of the French Right), and the historical framework is rendered as much by the activities of the fictional characters as by the historical ones: next to General Boulanger there is the fictional *boulangiste* Sturel; next to Clemenceau there is the fictional politician Bouteiller (modeled on the real politician Burdeau), etc.

The most obvious, but for my purposes the most pertinent, difference between fictional and historical characters in a novel is that the latter impose greater constraints on the novelist who wants to be a "painter of his time." He cannot make Napoleon die—or win the battle—at Waterloo, just as he cannot make Hugo the court poet of Napoleon III, Zola an *antidreyfusard,* or Trotsky the confidant of Stalin. And if the novelist chooses to place in the foreground events as well-known and as public as the Boulanger affair or the Panama scandal, then he will have to bend to similar constraints even as far as the activities of the *fictional* characters are concerned. Finally, he will have very little freedom of manoeuver, and the framework will invade the painting.

This is precisely what happens in Barrès' trilogy, where the invasion of the fiction by history introduces some interesting perturbations in narrative structure. *L'Appel au soldat,* which deals with Boulanger, and *Leurs Figures,* which deals with Panama, both realize the confrontation model, but in a "perturbed" way. Since the young men are introduced in *Les Déracinés,* however, we must begin there.

In *Les Déracinés,* fiction predominates; the novel realizes, in a fairly nonproblematic way, the structure of apprenticeship. It tells the intertwined stories of seven "jeunes Lorrains" who leave their native region to seek their fortunes in Paris. In terms of Barrès' thesis this is a highly dangerous and potentially disastrous step; indeed, the young men have been beguiled by an "outsider," their brilliant but nefarious *lycée* professor, Bouteiller. Bouteiller, an ambitious product of Jules Ferry's educational system, is described by the omniscient narrator as a "son of reason, a stranger to local or family traditions."[24] He will soon abandon teaching to become one of the leaders of the *parti radical*. In the meantime, however, he has taught his young disciples to reject their family roots for an abstract universalism; he has detached them from their native ground, has made them "young self-destroyers [who] aspire to rid themselves of their true nature, to uproot themselves" ["aspirent à se délivrer de leur vraie nature, à se déraciner"—*D*, 46]. Bouteiller thus plays, in the context of the novel, the role of a false or pseudo-donor, analogous to the role of Joseph Monneron in *L'Etape*.

Having stated Bouteiller's role in the very beginning, the novel—and indeed the whole trilogy insofar as it realizes the structure of apprenticeship—unfolds in a predictable way: those of Bouteiller's disciples who have the force, the intelligence, and the necessary circumstances to free themselves from his influence (and it is made clear that Bouteiller himself is but an "agent of transmission," his ideas being those of "l'état républicain")[25] end up "saved." The others—the majority—are not saved; we recognize here the narrative structure of the "antithetical brothers."

There is no need to recount the seven stories in detail. Suffice it to say that four of the young men end up badly; two of them end up well. The remaining one, Sturel, is more problematic, and I shall concentrate on him. But before that, a word about the others.

First, the negative series: Racadot becomes a murderer and is guillotined; his story takes up most of the last part of *Les Déracinés*. Mouchefrin, his accomplice, escapes the guillotine, and turns up in the later volumes of the trilogy as an *agent provocateur*, a police informer (*mouchard*—a destiny no doubt already inscribed in his name), and a blackmailer (*AS*, 57, 85–86; *LF*, 312, 358). Renaudin becomes a corrupt journalist, and then a publicity agent: the omniscient narrator calls him a "Parisian hoodlum" (*voyou parisien—AS*, 462). Suret-Lefort, outwardly successful, ends up, in a sense, worst of all—he becomes a Radical politician![26] In the next-to-last chapter of *Leurs Figures*, we see him plotting to displace Bouteiller as the leader of the radical Left; in the last chapter, we see him hailed as the new leader in the National Assembly. According to the narrator, Suret-Lefort is worse than his mentor: Bouteiller, at least, is sincere in his profession of republican ideals—he belongs to the "first truckload of republicans, among whom there were some statesmen" (*LF*, 349). But Suret-Lefort, the "cynical Suret-Lefort" (*LF*, 335), is merely an opportunist; he makes and unmakes alliances, "interested only in furthering his own interests" (*LF*, 14); he is a being "absolutely foreign to the notion of truth" (*LF*, 22). His worldly success is thus defined, in terms of the novel's ideological supersystem, as a series of degradations.

These four negative exemplary stories function in the trilogy as a "proof" of the *déracinement* thesis. The interpretation of each in terms of the thesis is explicitly formulated by the omniscient narrator, as well as by his fictional spokesman, Saint-Phlin.[27] It is quite remarkable, incidentally, that all of the four negative protagonists belong to the nonpropertied classes: Racadot is the son of a peasant and the grandson of a serf; Mouchefrin's father is a photographer who barely ekes out a living; Renaudin is the orphaned son of a "modest tax collector"; Suret-Lefort's family, once prosperous, now lives in a poor rented flat. We see here what Thibaudet called the "fils de famille" (today we would say the "héritier") side of Barrès' philosophy:[28] it would seem that in order not to suffer from *déracinement*, one has to *own* the ground as well as live on it.

The stories of Roemerspacher and Saint-Phlin, the two positive exemplary protagonists, also function as "proofs" of the thesis, but in reverse. These two young men both reject Bouteiller and find themselves new mentors (donors), and they both affirm themselves as "de plus en plus Lorrains." Saint-Phlin, the son and grandson of small landowners, leaves Paris after a few months and retires on his land. He becomes a disciple of the conservative social theorist Le Play, founds a family, and teaches his son "la discipline lorraine" (*LF*, 288). He is the one who, toward the end of the trilogy, formulates the "law" it is designed to illustrate: "the human plant flourishes, vigorous and fertile, only as long as it remains subject to the conditions that formed and maintained its species over the centuries" (*LF*, 283).[29]

Roemerspacher's story, although different in its details, illustrates the same thesis. Roemerspacher remains in Paris, but spiritually and ideologically he too is a true son of Lorraine. He chooses as his masters Taine and Jules Soury (a historian of religions and naturalist known for his nationalistic and anti-Semitic views), keeps in mind the earthy wisdom of his grandfather, and in his thirtieth year marries a young *Lorraine*. Saint-Phlin says of him: "there's a man, because he remains profoundly *lorrain* and instead of letting himself be dominated by the Parisian elements, he dominates them, uses them for his purposes" (*LF*, 282). Roemerspacher's story thus "repeats" and complements Saint-Phlin's, showing that one need not actually be in Lorraine in order to remain "subject to the conditions of the species." All one has to do is have the right ideas and reject all "foreign" influences.[30]

The stories I have summarized so far all conform without problem to the exemplary apprenticeship model—each one is unambiguously positive or negative, and they all teach the same "lesson." The most interesting story, however, is the problematic one having Sturel as protagonist. It is the most fully developed story in the trilogy, and realizes both the apprenticeship model and, in the last two volumes, the confrontation model. In both cases, however, the complete realization of the model falls short, or, more exactly, is short-circuited. It is this short-circuit phenomenon and the historical reasons that account for it which I shall now consider.

First, the apprenticeship. Unlike the other young men, Sturel fits fully neither into the positive nor the negative mold; his story can be read in either perspective. At the end of the trilogy, Sturel is a thirty-year-old man who has not yet found his way in life, despite his feverish involvement in two "good" causes. Whereas Roemerspacher and Saint-Phlin have defined themselves once and for all, in a way that allows for no future changes (since their self-definition is in total accord with the novel's ideological supersystem, the lack of change is a positive thing), Sturel has still not arrived at an authentic sense of self nor defined for himself a positive sphere of action.

This is partly due to his inability to find himself a suitable mentor. Saint-Phlin abandons Bouteiller for Le Play, Roemerspacher for Taine and Soury. But Sturel, despite his gradual disillusionment with his old teacher—a disillusionment that eventually turns to hatred—never succeeds in freeing himself completely from his influence. The link that persists between the two men, despite their political and ideological divergences, is emphasized in the last chapter of the trilogy: we see Sturel and Bouteiller, each of them alone after having suffered a personal and political defeat, walking up and down along parallel tracks in the gardens of Versailles. The narrator underlines the similarities between them by his commentary:

> Après avoir été une cause de déracinement et la doctrine même du déracinement, Bouteiller avait failli retrouver la continuité française. . . . Il y avait échoué. Ayant été presque un homme d'Etat, il retombait au "chacun pour soi." Quant à Sturel, séparé de l'innéité française par son éducation, il avait su, d'une manière mystérieuse pour lui-même, ressaisir ses affinités et s'enrôler avec ceux de sa nature ethnique, mais voici que pour la seconde fois ils venaient de se disperser, et, comme Bouteiller, il était rejeté dans un dur "chacun pour soi." (*LF*, 370)

> [After having been a cause of uprootment and the very doctrine of uprootment, Bouteiller had almost succeeded in rediscovering French continuity. . . . He had failed to do so. Having almost been a statesman, he had now fallen back to "every man for himself." As for Sturel, separated from French innateness by his upbringing, he had succeeded, in a manner mysterious to himself, in recovering his affinities and enlisting with those of his own ethnic nature, but now for the second time they had dispersed, and,

like Bouteiller, he was thrown back into a harsh "every man for himself."]

The sentence about Sturel summarizes in a sense the whole problem of the trilogy, and I shall come back to it. For now, let us note that the phrase about Sturel's unfortunate upbringing alludes not only to Bouteiller's influence but also to Sturel's *éducation sentimentale*. His first mistress, who initiated him into the realm of love the way Bouteiller initiated him into the realm of thought, was not only an outsider, but worse still, a foreigner. Astiné Aravian, "la belle Asiatique," not only taught her young lover about the ways of the flesh, but charmed him with her tales of the Orient with its "odor of death and roses" (*D*, 121). Playing sultan to her Scheherazade (*D*, 111), Sturel received from her lips a "cup of poison" he would always carry inside him. His system, already "weakened" by Bouteiller's teaching, was further weakened by the "dangerous foreign elements" Astiné "poured" into it. Her words had the effect of "turning him away from all realities, or at least from the interests of French life" (*D*, 125–127).

Although Astiné is eliminated from the trilogy in *Les Déracinés* (she is the victim of the two young murderers, Racadot and Mouchefrin), her spiritual and moral influence on Sturel is evoked at several crucial points even in the later volumes.[31] Sturel remains throughout the trilogy an "être nerveux et imaginatif," incapable of dealing with "concrete details" and following, at critical moments, only his personal whims. Toward the end of *Leurs Figures*, he diagnoses his own ill by comparing himself with Roemerspacher: "Roemerspacher will strike a just balance with emotionality, whereas I will let myself be invaded and destroyed by it" (*LF*, 334).

All of this would seem to make Sturel a candidate for negative status as the subject of an apprenticeship story. However, such a reading leaves out too many other elements to be satisfactory. Of all the young men, Sturel is the one who feels most strongly the need to recreate "l'esprit national"; as early as 1883 (in *Les Déracinés*), he calls for a Napoleonic "homme-drapeau" behind whom all Frenchmen can unite. Three years later, he recognizes his "homme-drapeau" in General Boulanger and becomes one of the General's first and most ardent supporters. Elected to Parliament on a *boulangiste* platform in 1889, he resigns a year later when he fears that he might turn into a "Parliamentary bureaucrat" (*AS*, 458). Ideologically he is a right-wing nationalist, virulently opposed to the parliamentary regime. When the Panama scandal explodes in 1892, he is part of the small group of *ex-boulangistes* who lead the battle against the corrupt deputies (including Bouteiller). Through the principles he defends and the causes he espouses, Sturel thus appears not only as the hero of a positive apprenticeship but also as the hero of two "holy wars": the battle for Boulanger and the battle over Panama, both of them having as an ultimate aim "the negation of parliamentarism" (*AS*, 51).

Here comes the problem, however: historically, neither one of these campaigns attained its aim. After his huge electoral victory in Paris in January 1889, Boulanger had a chance to seize power and topple the regime. But he hesitated, and was lost.[32] Very quickly, the Boulanger movement lost ground. The general himself went into exile in Belgium; in October 1891 he committed suicide over his mistress' grave. As for the Panama campaign, it put a temporary halt to the careers of some radical deputies like Clemenceau, but it did not topple the Republic. Barrès, who was himself elected as a Boulangist deputy in 1889 (unlike Sturel, he never resigned), was writing *L'Appel au soldat* and *Leurs Figures* during a national crisis which was far graver than Panama, but which still did not succeed in overthrowing the regime. Concerning the events he was narrating, Barrès therefore had the perspicacity of hindsight. That is what explains, I think, his ambivalence towards Sturel, the young Boulangist and anti-republican who, being understandably less clairvoyant than his creator, maintains his illusions far longer. One can say without exaggerating that if Sturel is "nerveux," "émotif," and unrealistic *in the fiction*, it is because the Boulangist movement and the anti-Republican campaign at the time of Panama did not succeed *in fact.*

The Russian Formalists already analyzed this kind of retrospective logic in narrative, which they called realistic motivation: if a story is heading for a *dénouement* in which the hero suddenly kills himself, realistic motivation requires that he be qualified *beforehand* as "melancholy," "impulsive," "an unstable personality," etc. What interests me here, however, is not the motivating device as such; it is too well known for that. Rather, it is the fact that in this instance the device was dictated not by verisimilitude, but by reality itself.

Let us take a closer look. In throwing himself into the Boulangist cause, Sturel was altogether on the "right" side in terms of the novel's thesis. Boulanger was the man who could "recreate the unity of sentiment" in France (*AS*, 51), the man through whom "l'esprit national" could affirm itself both against France's external enemies (i.e., Germany) and against its internal ones (foreigners, corrupt politicians, the parliamentary system itself). The Boulangist campaign thus had, potentially, all the makings of a holy war. That is how Sturel sees it, and the fact that the very positive Saint-Phlin agrees with him lends weight to his judgment. For Sturel, Boulangism is much more than a political movement: it is a "precious occasion for France to fulfill her duty . . . : for our general task is to maintain French nationalism" (*AS*, 319).

The Boulangist movement failed, partly because of the general's lack of daring, partly because of the lack of unity among his followers. Barrès masks neither of these facts; on the contrary, he renders them quite faithfully. But precisely for that reason, his story cannot conform fully to the model of confrontation. Two crucial elements for the realization of the model are missing: the presence of a united heroic group that believes in the absolute rightness of its action and in the ideals it pursues, and the nondefinitive defeat of the hero. After Boulanger's suicide, there remained only a handful of faithful in the movement, Barrès among them. For them, the possibility of a *revanche* was not excluded, and according to their perspective the short-term defeat could yet give rise to a future victory. But ten years later, when Barrès was writing *L'Appel au soldat,* this future victory was no longer conceivable: Boulangism was dead and buried. Drieu La Rochelle, as we have seen, did not hesitate to invent for his antagonistic hero a "new military and religious order" that may have had only a single member. But that is the mythic solution, which maintains the structure of confrontation at the expense of both veriisimilitude and historical reality. Barrès preferred a more historically accurate solution. It is therefore to Sturel, the young man he would no doubt have liked to make into a hero, that he assigned the task of formulating the promise of future victory:

> —Ils [the General's mourners, assembled around his grave] répètent encore: "Vive Boulanger" remarqua Thérèse de Nelles, mais, dans un an, qui se souviendra!
> —Dans un an! répliqua Sturel, pâle de tant d'émotions, dans un an il sera vengé. (*AS,* 504)

> [—"They are still repeating 'Long live Boulanger,' remarked Thérèse de Nelles, "but in a year who will remember!"
> —"In a year," replied Sturel, pale from so much emotion, "in a year he will be avenged."]

We remember that the speaker is an "être nerveux et imaginatif."

The fictional time of *L'Appel au soldat* ends in October 1891. That of *Leurs Figures* starts in June 1892, at the moment when the Panama scandal began to break. The facts were the following: the Panama Canal Company, in grave financial difficulties, had distributed sums of money (actually, checks) to a number of influential deputies in 1888, in order to buy their vote for a law authorizing a lottery loan to the company. Shortly thereafter, however, the company went bankrupt. In November 1892 one of its financial agents, the baron de Reinach (both he and another agent, Cornelius Herz, were Jewish) committed suicide. At that point, the right-wing deputies, sup-

ported by the extreme Left, succeeded in having a parliamen-
tiary commission set up to investigate the business of the bribes.
A trial took place in March 1893. According to the historian
Jean-Marie Mayeur, "with the Panama scandal, nationalists,
anti-Semites, and Boulangists tried to topple the regime."[33]
But the attempt failed. With the exception of a single deputy
who confessed, all the others were acquitted for lack of sufficient evidence. "In sum," Mayeur writes, "the campaign against
'les chéquards' . . . had not overthrown the regime as people
like Delahaye, Drumond and Déroulède had hoped . . . The
ministerial crisis once again played its cathartic role."[34]

Mayeur could have added Barrès' name to the list of those
who had hoped for a toppling of the regime. *Leurs Figures* is a
ferocious indictment of parliamentary politics and of those
who, according to Barrès, were its very incarnations: the Op-
portunists and the Radicals, Clemenceau first of all. But behind the corrupt politicians, there loomed an even worse enemy: the "foreign agents," "Jews born in Frankfurt," whose
money and influence corrupted France. A political cartoon of
the period, reproduced on the cover of the current Livre de
Poche edition of *Leurs Figures*, shows Clemenceau as a "balle-
rina," dancing with moneybags in his hand; the conductor, in
the lower right-hand corner, is a hook-nosed and bearded figure. The caption reads: "Clemenceau: le pas du commandité"
("the dance of the active partner"). *Leurs Figures* was dedicated
to Edouard Drumond, the author of *La France juive*. In its
conflation of anti-Semitism, anti-parliamentarism, traditionalism, and patriotism, *Leurs Figures* "fits" the confrontation model
perfectly.

What interests me here, however, is that despite its simple
divisions, *Leurs Figures* short-circuits the model the same way
as *L'Appel au soldat*—and for the same reason. Toward the end
of the novel (but one can ask whether the term is appropriate,
so massive is the presence of public events and characters in
the work), Sturel, who had taken a feverishly active part in the
campaign against "les chéquards," decides to publish a list that
provides incontestable evidence against the corrupt deputies—

a list that he alone possesses. But he is dissuaded at the last minute—not by the political arguments of Suret-Lefort and Bouteiller, who go to see him, but by the personal plea of a former mistress, whose husband's name is on the list. The narrator comments: "Moved by a woman's sighs, here was that avenger of public morality, obeying nothing but his own whims" (*LF*, 333). Two pages later, the narrator calls this incident "the triumph of the absurd and of aesthetic motives over reasoned arguments" (*LF*, 335).

The reason why Sturel succumbs to a woman's sighs must be sought elsewhere than in his "emotional" character, however. The publication of his list, which we are told would have brought down the regime, was simply a historical impossibility.

One may wonder why, knowing this, Barrès invented the episode of the abortive publication in the first place. Whatever his actual intentions, one can see in this episode both a short-circuiting of the confrontation model by historical circumstances and an *a posteriori* justification of the anti-republican campaign. The projected publication of "incontestable evidence" is presented in the fiction as a danger for the regime; such a publication would therefore have fit perfectly into a confrontation story with Sturel as its hero. But Sturel, as we already know, cannot be altogether a hero: he possesses the right values, he is passionate, combative, energetic; he has even succeeded, as the narrator states in a comment I quoted earlier, in "enlisting with those of this ethnic nature." But "circumstances were against him" (*LF*, 364). Circumstances were against Barrès too. If he could not give his near-hero the victory he sought, however, the novelist could at least evoke its possibility as an unrealized desire. Whence the existence, *in the fiction*, of incontestable evidence against "les chéquards"—evidence that neither the hero nor the novelist could use, the former because of his "character," the latter because of his respect for historical fact. Between the rule of the confrontation model, which requires a determined hero who won't back down, and the rule of historical accuracy, the latter carried the day. But the trace of desire remains: if only the circumstances had been different.

Does this means that the trilogy ends with an admission of defeat for its own anti-parliamentary thesis? In that case, *Le roman de l'énergie nationale* (or at least *Leurs Figures*) would be a *roman à thèse* that modifies its thesis in the process of illustrating it, and thereby subverts it. Such a reading is in fact possible: after the failure of Boulangism, after the failure of various attempts to overthrow the regime, to continue the struggle would have been to risk political disorder and anarchy. It is one of the author's spokesmen, the very reasonable Roemerspacher, who formulates, at the end of *Leurs Figures,* what might be called the modified thesis of the novel. Speaking to Sturel, he says:

> Que ces parlementaires soient des voleurs et des êtres bas, vulgaires, nuisibles, tout à fait méprisables, cela n'est point douteux. Mais ils sont la force, et la société est intéressée à ne pas disjoindre d'eux l'idée de justice, tant qu'elle n'a pas un autre personnel, aussi fort, entre les mains de qui transporter la justice. Au 27 janvier [1889], j'admettais que Boulanger chassât les parlementaires, parce qu'il pouvait assurer l'ordre pour le lendemain, mais dans l'état des choses, quand tu t'appuies sur des Fanfournot,[35] tu n'as évidemment aucune chance d'être le plus fort et de devenir le pouvoir légal: tu poses une bombe; tu es un anarchiste. (*LF,* 338)

> [Granted, these politicians are thieves and base creatures, vulgar, harmful, altogether despicable. But they are in power, and it is in society's interest not to divorce the idea of justice from them as long as it lacks an alternative group, equally strong, to whom it can entrust justice. On January 27, 1889, I was in favor of Boulanger's throwing out the politicians, because he could insure order for the morrow; but in the present situation, when you are leaning on people like Fanfournot, you obviously have no chance of being the stronger and of becoming the legal power: you are throwing a bomb; you are an anarchist.]

Sturel does not plant his bomb. If the choice is between a republic that "deracinates" and an anarchism that threatens to blow everything up, he chooses—like Barrès himself, who was not an *héritier* for nothing—the former.

It would be an exaggeration, however, to read the end of

Le Roman de l'énergie nationale as an apology, even a reluctant apology, for parliamentarism. The nationalist and anti-republican thesis of the work remains consistent; it is the final call to action that is modified by "circumstances." Instead of a collective action, which for the moment has no chance of succeeding, the trilogy ends by proposing an individualistic solution, a personal waiting period. "My task," Sturel declares to himself at the very end, "is to make myself more and more of a *Lorrain,* to be [the province of] Lorraine so that it might remain intact in this period when France, headless and disjointed, seems to be suffering from total paralysis" (*LF,* 369). It is in similar terms that Barrès explained his own position to his friends in the Action Française in 1901: "If the soldier and the favorable circumstance do not arise to create a harmonious France, let us at least create that France in ourselves: it will already be fortunate if our brains escape from this anarchy, this unbearable moral disorder in which we have been living for so many years."[36]

The last refuge of political losers is self-contemplation. While waiting for better days, one can always fall back on the *culte du Moi.*

The Model Relativized: Malraux's *L'Espoir*

Although Barrès' version of the confrontation model contains "local" perturbations that are interesting for both theoretical and historical reasons, one's dominant impression in reading the trilogy is that the model is maintained in all its simplicity. A respect for historical fact obliged Barrès to come to terms with the republic, but his view of the forces opposing each other in French society remains, in the trilogy, schematic and Manichean. Above all, he allows no elements to enter the fiction that might seriously question its "truths."

This is another way of saying that *Le Roman de l'énergie nationale,* like *Le Cheval de Troie,* like the *roman à thèse* in general, is monological in the extreme. "In the monological world,

tertium non datur: a thought is either confirmed or negated." [37]
The structure of confrontation, with its stark dichotomies that
admit no middle term and its organization of events into antagonistic patterns, can be considered as the generic deep
structure of the *roman à thèse*. In effect, this structure underlies stories of apprenticeship as well as stories of confrontation. In an exemplary apprenticeship story, the real adversaries are the donor and the pseudo-donor, with the protagonist
himself as the "prize"; in a confrontation story, the latter has
already been won over and is fighting for the Good. The presence of this single deep structure explains why, in both cases,
the novel polarizes reality (or rather, the representation of
reality): the confrontation between adversaries who are not
equals in right requires such polarization.

Still, one may suppose that there exist variations in kind
and degree even within the monologistic, polarized world of
the *roman à thèse*. After the massive monologism of Nizan and
Barrès, I shall therefore turn to an ideologically more complex (or, if one prefers, "less monological") work that nevertheless realizes the structure of confrontation: Malraux's
L'Espoir (1937). Concomitantly, my earlier question about the
constraints of history will be enlarged to the following: how
can a work both maintain the confrontation model and "dialogize" or relativize it?

Despite a narrative technique that emphasizes fragmentation and the multiplicity of points of view (a technique that
in principle acts against monologism), the primary structure
of *L'Espoir* is that of a simple confrontation: the Republican
side is massively and unproblematically right and good in its
fight against Franco. No matter how confused and "em-
brouillés" the details may be, the overall meaning of the war
is clear. Every time one of the Republican heroes expresses his
views on why he is fighting (from the simple peasant Barca,
who states that "the opposite of humiliation is brotherhood"
to the Catholic intellectual Guernico, who says: "I've *seen* the
Spanish people. This war is their war, whatever happens; and
I shall stay with them,") [38], his words must be taken as a privi-

leged interpretation. Indeed, over and above individual and political differences (which I will get to in a moment), there is virtual unanimity within the heroic group concerning the values for whose triumph the struggle is being waged: human dignity, human brotherhood, social justice. The Republicans are on the side of the Spanish people. Franco's forces hate the people (cf. the bombardment of Madrid); the values they represent are those of oppression and humiliation.

Insofar as its absolute division between the "good" and "bad" sides is concerned, *L'Espoir* conforms, then, to the confrontation model in a quite simple way. It also realizes the model through the collective hero and the actantial configuration.[39]

All this may seem too obvious to be worth mentioning. Yet, some of the better known critical interpretations of the novel, by playing down the importance of this primary confrontation structure, end up curiously skewed. Lucien Goldmann, for example, places exclusive emphasis on what he calls Malraux's "Stalinist perspective"; W. M. Frohock sees a conflict between Malraux's "intentions as artist" and his "intentions as propagandist."[40] These interpretations focus on what I call a secondary, "relativized" confrontation—but, paradoxically, they treat this confrontation as an antagonistic one; and they underestimate the importance of the primary (antagonistic) confrontation that is its context.

The secondary, "relativized" version of the confrontation model is realized in the ongoing discussion that occurs within the Republican ranks, concerning the problem of means *versus* ends. This discussion takes place essentially between the Communists, who argue for the primacy of organization and discipline, and the anarchists and Catholics, who argue for the primacy of ethics and spontaneous human feeling. The fact that the discussion is given emphasis in the novel constitutes a perturbation in the primary antagonistic structure. As we saw, the antagonistic model requires a heroic group that is ideologically united. By recognizing the existence of serious divergences within the Republican ranks, *L'Espoir* yields to the pressure of historical fact: the Republicans *were* divided.[41] For some observers like Orwell, the internal strife between anarchists, Trotskyists, and Communists became in a sense the primary event of the war. Malraux tries to minimize the internal strife by suggesting that everyone is in agreement about the ultimate values for which the war is being fought, and by emphasizing the necessary union of the rival factions in the face of the enemy.[42]

The primary confrontation structure is perturbed, then, by a secondary confrontation between members of the heroic group. But this secondary confrontation is not at all simple nor antagonistic. Admittedly, the novel leaves no doubt that the defenders of organization and discipline are "right." That is why Goldmann accuses Malraux of having adopted, in this instance, a deplorably Stalinist perspective. According to Goldmann, the novel's thesis can be summed up as follows: "Everything that is immediately and spontaneously human must be banished and even abolished in the name of an exclusive concern for efficiency."[43] In terms of such a reading, Manuel's gradual transformation into a hard-bitten military chief is a positive exemplary apprenticeship that proves the thesis of "efficiency" (*efficacité*): Manuel's troops are in large part responsible for the major victory at Guadalajara, with which the novel closes. Conversely, the Catholic officer Hernandez, who commands the Republican forces at the siege of Toledo and tries to put ethics before discipline (he allows the besieged Francoist general Moscardo to send a letter to his wife), pays for his lack of efficiency with his life. The defeat of the Republicans at Toledo shows that without disciplined and organized leadership, even a good cause is doomed to fail. Hernandez himself recognizes, on his way to the fascist firing squad, that "to be generous is to be the victor" (*la générosité, c'est d'être vainqueur* . . . p. 230).

Goldmann cites a large number of statements by various characters as evidence that the "Stalinist" argument in favor of discipline ("organiser l'Apocalypse," "transformer la guérilla en armée," etc.) is massively supported and illustrated in the novel. What he does not sufficiently emphasize, however, is that this argument is itself only the minor premise of a larger argument whose major premise is as follows: "This is a war which *must* be won by the 'good' side." The necessity of discipline is presented as a necessity *of the moment*. It is the context and the pressure of the war—which is a "holy war"—that makes even certain non-Communist characters, whose profound values are not those of hierarchy and discipline, bow to that necessity. Goldmann, in other words, overlooks the importance of the primary confrontation in the novel. This leads him not only to place exclusive emphasis on what he considers a pernicious argument, but also to ignore the complex and altogether relative way in which it is presented.

If the novel presents a "Stalinist" thesis, one can only say that it does so reluctantly. It is significant that the most consistent spokesman for the thesis of efficiency, the commander Garcia, is not a Communist (Goldmann refers to him as "le communiste Garcia")[44] and has only a grudging admiration for the Communists. In one of the major discussion scenes, when a Communist bureaucrat tells an anarchist that "concretely, there can be no politics with your ethics," Garcia intervenes: "The complication, and maybe the tragedy of the revolution is that there can be none without it either" (p. 184). At the end of the novel, after the "transformation of the guerilla into an army" promises an ultimate victory for the Republicans, the aviator Magnin, another non-Communist, asks Garcia what he thinks of the Communists. Garcia replies: "My friend Guernico says: 'They have all the virtues of action—and those alone!' But right now, it's action we are dealing with" (p. 439). Garcia is thus presented not as a Stalinist ideologue, but as a combatant in a just war who *must* choose efficiency and effectiveness ("efficacité" has both meanings) over generosity or nobility of heart, even while recognizing the moral superiority of the latter.

This choice, while affirmed as necessary, is also seen as tragic—not only by Garcia, but by others who defend the thesis of efficiency, including Manuel, who is a Communist. On his way to becoming an effective commander, Manuel becomes increasingly aware of the price he is obliged to pay. Toward the end of the novel, after having ordered the execution of two deserters, Manuel tells his former commander, the Catholic officer Ximénès: "I take responsibility for those executions: they were done in order to save the other men, our own. But listen here: every single step I've taken toward greater efficiency and better leadership has separated me more from my fellowmen" (p. 357). One of Garcia's earlier remarks, made during a lengthy discussion between him and the art historian Scali, can be seen as an anticipatory comment on Manuel's tragic self-perception. Garcia tells Scali:

"Du moment que nous sommes d'accord sur le point décisif, la résistance de fait, cette résistance est un acte: elle vous engage, comme tout acte, comme tout choix. Elle porte en elle-même toutes ses fatalités. Dans certains cas, ce choix est un choix tragique, et pour l'intellectuel il l'est presque toujours, pour l'artiste surtout. Et après? Fallait-il ne pas résister?" (p. 349)

["As long as we agree about the crucial point, the fact of resistance, that resistance is an act: it commits you, like any act, like any choice. It carries in itself all of its necessary consequences. In certain cases, this is a tragic choice, and for an intellectual it is almost always a tragic choice, especially for the artist. So what? Does that mean we shouldn't have resisted?"]

This comment strikes me as crucial, not only because it presents a highly self-conscious and relative justification for the thesis of efficiency (efficiency is not affirmed as a *value*), but also because it functions as an internal commentary on the simple articulations of the confrontation model itself, as it is realized in the novel. To the intellectual and the artist, the mythic oppositions of the confrontation model must appear simplistic. Yet, in a just war one cannot elude the necessity of making simple choices; one is obliged to act, and "all action is Manichean" (p. 345). Like the artist Lopez in the novel, whose frescoes speak "a language of man in battle" (p. 46), *L'Espoir* simplifies and perhaps mythifies historical reality; but it also suggests that there are times when such simplification is obligatory—and good.

The running dialogue between various members of the heroic group (and the important point is that it *is* a dialogue, despite the fact that under the circumstances one of the positions appears more "correct" than the others), as well as the internal dialogue that takes place within characters like Garcia and Manuel, who seek justifications for their own positions to themselves, suggests that Malraux was fully aware of the problems posed by the pro-Communist efficiency argument, but was willing to advance it as the only way to win the war. By ignoring the complexities of its presentation and the context of the primary confrontation which makes it justifiable, Goldmann flattened out the argument into a straightforward apology for Stalinism.

W. M. Frohock's reading of *L'Espoir* is more subtle, but I think that he too tends to underplay the significance of the primary confrontation. According to Frohock, the novel presents a "propaganda thesis" which consists in negating ethical values in favor of efficiency (this is identical to Goldmann's reading); but this thesis is contradicted, Frohock claims, by Malraux's "art," since the most emotionally charged scenes in the novel suggest that it is the ethical values that really matter. Frohock's prime example is the famous "descent from the mountain," where the wounded aviators are carried down in an atmosphere of solemn communion with the population. According to Frohock, "this scene glorifies the fraternity of men, precisely the fraternity which, according to the propaganda thesis of the novel, will not and cannot win revolutions! . . . the emotional effect on the reader . . . is directly opposed to the conclusions to which, as a propaganda piece, *Man's Hope* should have led him."[45]

This is a very subtle argument, and one could construct a similar one for many a *roman à thèse* (I myself present an argument along somewhat similar lines in chapter 5). But as far as *L'Espoir* is concerned, the argument seems to me unjustified. The contradiction in this novel is not "between" Malraux's thesis and his art. It is not the art that affirms or "glorifies" the value of fraternity while the thesis affirms the value of efficiency. It is the thesis, indissociable from the "art," that affirms both—arguing that in order to make human fraternity triumph (fraternity is *the* value of the Republican side), one must first win the war. The descent from the mountain is a reminder of what the war is all about (significantly, it takes place just before the victory of Guadalajara); the story of Manuel's evolution and Garcia's arguments for efficiency are a reminder that the war must be won.

The relativized, dialogical confrontation within the Republican ranks appears, finally, as only a "local" perturbation in the primary confrontation structure. Malraux avoids the really vexing issues between the Communists and the other political groups, and suggests that all the differences between them can be subordinated to the cause of winning the war. They did not win the war, and according to historians one reason for their defeat was precisely their lack of cooperation. This fact, however, does not invalidate Malraux's argument, and it certainly does not imply, as Goldmann suggests, that the argument itself "led not to victory, but to defeat."[46] The argument itself was a hope, a call for unity that did not materialize. *L'Espoir,* like any novel of confrontation, masks some contradictions and prevents some questions from being asked.

The dialogism (admittedly a limited one, for after all the defenders of efficiency have the last word) that characterizes the confrontation within the Republican ranks is due to the fact that the adversaries are all ultimately on the "right" side. That is why, in relation to the primary antagonistic confrontation, this secondary one is only a "local" perturbation. There exists, however, another perturbation in the novel's primary confrontation structure that is more than local; it is the presence of a muted suggestion that the "holy war" itself may not be all important. According to the confrontation model, nothing can take precedence over the fight for a just cause. That is why the confrontational hero must be subordinated to the heroic group. Malraux, however, allows the old art historian

Alvear to affirm even in the midst of the bombardment of Madrid: "I want a man to be responsible to himself and not to a cause, even if the cause is that of the oppressed" (286)—an idea that puts into question, or at least into an "other" perspective, the whole enterprise of confrontation.[47] One of the most often quoted sentences in the novel, Garcia's statement that the best thing a man can do with his life is "to transform into consciousness the widest experience possible" (p. 348), has a similar effect, since it subordinates the holy war to individual experience. Even Manuel, who has totally accepted the necessities of military action and the price it costs him, is able to envisage a future where confrontation will no longer be a pertinent category ("One day there would be peace. And Manuel would become another man, unknown to himself . . ." p. 445). Finally, the very discreet narrator himself suggests that there are certain things more important than even a just war. The novel closes with Manuel listening, during a momentary pause after the victory of Guadalajara, to Beethoven's music:

> Ces mouvements musicaux qui se succédaient, roulés dans son passé, parlaient comme eût pu parler cette ville qui jadis avait arrêté les Maures, et ce ciel et ces champs éternels; Manuel entendait pour la première fois la voix de ce qui est plus grave que le sang des hommes, plus inquiétant que leur présence sur la terre:— la possibilité infinie de leur destin: et il sentait en lui cette présence mêlée au bruit des ruisseaux et au pas des prisonniers, permanente et profonde comme le battement de son coeur. (p. 445)

> [Those musical movements that succeeded each other, rolled up in his past, spoke the way that city which long ago had stopped the Moors might have spoken, and that sky and those eternal fields; Manuel was hearing for the first time the voice of what is graver than the blood of men, more disquieting than their presence on earth:—the infinite possibility of their destiny; and he felt in himself that presence joined to the sound of the running streams and to the march of the prisoners, permanent and deep like the beating of his heart.]

If the infinite possibility of human destiny is graver even than the blood of men (one section of *L'Espoir* is entitled "Sang de gauche"), then the open-endedness of this novel is *qualitatively* different from the potential open-endedness of any confrontation story: it is the difference between radical, unforeseeable change and mere repetition-with-variations.[48]

To conclude: I think that *L'Espoir* is a *roman à thèse*s, with the emphasis on the plural (it presents at least two theses: the necessity of fighting against fascism, and the necessity for discipline in order to win); at the same time, it is conscious of the difficulty of certain choices, and makes this difficulty one of the privileged subjects of the fiction. In less complex (or more simply monological) *romans à thèse,* the "right" choice is never problematic—even if some people are unable to make it—for the values involved are absolutes. In *L'Espoir,* the struggle against fascism is an absolute value; but after that the choices become more complicated, and even the "right" choice is affirmed as problematic—literally, it poses problems. Furthermore, this choice is not seen as a way of acceding to an authentic being or selfhood. Manuel's being remains open to the infinite possibility of his destiny—he is not defined as a "chief" once and for all.[49] In its openness to the future and in its recognition of the complexity of certain choices, *L'Espoir* can be considered a *roman à thèse* that redefines, in a sense, the rules of the genre.

The Role of the Reader

One of the assumptions underlying our analyses until now has been that the role of the reader in the *roman à thèse*—whatever the particular narrative structure it realizes—is strongly "programmed." The assimilation of the *roman à thèse* to the broader category of "exemplary" narratives furnished a theoretical basis for this assumption. It is now time to look more closely at the role of the reader, taking account of the specificity of the structure of confrontation and of the structure of apprenticeship, as well as of the realist orientation of the genre.

As far as a single work is concerned, only a detailed stylistic and narratological analysis can determine the exact role assigned to the reader—more precisely, to the extradiegetic narratee, or the work's inscribed reader[50]—in that work. The role varies according to the number and kinds of utterances addressed directly to the extradiegetic narratee, according to whether he (or, as the case might be, she) is treated as a friend or an adversary, as someone well-informed or as someone to whom everything must be explained, and so on. This type of analysis, which must be repeated for each work, is not what concerns me here. The role of the reader I am dealing with is a more general, generic one.

We recall that in a *roman à thèse* which realizes the apprenticeship structure, the reader is called upon either to "repeat" the protagonist's evolution toward the "right" doctrine (positive exemplary version), or to reject the protagonist's evolution *in the name of* that doctrine (negative exemplary version). What is involved in both cases is the reader's virtual identification with the protagonist of the story, the difference being that in the negative version this identification is transformed in the course of the narrative into a *refusal* to identify with the failed subject. In both cases, however, the reader is presumed to undergo an ideological evolution, which can even be a total conversion. This model presupposes a reader who at the outset is not convinced, or who may perhaps be downright hostile to the novel's thesis, for it is only in relation to such a reader that one can speak of a genuine persuasion exercized by the novel. But of course the model cannot exclude readers who are already convinced at the start. In their case, the rhetoric of the work functions less as persuasion than as *confirmation:* the novel reinforces the reader's adherence to the "right" doctrine, by providing him with the opportunity to judge the protagonist's actions according to his own criteria, which are also those of the work's ideological supersystem.[51]

In a *roman à thèse* that realizes the confrontation structure, the effect as far as the convinced reader is concerned is essentially the same: the novel confirms the "right" values by recounting the heroic struggle of those fighting for them. As for the unconvinced reader, the effect aimed for is also that of persuasion, but there is a significant difference—at least at first glance—in the rhetorical means employed. Whereas in an exemplary apprenticeship story the reader's evolution is designated, so to speak, as the desired effect, since it is reflected within the fiction by the evolution of the protagonist (regardless of whether the latter is positive or negative), in a story of confrontation the reader's evolution is placed between parentheses: the reader, like the hero himself, is presumed to be *already* on the "right" side when the story begins. If this fact is not explicitly signaled in the narrative, it is because it is presupposed: a confrontation story is always told from the point of view of the subject-hero, not from that of the anti-subject; the anti-subject is the (inimical) Other. The values for which the hero fights are neither questioned nor even discovered in the course of the story. They are given from the start, so that the enunciation of these values in the course of the story functions as the explication of already known truths rather than as a new discovery.

This means that the reader is immediately placed in the position of someone who shares the hero's values and desires the latter's victory. The rhetorical strategy consists not in leading the reader gradually toward a predetermined truth, but in treating him from the start as a possessor of that truth, or at least as someone whose sympathies are on the side of those who possess the truth and are fighting in its name. One might call this strategy persuasion by cooptation: the reader, coopted from the start into the ranks of the hero, finds himself structurally—that is, necessarily—on the "right" side. He *must* desire the triumph of the hero, and hence of the latter's values. Only a "perverse," that is to say recalcitrant, reader would prefer the triumph of the enemy over that of the hero. But the perverseness—or the revolt—of the reader is not a possibility recognized by the genre.

Despite the apparent difference between the two types of stories, a closer look reveals that even in an apprenticeship story, persuasion involves an attempt to coopt the reader. The clearest example of this is found in novels with an overtly tendentious omniscient narrator. The latter's judgments or didactic generalizations are an attempt to coopt the reader even before the end of the story that is supposed to convince him. Thus, when the narrator of *L'Etape* calls a meeting hall a "den of socialists"; when the narrator of *Les Déracinés* refers to an actantially negative character as a "serf" or as a "Parisian hoodlum"; when the narrator of *Antoine Bloyé* speaks of the "plot of those in power" [*complot du commandement*] and compares the directors of a railroad company to "calculating spiders," he places—or attempts to place—the reader in an immediate position of complicity and of tacit agreement with his values. The didactic orientation of the story as a series of events leading to an univocal meaning is here doubled by an interpretive discourse which, through its choice of metaphors or epithets, betrays (or reveals) its prejudices, hoping (or perhaps feigning to assume) that those prejudices will be shared by the reader. This is a risky game, to be sure, for a discourse that is too obviously prejudiced can provoke an *actual* reader (especially one who does not share the prejudices) into contesting the narrator's right to narrate and into rejecting the story itself as "unfairly loaded."

The actantial role assigned to the reader of a confrontation story is that of a pseudo-helper: he does not participate as an actor in the story (to be extradiegetic is the sad lot of any reader), but as a witness to the struggle being waged by the hero, he is not indifferent. At the outer limit, one can even imagine the transformation of the reader into a "real" (that is, a pseudo-intradiegetic) helper. What I mean by that is that the reader might continue in his own life the struggle recounted in the novel. One of the effects manifestly intended by *L'Espoir* was to provoke the real support—whether financial, physical (cf. the International Brigades), or political—of its readers for the Spanish Republican cause. The world of the fiction rejoins here, to the point of merging with it completely, the world of contemporary history as it is actually experienced. In 1937, the "good" reader of *L'Espoir* was someone who became transformed in the course of the reading into a genuine actor—a character in a "true story" whose ending was not yet written.

L'Espoir is a rare case, since the conflict it recounted was a real one, and was furthermore not yet ended when the book was published. A contemporary reader of *L'Espoir* could thus literally "act out" the fantasies inspired by it, attempting to influence by his action the end of the story told in the novel. This was a short-lived privilege, to be sure, that readers after 1939 no longer enjoyed. It was also an exceptional one, since the great majority of novels dealing with a historical conflict are written after, not during, the war (*War and Peace* is a prime example).

The singularity of an example does not prevent its indicating more general tendencies, however. Because *L'Espoir* is a special case, it puts certain generic traits into greater relief. The status of the reader as a pseudo-helper is a generic trait characteristic of confrontation stories.[52] This status remains the same even if the conflict in question is in the historical past, or else invented. The difference is that in the latter instances everything takes place on the imaginary level. By saying "I want the hero to win," the reader is no longer expressing a desire that can be realized in the real world as well as in the fiction; he knows that his desire functions only as a fiction, or else retroactively, but his inscription in the novel requires that he formulate the desire nevertheless. A reader today who reads *L'Espoir* may desire the victory of the Spanish Republicans, even knowing full well who actually won in 1939.

Similarly, "acting out" on the reader's part remains a virtuality, whatever the status—real or fictional, present or past—of the conflict recounted. To the extent that the particular conflict is but an episode in a long-standing war (as in *Le Cheval de Troie*), or else a battle which, although now over, could flare up elsewhere in different circumstances (Zola's *Vérité*), the way is open to future action. Even in *Le Roman de l'énergie nationale*, where the lag between the time of the story and the time of writing perturbed the generic model, the future action of the reader is not excluded. It will not be in the Boulanger affair or in the Panama scandal, to be sure. But given the nationalistic and xenophobic thesis of the novel, it seems evident that the waiting period proposed at the end is but a latency period from which the hero—and potentially the reader—will emerge at the first opportunity.

Leading the argument a step further, one can suggest that the possibility of "acting out" inscribed in the *roman à thèse* indicates a more general tendency inherent in the genre: the tendency to join the fictional world of the work to the experienced world of the reader, so that one becomes the extension or continuation of the other. This tendency is that of the *exemplum,* where the fiction is always designed to lead to a *prise de conscience,* and eventually to an action on the part of the reader or listener. In the *roman à thèse* this tendency is reinforced by the fact that the fictional matter is not allegorical or fantastic, but "realistic." The junction between fiction and life does not occur only on the level of the interpretation which formulates the "moral of the story"; it also occurs on a more immediate level, since the world of the fiction is recognized as being "the same" (or at least of the same kind) as the world experienced by the reader. The *roman à thèse* thus combines two traits belonging to different genres: verisimilitude, or an intersection between the *matter* of the fiction and the historical-cultural reality of the reader, characteristic of realist fiction; and didacticism, or an intersection between the *interpretation* of the fiction and the real world of the reader, characteristic of allegory and of "exemplary" narratives in general.

Using a distinction proposed by Georges Lavis and recently reiterated by Linda Hutcheon, we might say that the *roman à thèse* tends to blur the difference between *fictive* referents (objects or events represented in the novel) and *real* referents, of which fictive referents are merely analogues.[53] The *roman à thèse* thus encourages the reader's "referential illusion," by attempting to eliminate the distance between fiction and life. This tendency would seem to place it at the antipodes of modern self-conscious fiction—what some have called metafiction—which emphasizes the constructed, artificial, fictive status of its referents. And yet, it is interesting to see how Linda

Hutcheon, an ardent defender of metafiction, concludes her discussion of the reader's role in metafictional works (in which, rather than being asked to "identify" with fictional characters, the reader is asked to become aware of the "act of reading itself" as a sense-making activity) by suggesting that the ultimate aim of such works may be to "seduce" the reader into action—"even direct political action."[54] It would seem that the maximal encouragement of the referential illusion, characteristic of the *roman à thèse,* and the maximal frustration of that illusion, characteristic of modern metafiction, both lead the reader via the book back into real life. One could argue that the *roman à thèse* does so in a "bad" way, by reinforcing the reader's naive inclination to confuse fiction with reality, words with things—to make the reader into a kind of Don Quixote or Emma Bovary, as it were. Metafictional works, on the other hand, would do so in a "good" way, by obliging the reader to recognize his own activity *qua* reader as a counterpart of the writer's activity, both of these taking place in the real world (and both of them being ontologically distinct from the activities of fictional beings).

I would not wish to make such a value-laden argument, however. Polarization in critical discourse is as ideological—and ultimately as undesirable—as polarization in fiction. What I would suggest is that because of its desire to close the gap between fiction and the real world, the *roman à thèse* is a perishable genre. Sartre once wrote that "The works of the mind are like bananas—they don't travel well."[55] If this *bon mot* is of doubtful validity as far as all the "works of the mind" (or even all bananas) are concerned, it applies rather well to the *roman à thèse.* Written in and for a specific historical and social circumstance, the *roman à thèse* is not easily exported. And even in its native land, it becomes "ancient history" as soon as the circumstance that founded it no longer holds. Certain circumstances remain alive longer, or age more gracefully than others: the Dreyfus Affair is probably closer to today's French readers (and even some non-French ones) than the anti-Republican battles that were contemporaneous to it. Nevertheless, one must admit that no reader today will read *Vérité* with the passion of a reader in 1903, or *L'Espoir* with the emotions of a reader in 1937.[56] For those readers, the Affair or the civil war in Spain were part of their immediate, historically experienced present; for us, they are more or less vivid, more or less borrowed memories.

Naturally, no reader today, or at any other time, reads any work of the past the way its contemporary readers did. Furthermore, there may be some readers today for whom the Dreyfus Affair, the Spanish Civil War—and who knows, perhaps even the campaign against the Republic—are burning issues. But our discussion concerns neither these exceptional beings nor the general rule that applies to all readers and all works. Alongside the general rule there is the specific rule of the *roman à thèse*, which states that the narrower the thesis—that is, the more closely it is tied to a specific historical circumstance—the more perishable the novel is *as a roman à thèse*. Its recuperation on a "higher" level is always possible: one can read Barrès for his style, the way one reads Pascal's *Les Lettres Provinciales*. But to read *Les Déracinés* for its style (or because one finds its overtly tendentious narration, let us say, "campy") is to negate it as a *roman à thèse*.

Paradox of this genre: the more closely a work conforms to it, and to it alone, the more the work is destined to disappear. The *romans à thèse* that survive their own period do so *despite* their belonging to the genre, not because of it. They are not read, afterwards, as *romans à thèse*—except perhaps by literary theorists and historians, who are not "natural" but professional readers.

And yet, the author of a *roman à thèse* (this may in fact be his claim to glory) will never say, like Stendhal, that he writes in order to be understood a hundred years later. He makes his peace with the ephemeral. The readers he writes for are those of his own time—those who, like the anonymous readers of the review *Iskra* whom Nizan quotes in his epigraph to *Le Cheval de Troie*, read not only in order to learn "where to begin" but also "how to live and die."

Chapter 4
Redundancy and the "Readable" Text

THE TITLE of this chapter alludes to the well-known distinction proposed by Roland Barthes in *S/Z*, between "readable" (*lisible*) and "writable" (*scriptible*) texts. In Barthes' value system, as set forth in *S/Z* and subsequent works, the "readable" and the "writable" came to define two diametrically opposed spaces or poles—the first standing for all that is traditional, systematic, analyzable, and ultimately of limited interest; the second for all that is modern, elusive ("about writable texts there may be nothing to say"[1]), and for that reason endlessly satisfying. The writable is playful, fluid, open, triumphantly plural and hence impervious to the repressive rule of structure, grammar, or logic; the readable is serious, closed, structured, constrained, authoritarian, redundant: it imposes meaning, it makes the reader into a consumer, not a producer, of the text.

This bipolar division—which, curiously, recalls the Manicheanism of the *roman à thèse*—would be worth analyzing as a cultural and critical phenomenon in its own right, characteristic of a certain strain of intellectual radicalism in France in the late sixties and early seventies. This was the heyday of the *Tel Quel* group's critique of structuralism, and in particular of the structuralist concept of the sign; it was also the heyday of the critique of realist or representational fiction (defined in its essence as "repressive" and "bourgeois"), and of the idealizing of an avant-garde, inherently subversive, "plural" *text*.[2]

Fascinating as this subject is, both theoretically and in terms of cultural history, it is not my subject here. What interests me, rather, is the possibility of using redundancy as a generic criterion of the *roman à thèse*. In *S/Z*, Barthes lays particular emphasis on the role of redundancy in "readable" texts (that is, in realist fiction), for it is by means of redundancy that plural meanings and ambiguities are reduced, with a corollary reduction of the number of possible readings. In the *roman à thèse*, where a single "correct" reading is required (or more exactly, is posited as a desired effect), we can expect that there will be a considerable amount of redundancy. The interesting question is: can we define *types* of redundancy characteristic of the *roman à thèse*, which can function as generic indicators? In order to answer that question (as well as the related question of the "amount" or degree of redundancy in a work or genre), we must be quite clear as to the meaning of the term "redundancy" (it is not necessarily pejorative); we must also have, as a point of comparison or as a background against which the particularities of the *roman à thèse* may be perceived, an inventory of the redundancies that characterize realist fiction in general. Finally, we can attempt to see how redundancy is linked to reading, and in particular to the problem of the evaluation of literary texts.

The Notion of Redundancy in Linguistics

In ordinary language, redundancy has a negative connotation. Webster's primary definition of "redundant" is "Exceeding what is natural, usual, or necessary; superfluous, as, a redundant foot in a verse; redundant words in a statement." To say, therefore, that a given discourse is redundant is to imply that it is full of things it could, and should, have done without.

Linguists and information theorists know better, however; in their vocabulary redundancy is a positive term, for without redundancy there can be no communication. There exists no language, either natural or artificial, including the language of computers, that is not obligatorily redundant. As the French linguist Jean Dubois explains, speaking of natural languages: ". . . communication never takes place under optimum conditions: there are 'noises' that invariably act as obstacles to communication, such as other voices, a lack of attention on the part of the listener, and so on. The listener finally hears only part of the message. All the elements of an utterance, regardless of their linguistic level, must be redundant; this redundancy is not a matter of choice on the part of the speaker, it is inherent in the language."[3] Redundancy "allows for the conservation of information that 'noises' may suppress." It is a "surplus of information," but a necessary surplus: "there is redundancy when the probability of the occurrence of a sign is maximal or equal or close to 1. In that case the sign carries little or no information, but can still be considered as a (compensatory) conservation of information."[4]

In natural languages, the principal causes of redundancy are "the constraints imposed in the choice of linguistic units and in their combination, their relationship to each other—in a word, *the organization of the language into structure.*"[5] Because of these constraints, which prescribe or else forbid certain combinations, and which, as Dubois mentions, function on all linguistic levels, the probability of occurrence of a sign in a given context varies from 0 to 1. For example, in the spoken French sentence, "Les petites filles sont bavardes" [leptitfijsõbavard—"Little girls are talkative"], the sign of the plural appears twice, the second time being totally redundant—that is, of a probability of 1 —after the first; the sign of the feminine appears three times. These are syntactic redundancies, or, in the case of the feminine, syntactico-semantic ones (cf. "filles"). The sentence also has some strictly semantic redundancies which A. J. Greimas and other structural semanticians have called *isotopies:*[6] thus the word (or, to use Greimas' terminology, the lexeme) "bavardes" necessarily contains the seme "animate," since it follows and qualifies the lexeme "filles," which contains that seme. In the position in the sentence occupied by "bavardes," a lexeme containing the seme "inanimate" (such as "émaillées" or "vernissées") is forbidden.[7] It is conceivable, of course, that a sentence like "Les petites filles sont émaillées" ("Little girls are enameled") might be found in a surrealist poem. But the poetic effect here would come precisely from the infraction of the code, which prescribes a semantic redundancy; the shock effect of the famous Chomsky sentence, "Colorless green ideas sleep furiously," comes from a similar infraction, as do metaphors in general.

In the above example the redundancies are obligatory, inherent in the code of French; the freedom of choice of the speaker is either limited (I can choose a different adjective than "bavardes," but certain adjectives are excluded) or else nonexistent (I have no choice at all about marking gender and number). The further up one goes on the scale of linguistic levels, the greater the freedom of choice on the part of the speaker: on the lexical level I have more choice (at least as far as the combination of words is concerned) than on the phonological level, which involves the combination of distinctive traits into phonemes. As for the discursive or textual level, which involves the combination of sentences into a discourse or text, the speaker's freedom is, according to the linguists, "very great."[8]

It would seem, in effect, that on the level of discourse or of the elaboration of texts, whether these are written or spoken, we are no longer dealing only with redundancies that are part of a linguistic code; we are also dealing with rhetorical or stylistic redundancies—precisely with those "excessive" or "superfluous" features that correspond to the ordinary notion of redundancy. Does this mean that on the textual level there are no constraints, no obligatory redundancies that would correspond to those on the level of the sentence? Certainly not. To the extent that redundancy is an essential means of conserving information and an equally essential means of creating syntactic and semantic *coherence*, it must necessarily function on the level of texts as well as on the level of individual sentences. As the theory of text grammars is at present a very incomplete one, we shall no doubt have to wait a while before anything like a general theory of textual redundancy is formulated. In the meantime, however, we could already begin to study certain *types* of texts and certain categories of discourse in terms of redundancy, that is, in terms of the greater or lesser degree of probability of occurrence of certain signs (signs being understood here in a very broad sense). For example, the category of discourse known as the "political campaign speech" can be defined largely in terms of the redundancies—both on the level of sound and of sense—that characterize it. Similarly for the category of texts known as "la dissertation française," characterized by the redundant triad: saying what you are about to say; saying it; saying what you have just said.

The important point here is that these are formal redundancies independent of the specific content of a given text, and independent as well of the purely individual, stylistic redundancies, characteristic of a specific speaker or writer, that a given text may contain. We might therefore call these *generic* redundancies, situated between the strictly obligatory redundancies of the language and the "free," noncoded redundancies of individual discourse.

The notion of generic redundancy seems to me to be of wide applicability, both in the analysis of "ordinary" discourse and in the analysis of literary texts. If one starts from the hypothesis that the *degree* and the *types* of redundancy in a given text are a manifestation of its genre, then it becomes possible to formulate generic definitions of texts using redundancy as one important criterion. Linguists might, with the help of speech-act theory, study in a systematic fashion the constraints, and therefore the redundancies, that characterize the various "genres" (prayer, order, request, promise, exhortation, thanks, etc.) of everyday language. As for the study of literary genres in terms of redundancy, it might serve not only literary theory, but might eventually contribute to a more general theory of text grammars—thus demonstrating once again the fruitfulness of the exchange between linguistics and poetics that Roman Jakobson so often and so persuasively argued for.[9]

Redundancies in Realist Fiction

The fact that realist fiction—and more generally, realist narrative—can be defined in terms of redundancy has not escaped the attention of contemporary theorists of narrative. According to Roland Barthes, one of the essential traits that distinguish the "readable" text from modern "plural" texts is its "obsessive fear of failing to communicate meaning"—whence its recourse to redundancy, which Barthes defines as "a kind of semantic babble" in which meaning is "excessively named."[10] We recognize here a somewhat pejorative version of the linguists' definition of redundancy as a means of conserving information. In effect, any text that aims at optimum communication or at a maximal reduction of ambiguity will tend to be heavily redundant, thus eliminating the interference of "noise." Since in reading a text of any length one of the most obvious kinds of "noise" is the reader's forgetfulness, we can predict that the longer the text the more it will need to multiply its redundancies.

But "readable" texts are not the only ones threatened by the reader's forgetfulness. Furthermore, we have seen that redundancy exists not only on the semantic level, but on all levels of a text. Consequently, even if modern texts are not redundant in the same way, or to the same degree, as the realistic novel, it is impossible that they be wholly devoid of redundancy. A systematic study of the redundancies that characterize modern "plural" texts (those of Philippe Sollers or Maurice Roche, for example) would perhaps show that the break between what Barthes calls the "classical" and the "modern" is not as radical as some have thought. At the same time, such a study would bring to light important differences (for it is not a matter of denying differences, but only of estimating their just measure), especially as concerns the problematic relation between redundancy and repetition. If there is one thing that modern texts make clear (and here the important example would no doubt be Gertrude Stein), it is that repetition does not necessarily imply discursive coherence, nor, for that reason, redundancy.[11] But from there to an explicit understanding of the difference between the two, and of the ways in which this difference may be exploited, emphasized, or on the contrary occulted by a given text or category of texts, we have yet a way to go.

As concerns the redundancies of realist narrative, which have received more attention, the most suggestive analyses to date, besides those of Barthes, have been those of Philippe Hamon. Hamon has argued, in several extremely interesting articles,[12] that the discourse of realist narrative—which he calls a "constrained discourse"—is characterized by multiple redundancies operating on the level of characters and their functions, on the level of narrative sequences, of descriptions, of "knowledge" to be transmitted, in fact on just about every level of the narrative. According to Hamon, "the realist undertaking is identified with the pedagogic desire to transmit information . . . , and thus to avoid as much as possible any 'noise' that might interfere with the the communication of information and the transitivity of the message." The "realist-readable" text is therefore characterized by "a hypertrophy of anaphoric devices and redundancy, aiming to insure the cohesion and the disambiguation of the information transmitted."[13]

Hamon illustrates his theoretical statements with numerous examples, drawn for the most part from the novels of Zola. He makes no attempt, however, to classify or to study systematically the types of redundancies that insure (and *how* they insure) the coherence and the "disambiguation" of realist narrative. Despite the fatigue and the occasional frustration (both for the analyst and his or her reader) that the establishment of inventories involves, the ungratefulness of the task is compensated for by the greater descriptive precision and by the new discoveries it makes possible. Gérard Genette, whose work in the domain of narratology is in this respect exemplary, speaks at one point in "Discours du récit" of "les disgrâces de la nomenclature." Indeed. But without the names that Genette invents for them, would we perceive and be able to identify the devices and figures whose complex interaction constitutes, as Genette shows, the infinitely varied discourse of narrative? Provided that one not consider, Casaubon-like, classification as an end in itself, it is not only excusable but necessary.

As the reader will undoubtedly have guessed, what follows is a classification. I propose, first, to classify the principal types of redundancy to be found in realist fiction (some of these being, of course, equally possible in other narrative genres as well, such as the fairy tale, the fantastic, etc.). After that, it will be possible to ask whether the prevalence of certain types of redundancy, as well as variations in degree of redundancy, can be used to distinguish the *roman à thèse* within the larger category.

In order to begin such a classification, one must have before one a schema, however simplified it may be, of the main constituents of a traditional narrative text. Using this schema, we can establish the possible redundancies between different levels of the text and between the elements existing on a single level. The following schema is based chiefly on the works of A. J. Greimas and Gérard Genette; I have occasionally modified their terminology (see schema 1).

The schema calls for a few comments. First, it acknowledges the by now canonical distinction between the level of story (*histoire*) or narrative content (which the Russian Formalists called *fabula*), and another level variously called the level of *discourse* (Todorov, Chatman) or of *récit* (Genette), which the Formalists called *suzhet*. With the help of this distinction— whose ancestor was perhaps the classical rhetorical distinction between *inventio* on the one hand, *dispositio* and *elocutio* on the other—one can define any narrative as the "putting into discourse of a story."[14] A story is constituted by *sequences* of events or actions (these sequences can be broken down into "kernels" and "catalyses," following the terminology suggested by Roland Barthes in 1966),[15] which follow upon each other logically and chronologically and which are experienced or accomplished by *characters* in a *context*.[16] The putting into discourse of the story is the way in which the story is presented to the reader or listener; more simply, it is the text as it appears or unfolds in a reading or listening experience. The three determinants of the process of putting into discourse are: 1) *narration* or narrative instance (who is telling the story, to whom, under what circumstances?); 2) *focalization* (from whose perspective(s) is the story "seen" or experienced?); and

Schema I
Principal Constituents of the Narrative Text

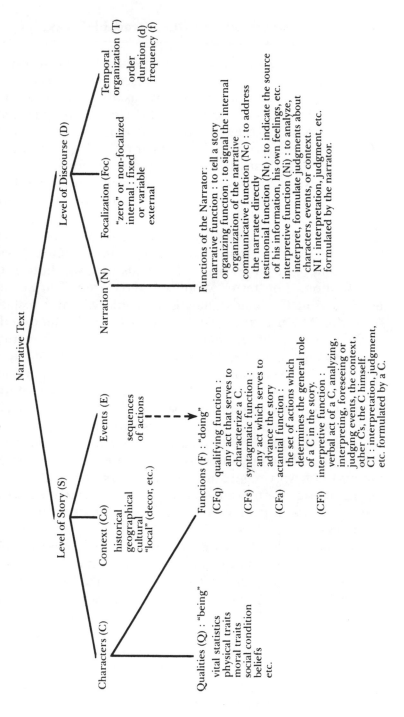

Narrative Text

Level of Story (S)

Characters (C)   Context (Co)   Events (E)

Context (Co)
historical
geographical
cultural
"local" (decor, etc.)

Events (E)
sequences
of actions   →   "doing"

Qualities (Q) : "being"
vital statistics
physical traits
moral traits
social condition
beliefs
etc.

Functions (F) : "doing"

(CFq)   qualifying function :
any act that serves to
characterize a C.

(CFs)   syntagmatic function :
any act which serves to
advance the story

(CFa)   actantial function :
the set of actions which
determines the general role
of a C in the story.

(CFi)   interpretive function :
verbal act of a C, analyzing,
interpreting, foreseeing or
judging events, the context,
other Cs, the C himself.
CI : interpretation, judgment,
etc. formulated by a C.

Level of Discourse (D)

Narration (N)   Focalization (Foc)   Temporal
organization (T)

Temporal
organization (T)
order
duration (d)
frequency (f)

Focalization (Foc)
"zero" or non-focalized
internal : fixed
or variable
external

Functions of the Narrator:
narrative function : to tell a story
organizing function : to signal the internal
organization of the narrative
communicative function (Nc) : to address
the narratee directly
testimonial function (Nt) : to indicate the source
of his information, his own feelings, etc.
interpretive function (Ni) : to analyze,
interpret, formulate judgments about
characters, events, or context.
NI : interpretation, judgment, etc.
formulated by the narrator.

3) *temporal organization* (the order, frequency, and duration of events as they are recounted in the discourse versus the order, frequency, and duration of events as they occurred in the story). In "Discours du récit," Gérard Genette has analyzed in detail the possible relations that can exist between the story and its putting into discourse. As for the logic of the story proper (independently of its putting into discourse), it has been studied most particularly by A. J. Greimas and Claude Bremond, in the tradition inaugurated by the works of Vladimir Propp.[17]

As concerns terminology, I have for the most part retained the terms proposed by Greimas and Genette, designating by letters in parentheses the terms that will figure in my classification. The terms "context" and "event," however, do not figure in Greimas's analytic vocabulary,[18] and instead of "character" he uses the term "actor." I have also modified one of the functions of the narrator enumerated by Genette. He proposes the term "ideological function" to designate "the narrator's interventions, direct or indirect, with regard to the story," these interventions taking "the didactic form of an authorized commentary on the action."[19] Even while retaining Genette's definition, I prefer to use the more general (and more neutral) term of "interpretive function." What it designates is, in effect, any interpretive commentary formulated by the narrator with regard to the characters, the context, or the events of the story. Similar interpretive commentaries can of course also be formulated by one or more characters within the story.

Finally, I should point out that in the classification that follows I have in mind chiefly the type of narration made by an "extraheterodiegetic narrator with zero focalization," in Genette's terminology—roughly corresponding to the traditional "omniscient" narrator. This does not, however, affect the classification of types of redundancy, for all of the redundancies I enumerate can in principle also be found in narratives with a different type of narrator (intradiegetic, who tells a story within a story; autodiegetic, who tells his own story, etc.), or with a different focalization.

In working out the classification, I found the use of formulas as a kind of shorthand notation helpful. To facilitate readability, however, I have given, under the heading of "Explanations and Remarks," verbal definitions corresponding to each formula. A reader may skip the formula and read only the definition.

*Classification of the Types of Redundancy Possible
in Realist Fiction*

Category A. *Redundancies on the level of the story* ($S = S$)

Formula	*Explanation and Remarks*
A.1.1. $C_1E = C_2E = C_nE$	The same event or same sequence of events happens to more than one character. This is a well-known form of narrative doubling or tripling.
A.1.2. $CE_1 = CE_2 = CE_n$	The same event or same sequence of events happens to a single character n times. This is another form of narrative reduplication. Cf. the "novel of failure," in which the protagonist fails n times—in love, in his career, in friendship, etc.
	Rem.: The "same" event designates events which have the same narrative structure. The specific circumstances can vary of course (and usually do).
A.2.1. $C_1Q = C_2Q = C_nQ$ $C_1Fq = C_2Fq = C_nFq$	Several characters have the same qualities or accomplish the same qualifying functions.
	Rem.: The absolute identity of qualities between two or more characters is excluded; the redundancy is, here as elsewhere, a partial one; e.g., C_1 is young, rich,

Formula	*Explanation and Remarks*
	ambitious, and a student; C_2 is young, poor, ambitious, and a student; C_n is young, rich, non-ambitious, and a student, etc.
A.2.2. $CQ_1 = CQ_2 = CQ_n$ $CFq_1 = CFq_2 = CFq_n$	A single character manifests the same qualities or accomplishes the same qualifying functions throughout the story.
	Rem.1: Characters who do not change at all in the course of the story are those E. M. Forster called "flat characters." But even "round" characters have certain qualities that do not change—e.g., name, vital statistics.
	Rem.2: A change in qualities, even the most basic ones such as name, is always possible: the coward becomes brave, X turns out to be really Y or changes his name to Y, etc. The only restriction is that in realist narrative any change in qualities of a character must be *motivated*.
A.3.1. $C_1Fs = C_2Fs = C_nFs$	Several characters accomplish the same syntagmatic function: e.g., two doctors operating, three war pilots on a mission, etc.
	Rem.: Two characters that have one or more syntagmatic functions in common can still differ in their qualities, their actantial functions, etc.
A.3.2 $CFs_1 = CFs_2 = CFs_n$	A single character accomplishes the same syntagmatic function several times; e.g., a doctor oper-

Formula

Explanation and Remarks

ates n times, a war pilot leaves on mission n times, etc.

Rem.: If a character has only a single syntagmatic function, or a very limited number of them repeated n times, then the syntagmatic function may merge with a qualifying function: the doctor "acts the doctor," the pilot "acts the pilot." Such a character is a minor character, even though he may be necessary to the action (e.g., a doctor who appears several times and serves to advance the action, even though he does nothing but "act the doctor").

A.4. $C_1Fa = C_2Fa = C_nFa$

Several characters have the same actantial function; i.e., a single actantial category is "occupied" by several characters, who are in that respect redundant with each other. Such an actantial category can be considered *overdetermined* in a given work.

A.5.1. $C_1Fi = C_2Fi = C_nFi$

Several characters pronounce the same interpretive commentary (judgment, analysis, prognosis) concerning an event, a context, a character, etc.

A.5.2. $CFi_1 = CFi_2 = CFi_n$

A single character pronounces n times the same commentary concerning an event, a context, a character (who can be himself), etc.

Rem.: The characters' commentaries can be expressed in exactly the

Formula	*Explanation and Remarks*
	same words from one time to another (which is rather rare), or else in different words which "mean the same thing." This poses the problem of the synonymity of nonidentical statements, which is an as yet unresolved linguistico-philosophical problem. Any theory of redundancy rests, however, on the supposition that verbally different statements can be synonymous.
A.6. $C = Co$	The context is metonymically redundant with a character; e.g., the baker in his bakery, the priest in his sacristy (example cited by Hamon), etc.
	Rem.: Certain characters can function as context in relation to others: the baker's apprentice, the choir boy for the priest, etc. If such characters have no other function, they can be considered as purely "contextual" characters.
A.7. $E = CI$	An event is redundant with the interpretive commentary made by a character (or several characters) concerning it.[20]
	Rem.1: The *order* of the redundant elements is pertinent here. If the commentary follows the event, its function is to "fix" or *name* the latter's meaning. If the event follows the commentary (e.g., a character says: "War is inevitable" and then the war breaks out), then the event confirms the commentary

Formula

Explanation and Remarks

and functions as a "proof" of its validity.

Rem.2: Certain characters "are always right"—i.e., their commentaries (prognoses, analyses, judgments) are always confirmed by events. Such a character functions as a "correct interpreter," or as a spokesman for the values of the implied author. Once such a character has been constituted, all of his commentaries will tend to function as authoritative commentaries in the work.

Rem.3: Inversely, there may be characters whose commentaries are never confirmed by events. Here, the *absence* of redundancy between event and commentary marks the character as a failed or false interpreter. From that point on, all his commentaries will tend to be discredited.

Rem.4: Since events are constituted chiefly by the actions of the characters, we can rewrite this type of redundancy as follows:

$$\left.\begin{array}{c} C_nFs \\ \\ C_nFa \end{array}\right\} = C_1I$$

In other words, the syntagmatic and actantial functions of a character C_n are redundant with the commentary that C_1 makes about them. C_1 and C_n may be one and

Formula

Explanation and Remarks

the same; in that case, the character comments on his own actions, or on his own role.

A.8. $C_nF_q = C_1I$

The qualifying functions of a character C_n are redundant with the interpretive commentary made about him by C_1; e.g., C_1 says about C_n: "He is a coward," and C_n acts in a cowardly manner.

Rem.1: C_n and C_1 can be the same character; in that case, the character comments on his own qualifying functions.

Rem.2: See Rems. 1–3 in category A.7.

A.9. $CFa = \begin{cases} CQ \\ CFq \end{cases}$

The actantial role of a character is redundant with his qualities or his qualifying functions; e.g., the subject-hero is handsome, generous, courageous, intelligent (or becomes that way in the course of the story); ditto for the helper and the donor. The anti-subject or false hero, as well as the hero's opponent, are not (really) handsome, generous, courageous, etc.

Rem.1: The opposition *being* vs. *seeming* is pertinent here. A character may not be what he seems, he may wear a mask, etc.

Rem.2: This type of redundancy is especially prevalent in popular or folk genres, where the characters tend to be heavily stereotyped; this redundancy is in fact a definition of stereotyping. In the novel (even

Formula	*Explanation and Remarks*
	in the *roman à thèse*, which sometimes exploits this type of redundancy), the redundancy is generally only partial; e.g., the hero is intelligent, not necessarily handsome, not always courageous or virtuous. The opponent is not wholly, or not always, cowardly, evil, etc.

Category B. *Redundancies on the level of discourse* $(D = D)$

B.1. $Nc_1 = Nc_2 = Nc_n$	The narrator maintains (or repeats) the same type of contact with the narratee: he is consistently "chatty," discreet, joking, moralizing, didactic, etc.
	Rem.: Stylistic analysis becomes pertinent here. This concerns in fact the "style" adopted by the narrator in his contacts with the extradiegetic narratee, that is, with the inscribed or encoded reader.
B.2. $NI_1 = NI_2 = NI_n$	The narrator pronounces n times the same commentary about a character, an event, or a context. Homeric epithets enter into this category, as do all other direct commentaries and characterizations made by the narrator. The narrator's commentaries can very in length and development.
	Rem.: See Rem., category A.5.2. above.
B.3. $Nt_1 = Nt_2 = Nt_n$	The narrator indicates n times "the source from which he obtained his information, or the degree of pre-

Formula

Explanation and Remarks

cision of his own memories or the feelings aroused in him by a given episode."[21]

Rem.1: This type of redundancy is found above all in auto (or homo)-diegetic narratives, but it is also possible in hetero-diegetic narratives—cf. the "testimonial" remarks of the omniscient narrator in Fielding's novels.

Rem.2: The testimonial function is linked both to the communicative function (the narrator's testimonial statements establish a type of communication with the narratee) and to the interpretive function (the testimonial statements can be part of a commentary about a character, an event, etc.)

B.4. $Foc(E_1) = Foc(E_2) = Foc(E_n)$

The focalization, of whatever type it is, is maintained throughout the narrative—e.g., a "non-focalized" narrative doesn't suddenly become internal or external, etc.

Rem.: Variations in focalization may be found in any narrative, as Genette, and especially Mieke Bal,[22] have shown. We are therefore dealing once again with a partial redundancy, but one which establishes the *dominance* of a certain type of focalization.

B.5.1. $f(E_1) = f(E_2) = f(E_n)$

The frequency (i.e., the number of times an event is told) tends to be consistent.

B.5.2. $d(E_1) = d(E_2) = d(E_n)$

The duration (i.e., the relation between the "length" of discourse

Formula

Explanation and Remarks

and the "length" of the event recounted) tends to be consistent.

Rem.: Here, more than ever, we are dealing with only partial redundancies, for variations in frequency and especially in duration occur in every narrative of more than minimal length. Yet, it seems safe to say that in most narratives the occurrence of a certain *kind* of frequency and a certain *kind* of duration becomes after a while highly foreseeable, hence redundant. The identical information conveyed in such cases is not semantic, but formal. In *A la recherche du temps perdu,* the reader learns to expect very long scenes, which are a phenomenon of duration. In Robbe-Grillet's novels, the reader expects every "event" to be told more than once (frequency). In the realist novel, the dominant frequency is generally singulative (each event is told once); as for duration, every text creates its own pattern. Consistency in duration (i.e., in narrative rhythm) is probably one of the chief determinants of a given text's narrative style.

Category C. *Redundancies between the level of story and the level of discourse* $(S = D/D = S)$

C.1. $E = f_{2-n}$

An event is told more than once (repetitive narration).

Rem.1: This type of redundancy should not be confused with type B.5.1. There, what recurred and

Formula

Explanation and Remarks

became highly probable was *a given type of frequency,* whichever it was: the recurrence functioned solely on the level of discourse. Here, the redundancy functions *between* the level of story and the level of discourse; this type of redundancy is found only in what Genette calls repetitive narration (*récit répétitif*), not the other two frequencies (singulative and iterative).

Rem.2: One should not equate every repetition of an event by the discourse with a redundancy of this type. Almost always in the *nouveau roman,* the repetition in the telling of an event establishes a "false redundancy," because each version of the "same" event contradicts previous versions. In order to have a genuine redundancy of the type C.1, each version of an event must unambiguously refer to that event and not to another. If contradictions exist, they must be motivated in terms of character, etc., (cf. *Rashomon*). The "false redundancies" of the *nouveau roman* might serve as a criterion of genre. They also suggest one possible difference between redundancy and repetition.

C.2. $E = NI$

An event is redundant with the interpretive commentary which the narrator makes about it (see category A.7).

Formula	*Explanation and Remarks*
	Rem.1: See *Rems.1–4,* category A.7. A narrator who "is always right" is generally an omniscient narrator; a narrator who is rarely or never right (what he says is not confirmed by events) is, using Wayne Booth's terminology, an "unreliable narrator."[23]
	Rem.2: An omniscient narrator who tends constantly to interpret the events he tells (either before, or after, or simultaneously with the telling) does what Barthes calls "excessively naming the meaning." He is a "talkative" or openly didactic narrator, in opposition to a "discreet" or taciturn one.
C.3. $CFq = NI$	The qualifying functions of a character are redundant with the interpretive commentary (or commentaries) which the narrator makes about them (see category A.8).
C.4. $CI = NI$	The interpretation pronounced by a character about an event, a context, or a character (who may be himself) is redundant with the interpretation(s) of the narrator.
	Rem.1: the order of the two interpretations is perhaps pertinent. In any case, the redundancy between them (which may be only partial, with only some elements repeated) acts as a reinforcement of both, one by the other ("echo effect").

Formula	*Explanation and Remarks*
	Rem.2: There may also be contradictions, or a total absence of redundancy between the two interpretations. In that case, if the narrator is omniscient, it is the character's interpretation that is discredited. If the narrator is not omniscient, subsequent events will "prove" one right. The one who is right may then become the implied author's spokesman.

I will not comment in detail on the categories of the above inventory, but merely emphasize some essential points. First, the inventory presents the principal types of redundancy possible in realist fiction; not all of these types are necessarily realized in any given work. Second, some of the redundancies mentioned can be found in other types of narrative as well: fairy tales, science fiction, etc. That is one reason why each narrative genre or sub-genre should be studied individually, in order to see whether it is possible to specify certain types of redundancy (or of non-redundancy) that characterize it in particular. Third, the redundancies mentioned above are *formal* redundancies, which function independently of the specific content or the specific style of individual works; these redundancies constitute, therefore, a system of formal constraints—that is, a code—which defines the rules of narrative coherence, and in particular the rules of realist narrative.

Finally, as I suggested in some of my explanatory remarks, one must certainly study the *absence* of redundancy as well as the redundancies themselves in analyzing a single work or a single kind of work. An artistic text is defined as much by its infractions of formal constraints, or its playing with and on formal constraints, as by its submission to them. Furthermore, if certain groups of texts manifest a number of specific and recurrent infractions of the realist code, these infractions can themselves serve as a classificatory criterion. In Robbe-Grillet's novels, for example, we know that a single name can designate, without any realistic motivation, a series of characters who are not the "same." This constitutes a play on the redundancies of category A.2.2. above, and this play (which eventually becomes highly probable, hence redundant in its own way) can in turn be considered as part of a code: the specific code (corresponding to the idiolect in linguistics) that regulates the novels of Robbe-Grillet.

Redundancies in the *Roman à thèse*

I have stated several times in the course of this work that the *roman à thèse* is characterized by "a great deal" of redundancy. The theoretical, classificatory detour we have just taken should allow us to define more precisely what that means. At the same time, it should allow us to test the theoretical hypothesis that redundancy can serve as a criterion of genre. It would be foolish, of course, to try to define the *roman à thèse*, or any other genre, exclusively in terms of redundancy. I am suggesting only that redundancy can serve as one criterion among others, or as one methodological approach among others. It is only by a series of successive approximations, or definitions in terms of converging criteria, that one can hope to pin down anything as complex and as unstable as a novelistic genre. Aristotle, who cannot be accused of lacking in method, said that every object must be studied with the precision appropriate to it. If the poetics of the novel can aspire to precision, one should not aim for greater precision than its object allows.

As concerns redundancy in the *roman à thèse*, my starting hypotheses are as follows: first, the *roman à thèse* manifests a very high *degree* of redundancy; second, it privileges certain *types* of redundancy; third, it *thematizes formal redundancies* in a particular way—in other words, it invests formal redundancies (or certain types of formal redundancy) with specific contents in a characteristic way. These three hypotheses are obviously interrelated, but it will be simpler to treat them separately.

"Highly Coherent Systems": Degree of Redundancy

In a general way, one can define the degree of coherence of a system (be it a statement, a text, a family, a political party, or whatever) as a function of internal contradiction. The fewer contradictory elements there exist in the system, the greater its degree of coherence, and vice versa. If contradictory elements within the system become too numerous, it eventually breaks up: the text becomes "unreadable" (or schizophrenic), the family splits up, the political party splinters. However, the total absence of internal contradiction may also have a negative effect on the functioning of the system. To the extent that contradictions introduce disruptive elements (every contradiction provokes a crisis of varying strength and duration), they allow the system to test and possibly to reinforce its own coherence. A crisis overcome (or "weathered") becomes in that case a sign of coherence; it is also a sign of the system's flexibility or "openness," since it obliges the system to integrate new elements without which it would run the risk of stagnating. If too much internal contradiction leads to a break-up, the total absence of contradiction leads to decay.

Reformulating the above in terms of redundancy, we can see that total redundancy (in other words, maximum coherence) in a system of communication would be as dysfunctional, although in a different way, as the total absence of redundancy. In fact, neither of these possibilities is wholly realizable: in order for communication to take place—or for a text to constitute itself—there must be both conservation of "old" information and the introduction of new information, both a certain predictability of signs and a lack of predictability. New information does not necessarily bring contradiction with it, but it does at least open that possibility. And in every case it complicates the message, by introducing new material to be processed; the complication might eventually act as a "noise" obstructing the transmission of an unambiguous meaning.

Obviously, certain systems, and certain texts, are more redundant than others—they tend to conserve information rather than increasing it. Within the broad category of realist narrative, the *roman à thèse* is such a system; but within this system itself, one will certainly find variations in degree of redundancy when comparing one text to another. It is by comparing two texts one intuitively knows to have different degrees of redundancy that one can arrive, without the use of quantitative methods involving a computer, at a more precise notion of what is meant by degree of redundancy. I shall therefore consider two novels I have discussed previously in different contexts—the first being my "model" *roman à thèse*, Bourget's *L'Etape*, the second a "problematic" *roman à thèse*, Malraux's *L'Espoir*. As I hardly need point out, an exhaustive analysis of redundancies in the two novels is impossible here; but for my purposes, a selective comparison will be sufficient.

In *L'Etape*, I shall concentrate on the way the novel constitutes one of its main characters, for this will allow us to understand how its general system of redundancies functions. In a realist novel, characters are the nodal points around which events, interpretive commentaries, actantial categories, and various contexts revolve—they are, in a sense, intersections where the multiple levels and components of the text meet. The more "major" a character is, the more elements are clustered around him, and vice versa. It is therefore by a somewhat circular process that one designates certain characters as "major" ones in a given work; or rather it is by a retrospective process, for it is only after having read the whole novel that one can fully distinguish major characters from secondary or minor ones. Once this judgment has been made, it is possible to return to the beginning and see how the novel constitutes the character, step by step, and how it inserts the character into a network of redundancies.

Let us look, therefore, at the way *L'Etape* constitutes the character of Joseph Monneron, who, it will be recalled, is the hero's father and plays a negative actantial role (that of a false or pseudo-donor) in the hero's story. Before actually appearing on the scene, Joseph Monneron is presented to the reader *in absentia* no less than four times: twice by the omniscient narrator, once by the "good" donor Victor Ferrand, and once by the subject-hero, Jean Monneron. These four presentations, which are in fact interpretive commentaries about the character, occur as follows (I have indicated in parentheses the symbols used in the preceding classification of redundancies):

1. First commentary by the narrator (NI_1), addressed to the extradiegetic narratee:
   a. JM, a lycée professor, is a "farmer's son" ("fils de cultivateur")
   b. His career represents the type of development promoted by the "doctrinaires of our democracy" (the narrator's irony is evident)
   c. He owes his career entirely to himself and the State
   d. He is proud ("Il est fier")
   e. He is an "absolute exemplar of a Jacobin" ("exemplaire absolu de Jacobin")
   f. He is "outside any kind of religion" ("hors de toute espèce de religion")[24]

2. Commentary by Victory Ferrand (C_1I), addressed to Jean:
   a. JM is a "déclassé"
   b. His career shows "the complicity of the State, as created for us by the Revolution"
   c. "His irreligiosity is, like his radicalism, a proof that he does not live with his dead" (i.e., his ancestors—"la preuve qu'il ne vit pas avec ses morts")
   d. He is proud ("Il est orgueilleux")
   e. He is the "son of a Jacobin"
   f. He has "broken with the tradition of his race"
   g. He is an "honest man with the ideas of a sectarian" ("un honnête homme avec les idées d'un sectaire") (1:25–28)

3. Commentary by Jean Monneron (C_2I), addressed to Victor Ferrand:
   a. "For all his distinction, the peasant is too close" ("Tout distingué qu'il est, le paysan est trop près")
   b. He is a Republican; he has "faith in the principles of '89"
   c. Separated from his family since childhood, he does not know anything about life ("il ne connaît pas la vie")
   d. He suffers from a voluntary blindness as far as his own family is concerned (Julie and Antoine)

   e. He is an unhappy man who won't admit his unhappiness to himself.

   f. He is a lover of literature ("un amoureux des Lettres")

   g. He is an idealist to the point of living in a dream-world ("un idéaliste jusqu'à la chimère") (1:47–48).

4. Second commentary by the narrator (NI$_2$):

   a. "a dreamy professor, willfully blind to truths that are too painful" ("Professeur chimérique, volontairement aveugle sur des vérités trop pénibles"—1:65).

Thus, in the first two chapters of the novel, and before he has made a single appearance in "flesh and blood," Joseph Monneron has been summed up and interpreted at least four times (for I have not noted *every* interpretive commentary about him)—this in a context where all the interpretations function as "correct" ones. The omniscient narrator speaks, by definition, with the "voice of Truth"; Victor Ferrand, before we hear his interpretation, has already been presented by the narrator in extremely positive terms (1:10–13), so that even if we overlooked the fact that his commentary "repeats" the narrator's commentary, he would function as a "correct" interpreter. As for Jean Monneron, he is not given from the outset as a correct interpreter (his immediate past, after all, is that of a republican, anticlerical *dreyfusard*), but since his commentary "repeats" the previous two commentaries and is addressed to Ferrand, who agrees with it, there can be no doubt as to its "correctness."

Superimposing the commentaries on each other, we note the following redundancies: the second commentary is redundant in relation to the first, not only because it characterizes Joseph Monneron in essentially the same way, but because it even repeats the vocabulary of the first. The individual vocabulary items are not combined in exactly the same way, however (e.g., "exemplaire absolu de Jacobin" vs. "fils d'un Jacobin;" "hors de toute espèce de religion" vs. "son irreligion;" "fier" vs. "orgueilleux"), thus allowing for a certain variation within the redundancies. More importantly, the second commentary introduces a new bit of information that was not present in the first: it characterizes Joseph Monneron as an "honnête homme," despite his sectarian ideas. Finally, Ferrand's commentary *develops* certain bits of information that were present in the narrator's commentary without being developed: it is Ferrand who establishes the links between irreligiosity, radicalism, and the break with tradition, thus inaugurating the demonstrative movement of the novel; it is also Ferrand who insists on the importance of "continuity with one's race," thus preparing the way for Jean Monneron's "return to his ancestors" by means of his religious conversion at the end of the novel.

As for the third commentary, by Jean, it repeats certain bits of information given in the preceding ones (elements a, b, c are redundant with elements a, b, c in the other two commentaries), but it introduces three (or perhaps four) pieces of new information: Joseph Monneron is "willfully blind" to what is happening in his family (this prepares the way for the stories of Julie's "shame" and Antoine's disgrace, of which the father is unaware until practically the very end); he is unhappy without admitting it (this may, however, be merely a variation on the preceding piece of information); he is "idealistic to the point of living in a dream-world"; finally, he is a lover of literature. This last piece of information may be considered as a variant on Ferrand's judgment that he is an "honnête homme," since it endows Joseph Monneron with a positive quality in addition to all his negative ones.

The fourth commentary, which is again by the narrator, repeats (and consequently reinforces) the new information contributed by Jean. Thus, *there is not a single interpretive element concerning Joseph Monneron that is not repeated at least once in the course of the four commentaries.*

Using our previous notation, we may formalize the redundancies among the four commentaries (keeping in mind, however, that we are dealing with partial redundancies, in which not *all* the elements are repeated from one commentary to the other) by means of the following chain:

$$\langle 1 \rangle \quad NI_1 = C_1I = C_2I = NI_2 \ldots$$

As the suspension points indicate, this is actually only the beginning of a chain, for the four commentaries occur at fifteen-page intervals in the beginning of the novel. A complete analysis would show that this interpretive chain is continued to the end of the novel, introducing other characters who repeat some of the previous interpretations, bringing in more interpretations by the narrator and by Ferrand and Jean, and so on. The degree of redundancy is thus determined by the *number of times* that an interpretation (and more generally, any piece of information) is given; but it is also determined by the *number of different "voices"* that formulate the interpretation, and the *number of levels* on (and between) which the redundancies exist. Thus, considering only our partial chain given above, we can see that its degree of redundancy is increased by the fact that three different voices formulate the "same" interpretation; it is also increased by the fact that one of these voices— the narrator's—is on a different level: the narrator's interpretations function on the level of discourse, while those of Jean and Ferrand function on the level of story.

We can push the analysis further: the chain we have been examining can itself be decomposed into simpler chains, since each of the interpretations is part of its own homogeneous series. We thus obtain three simple chains as follows:

$$\langle 2 \rangle \quad NI_1 = NI_2 = NI_3 \ldots$$ Interpretations of the narrator concerning Joseph Monneron

$$\langle 3 \rangle \quad C_1I_1 = C_1I_2 = C_1I_3 \ldots$$ Interpretations of C_1 (Victor Ferrand) concerning Joseph Monneron.

$$\langle 4 \rangle \quad C_2I_1 = C_2I_2 = C_2I_3 \ldots$$ Interpretations of C_2 (Jean Monneron) concerning Joseph Monneron

Each of these interpretive chains is redundant within itself (its elements are redundant with each other), and is also redundant with the other chains. The redundancies between $\langle 3 \rangle$ and $\langle 4 \rangle$ function on the level of story; those between $\langle 2 \rangle$ and $\langle 3 \rangle$, and $\langle 2 \rangle$ and $\langle 4 \rangle$ function *between* the level of discourse and the level of story. Thus:

$$\langle 2 \rangle \quad NI_1 = NI_2 = NI_3 \ldots \qquad \text{(level of discourse)}$$
$$\langle 3 \rangle \quad C_1I_1 = C_1I_2 = C_1I_3 \ldots \qquad \text{(level of story)}$$
$$\langle 4 \rangle \quad C_2I_1 = C_2I_2 = C_2I_3 \ldots \qquad \text{(level of story)}$$

Reading the redundancies vertically (or along the slanted lines, as between $\langle 2 \rangle$ and $\langle 4 \rangle$), we obtain complex chains like chain $\langle 1 \rangle$, whose redundancies I have indicated above with heavy lines.[25] Reading the redundancies horizontally, we obtain simple chains. The more links there are within the simple chains and between them, the greater the degree of redundancy in the text. One might even assign different "weights" to the various links, giving more weight to a vertical link than to a horizontal one, more to a link between elements belonging to different levels than to one between elements belonging to the same level. At that point the use of a computer would become indispensable—alas, or perhaps fortunately (if one wanted to go that far)!

But we soon realize that the analysis has only begun, for interpretive redundancies (whether simple or complex) are only one possible type among others: actantial redundancies, redundancies of events, of context, of qualities, of focalization . . . The network of redundancies produced by the combination of these different types is potentially so complex as to defy any attempt at analysis—at least without highly sophisticated mathematical methods. But even if we stick to analysis of a more homespun variety, we can go further; as concerns Joseph Monneron, for example, we can study the way he is presented when he finally appears on the scene; his actantial function; his various qualities, qualifying functions, and syntagmatic functions; his characteristic context; and see whether these are redundant with each other. Thus, when he appears on the scene, we note the following: the text first describes his context, that is, his "habitat" and the characters who surround him (his wife, his children other than Jean); next, we find a physical description of the character; finally, we hear him speak. Now *all of these indications confirm and repeat the previous interpretations* by the narrator, by Ferrand, and by Jean. Joseph Monneron lives in an apartment full of disorder, of a "bohemianism with nothing picturesque about it" ("confirms" his *déclassement*); on the walls of his dining room, there are engraved portraits of Hugo, Michelet, Jules Ferry, and Gambetta, heroes of the Republic; Monneron's favorite place is his study, where he sits surrounded by books ("confirms" his love of literature, his escape from painful realities); his wife is vulgar, a bad housewife; their youngest son, whom he spoils terribly, looks like a little hoodlum ("voyou"—the wife and youngest son are purely contextual characters, having no other function than to signal, redundantly, Monneron's *déclassement* and unhappiness); Monneron's physique (he is short, of powerful build) indicates his "plebeian" descent, but his eyes are sensitive and intelligent; finally, the first words we hear him pronounce indicate his "fanatical irreligiosity," since he tells Jean that the Republic ought to abolish All Souls' Day and substitute for it a Republican holiday honoring the dead who are buried in the Pantheon (1:74–82).

As far as Joseph Monneron is concerned, then, there is not a single piece of information given in this opening scene that does not confirm and reinforce the previous commentaries by the narrator, by Ferrand, and by Jean. The narrative advances, to be sure; it introduces new characters, a new context, new dialogue, and new actions; but these new elements merely repeat, in their own way, what we knew already. Whatever he says or does, whatever happens to him from now on, Joseph Monneron will never be anything other than a man "willfully blind to truths that are too painful," an *"honnête homme* with the ideas of a sectarian," an "idealist to the point of living in a dream world," an "unhappy man who won't admit it to himself," and above all a man who has ruined his life by his irreligiosity and his radicalism, signs of a too rapid rise in a society "created for us by the Revolution." If we recall, in addition, that Joseph Monneron plays a negative actantial role in the novel (as a negative exemplary subject in his own story, and as pseudo-donor in Jean's story), we can see just how perfectly consistent, how perfectly "readable" a character he is, caught in (created by) a network of interlocking chains of redundancy that allows for no deviations and no surprises. In an extremely elementary way, we can represent this network as a single complex chain:

$$\langle \tilde{5} \rangle^{\circ} NI_n = C_1I_n = C_2I_n = CFq = CFs = CFa$$
$$\|$$
$$Co$$

where NI_n are the repeated interpretations of the omniscient narrator

C_1I_n are the repeated interpretations of Victor Ferrand
C_2I_n are the repeated interpretations of Jean Monneron
CFq/Fs/Fa are the qualities and qualifying functions, syntagmatic functions, and actantial functions of Joseph Monneron; and
Co is Joseph Monneron's context (where he lives, characters who surround him, etc.)

In a word: nothing is left to chance. We see here what Barthes called the readable text's "obsessive fear of failing to communicate meaning" move from a neurotic to what might be called a pathological state. The text succeeds so well in becoming "readable" that it ends up (or at least comes close to) closing off all openings, preventing any gap in its network of redundancies.[26] But, by a supreme irony, it may happen that a reader, caught up in this hermetically closed space, will want at any cost to get out of it. Rebelling against a meaning whose communication is all too clear, this reader may say to the text what Gide said to Barrès about *Les Déracinés:* "Your too constant affirmation makes us want to contradict you."[27] At this point, the extreme coherence of the *roman à thèse* turns against itself, becomes dysfunctional: by an excess of "readability," the text risks becoming unreadable—or at the very least, unread.

Possibly *L'Etape* is itself too clear an example: not every *roman à thèse* is as redundant, or as "constant in its affirmations," as this one. But variations among novels in their degree of redundancy do not invalidate the general principle I am discussing. This is confirmed if we look at *L'Espoir,* which is more widely read today (and no doubt more readable in the ordinary sense of that word) than *L'Etape.*

The general degree of redundancy in *L'Espoir* is less than in *L'Etape* (for reasons we shall see in a moment). But as far as the Communist thesis of discipline is concerned ("in order to win the war against Franco, the Left needs disciplined leadership, which the Communists can provide"), its degree of redundancy is quite high. Indeed, this thesis is formulated, more or less completely or explicitly, but always unmistakably, by *six* different characters (hence six different voices), from one end of the novel to the other.[28] Furthermore, one variant of this thesis is expressed in one instance by the narrator, even though the latter is of the extremely "discreet" variety in this novel.[29] This makes for a total of seven different voices redundant with each other; and since one of these voices, the narrator's, is on the level of discourse, that adds a "heavier" link to the redundancies. We therefore obtain the following complex chain:

$$\langle 6 \rangle \quad C_1 I = C_2 I = C_3 I = C_4 I = C_5 I = C_6 I = NI$$

But there are more interpretive redundancies than this, for some of the six characters repeat their interpretations at various times: Garcia (C_2) states his five times, which confirms one's intuitive sense that he is the novel's principal "correct interpreter" or authorial spokesman; Heinrich and Ximénès (C_5 and C_6) state theirs twice each. As for Manuel (C_4), he not only states the thesis; he *lives* it, since part of the story told in the novel is precisely the story of his positive exemplary apprenticeship as a military chief. Manuel learns the necessity of discipline through personal experience, which introduces a major redundancy: all of Manuel's story can be considered as a "proof" of the thesis stated by Garcia and the others (including Manuel himself).

Besides Manuel's story taken as a whole, there are other events that function as "proofs" of the thesis: the victory of Guadalajara is the conclusive proof (at least in the novel, for it ends with this victory) that in order to win, the Republicans must be organized and disciplined. This victory is the work of troops commanded by Manuel and Heinrich, with the strategic help of Garcia—in other words, it is the work of those characters who have all along stated the "correct" view. There is, as well, a major *a contrario* proof toward the beginning of the novel: the defeat of the Republican forces at Toledo, due to an absence of organization and discipline. Considering all of the above, we obtain the following complex chain of redundancies:

$$\langle 7 \rangle \ E_1 = E_2 = E_3 = C_1I = C_2I_5 = C_3I = C_4I_2 = C_5I = C_6I_2 = NI$$

where E_1 is Manuel's apprenticeship story, E_2 is the victory of Guadalajara, E_3 is the defeat at Toledo (proof by negation), and where the number of interpretive statements (regarding the necessity of discipline) made by each character is indicated by the subnumerals.

As concerns the discipline thesis, then, *L'Espoir* manifests a quite high degree of redundancy. However, the general degree of redundancy in the novel is not as high as in *L'Etape*, for two main reasons: first, *L'Espoir* does not exploit certain types of redundancy (for example, the narrator's interpretations are extremely rare), which reduces the number of links and the number of chains in the network; second, as we saw in the preceding chapter, *L'Espoir* allows *other* interpretive voices to enter into a dialogue with the exponents of discipline—indeed, these "other" voices belong sometimes to the same characters (as in the case of Manuel and Garcia). These contradictory voices are not strong enough to break up the system (in this case, a break-up would mean that no single view predominates), for despite their presence, the discipline thesis remains dominant. But they do introduce a certain tension, or to change metaphors, they leave certain openings open. Paradoxically, it may be these very openings that make a reader "swallow" the thesis: the reader's desire to contradict is attenuated when the affirmations of the text are less constant.[30] This leads to the conclusion that even in "highly coherent" texts, a little internal movement does no harm. Nizan remarked, in reviewing one of Malraux's novels, that "the reader adher[es] to the work of art to the extent that he gains in consciousness what he loses in facility"[31]—which is another way of saying that what is easy to understand is not always what gives the most pleasure; perhaps the reader gains in pleasure what he loses in "readability."

Privileged Types

As the foregoing discussion has suggested, the degree of redundancy is partly a function of the *types* of redundancy present in a work: the more different types are present, the higher the degree of redundancy. In addition, we may suppose that certain types of redundancy are by their nature such that their presence or absence will tend to increase or diminish the degree of redundancy in a work. A work like *L'Etape*, which has a long chain of redundant interpretations by the omniscient narrator, whose commentaries announce or confirm the meaning of events and of the characters' various functions, will possess a higher degree of redundancy than a novel like *L'Espoir*, where the narrator's interpretations are extremely rare, or a novel like *Le Noeud de vipères*, where there is no omniscient narrator at all.

Nevertheless, it seems clear that certain types of redundancy must be found in all *romans à thèse*, even in the most discreet ones; without such redundancies, there would be no "thèse." I will discuss five privileged types; some of them are, as it were, optional; others are part of the "rules" of the genre. The first two are as follows:

type 1. $\left.\begin{array}{l} \text{E} \\ \text{CFqsai} \end{array}\right\} = N_x I$ N_x: omniscient narrator (see categories C.2 and C.3 above)

type 2. $\left.\begin{array}{l} \text{E} \\ \text{CFqsai} \end{array}\right\} = C_x I$ C_x: correct interpreter or spokesman character. There may be more than one in a work. (See categories A.7–A.9 above)

In other words: the events and the characters' various functions (qualifying, syntagmatic, actantial, interpretive) are redundant with the interpretive commentary made about them by the omniscient narrator (type 1) or by a "correct interpreter" within the story (type 2). If the commentary precedes (i.e., announces) the event, then the latter confirms the commentary and constitutes a "proof" of its validity; if the commentary follows the event or unfolds simultaneously with its telling, then the commentary "fixes" the event's meaning by eliminating other interpretations.

Obviously, the two types can (and usually do) coexist within a single work; that is the case in *L'Etape,* in *Le Roman de l'énergie nationale, Le Cheval de Troie, Les Beaux Quartiers,* and to a lesser degree in *L'Espoir* (although he is very discreet, the narrator, who is omniscient since he knows what goes on in every character's head, does make interpretive comments from time to time). Similarly, the number of times that a redundancy of either type 1 or type 2 occurs, as well as the frequency of the two types, can vary from work to work. What is required, however, in order for the work to function as a *roman à thèse* is that there be at least one redundant interpretation (whether of type 1 or 2) that functions on a global level—in other words, that accounts for the "whole story" told in the novel. This kind of global interpretation is precisely what defines the *exemplum,* where the story in its entirety exists only in order to be interpreted. The canonical form of such an interpretation is the "moral" which follows the story and sums up its "lesson" for the reader or listener.

But a novel is much longer than an *exemplum*. That is why we can be fairly certain that the number of *romans à thèse* that contain only a single redundancy of type 1 or 2 is extremely small, not to say zero. The length of the text and the large number of events and actions of all kinds require frequent commentaries that will prevent the meaning from "scattering," losing its solidity. Furthermore—but here we move to the question of the semantic investment of formal categories—in the *roman à thèse* the interpretive commentaries refer, most often explicitly, to the work's governing ideology or doctrine.

In a formal perspective, the point that must be emphasized is that the *roman à thèse* is a narrative genre in which actions and events are continually doubled by interpretive commentary. It is a "talkative" genre. Whether the "talk" be by the narrator or by privileged characters or by the two in alternation, there is a great deal of it, reminding us of Barthes' definition of redundancy as a "semantic babble." In this instance, however, the "babble" has precise ends in view: to analyze, to judge, to persuade, to impose a conviction and a line of action on the interlocutor, both inside the fiction and outside it. *L'Espoir* is a good case in point: in this war novel, where action would seem to predominate, scenes of discussion and reflection—philosophical, strategic, tactical—are more frequent, and more memorable, than scenes of battle.

The primacy of interpretive discourse in the *roman à thèse* is indicated by the next two privileged types:

type 3. $N_x I_1 = N_x I_2 = N_x I_3$ N_x: omniscient narrator (see category B.2.)

type 4. $C_x I_1 = C_x I_2 = C_x I_3$ C_x: correct interpreter or spokesman character (see categories A.5.1. and A.5.2.)

There exist in the *roman à thèse* series of interpretive commentaries made by the omniscient narrator (type 3) or by one or more spokesman-characters (type 4), or by both (alternation of types 3 and 4), such that an interpretive "line" is established which runs from one end of the narrative to the other. These commentaries are at least partially redundant with each other; their function is to reduce the ambiguities of the story, imprinting the latter with a single meaning. What is especially important is not the number of commentaries (which can vary from work to work), but their redundancy, or more precisely the *absence of contradiction* between and within them. In Balzac's novels there are enormous numbers of interpretive commentaries made by the narrator, but their function is less to imprint an interpretive "line" on the story than to furnish realistic motivations for actions or events that might otherwise appear *invraisemblables*. Balzac's commentaries, as Genette has shown, have an *ad hoc* quality about them: Does a particular action appear too arbitrary, inconsistent with what went before? The Balzacian narrator immediately invents a psychological or social "law" that will explain the action and give it verisimilitude.[32] But the Balzacian narrator shows no particular concern for the consistency or continuity of his "laws." Indeed, one "law" may contradict another, formulated a few pages earlier or later to explain a different action. In the *roman à thèse*, on the other hand, such *ad hoc* use of commentary as a device of verisimilitude is subordinated to a premeitated didactic and persuasive function.

I spoke in a previous chapter of the ideological supersystem that characterizes the *roman à thèse*, and more generally any strongly monological genre. We can now understand that this supersystem is the result of interpretive redundancy: it is the dominant interpretive "line" in the work that establishes a hierarchical structure, integrating the partial systems of individual characters into the work's supersystem, where each has its proper place.

There may be *romans à thèse* from which type 3 is absent—either because there is no omniscient narrator, or because the latter is extremely discreet. In *L'Espoir*, we cannot speak of a veritable series of redundant commentaries by the narrator, for he intervenes very little. It may be in order to compensate for this discretion that *L'Espoir* has so many talkative characters: the "voice of Truth" is here distributed among the actors of the story; we might even say that it is fragmented, but fragmented or no, it is still present.

It seems certain, however, that novels in which the narrator leaves most of the interpretive talk up to the characters have more potential for internal contradiction or for "gaps" in meaning than those in which the narrator himself speaks with the voice of Truth. In *L'Espoir*, the characters who formulate the Communist thesis engage in fairly frequent dialogues with other characters—such as Captain Hernandez, or the old art historian, Alvear—who defend either opposing values or altogether other ones (Alvear voluntarily excludes himself from politics, and his values have literally "nothing to do with" the major preoccupations of the heroic group). To the extent that these other characters are given the right to speak—in a context that does not devalorize their discourse *a priori*, as is the case, say, when Joseph Monneron speaks in *L'Etape*—the Communist thesis is relativized, or at least put in its place. It is presented not as an absolute truth, but as a valid tactic in the precise circumstances of the war. The result is a certain degree of dialogism, which, as we saw in chapter 3, makes *L'Espoir* a more complex *roman à thèse* than some others. But it nevertheless remains a *roman à thèse*—or perhaps it would be more exact to say that it lends itself to being read as a *roman à thèse*—both because of the clear ideological division between the adversaries in the confrontation story (Republicans vs. fascists) and because within the Republican forces it is the Communists who have the last word. We shouldn't forget, after all, that Hernandez, a Catholic humanist for whom discipline is less important than ethics, pays for his "wrong" interpretation with his life: he is captured and shot by the enemy after the defeat at Toledo, which took place under his command.

The fifth type of redundancy privileged by the *roman à thèse* is the following:

type 5. CFa = CQ (See category A.9.)

In other words, the actantial function of the characters is redundant with their qualities (or with their qualifying functions). As I noted earlier, this type of redundancy is found above all in popular and folk genres, where the characters generally function as cultural stereotypes or as the carriers of accepted cultural values. But a partial redundancy between a character's actantial function and his qualities, between what he "does" and what he "is," exists in any realist narrative, and this redundancy is particularly exploitable—as well as particularly exploited—by the *roman à thèse*. Since what is involved here is the semantic investment of a formal category, I will treat it in detail below.

Semantic Investment of Formal Categories:
The Technique of the Amalgam

Earlier, in discussing the structures of apprenticeship and of confrontation, I noted that the specificity of the *roman à thèse* resides in its appropriation of a narrative structure by a particular mode of discourse. The same is true as concerns redundancy: the *roman à thèse* is characterized not only by its high degree of redundancy and by the types of redundancy it privileges, but also by the specific contents with which it invests formal redundancies. The interpretive commentaries that accompany the action, for example, are, as we saw, not haphazard. The interpretive "line" they create constitutes precisely that doctrinal element which we defined as a distinguishing feature of the genre. However, this doctrinal element does not reside only in commentary, which is the obvious place we would expect to find it. It is also present in the way the novel structures events and characters, independently of any commentary. We can see this by expanding the analysis of our fifth privileged type of redundancy. It is appropriate to deal with the question of semantic investment in terms of the characters, for in the *roman à thèse*, as in all traditional fiction, it is the characters who function as the chief carriers and organizers of meaning.

In popular and folk genres, the characters' qualities are stereotyped, as are their actions. The semantic investment here usually emphasizes the physical attributes and the culturally recognized moral attributes of a character: is he handsome or ugly? strong or weak? neat or ill-kempt? courageous or a coward? honest or dishonest? manly or "effeminate"? (For a female character, the questions would turn around her beauty and her "virtue".) The greater the redundancy between the various qualities of the character, the more predictably he tends to function as a stereotype; thus the male character who is ugly, ill-kempt, a coward, dishonest, and "effeminate" is more stereotyped, and hence more predictable in his actions (he will surely be a villain) than a similar character who is endowed with at least a few culturally positive traits. When a reader says about a fictional character that she is "too negative" or "too perfect," or else that the author is too obviously prejudiced against (or for) her, the reader is expressing in intuitive terms a judgment about the degree of redundancy among the character's qualities. In realist fiction, readers are generally less ready to tolerate charactets who are "all of a piece" than they are in fairy tales, mass-market thrillers, or other mythic genres. This is no doubt due to the criterion of verisimilitude, which requires that characters be more complex, psychologically more believable (and therefore less consistent) in works that claim to represent reality than in works in which the real is not pertinent.

We see here one of the potential weaknesses—or at least one of the potential problems—of the *roman à thèse* as a realist didactic genre. The problem is that of the double bind: to the extent that the didactic demonstration is clearer when the characters and their story are simple and without internal contradictions, the *roman à thèse* will tend to eliminate precisely those aspects of the character and of the story that contribute to making them verisimilar. In doing so, the novel necessarily weakens its own credibility as a representation of the real. Whence the paradoxical situation that defines the dis-ease of the genre: the more a *roman à thèse* is faithful to its didactic calling, the less it succeeds in making itself believed, that is, accepted as a reliable, truth-telling witness. Authoritarian regimes, in literature as in politics, are fatally lacking in legitimacy.

To return to our fifth type of redundancy, we may re-write it as follows:

type 5a. $Cfa = CQ_{a=b=c=n}$

where a, b, c, n are specific qualities that either valorize or devalorize the character in the axiological system of the work. As we have just seen, in popular or folk genres these qualities are expressed chiefly in terms of the physical and moral categories considered important by a given culture. Besides these categories, a character may be defined in terms of profession, nationality, social class, religion, political and philosophical ideas, etc. These latter categories are particularly emphasized in serious fiction, but they can also be found in popular genres like the western or the thriller.

What I call the technique of the amalgam consists in the following: a character is constructed in such a way that his or her culturally negative qualities are redundant with qualities whose pertinence is specifically ideological—understandable in reference to a specific ideology or doctrine. The result is that the character is doubly damned: the culturally negative traits and the ideologically negative traits reinforce each other. The technique of the amalgam is one of the more transparent devices of propaganda literature (it is what accounts for the fact that in socialist-realist novels, for example, the villain must be not only unattractive, but must have capitalist affinities); but it is also a permanent temptation (or an inherent tendency) of any *roman à thèse*, even of those that belong to "good" literature.

I have studied this technique in some detail in Drieu La Rochelle's novel *Gilles* and will refer to that example here.[33] About halfway through the novel, there appears a female character who plays an important role for about fifty pages, then disappears. Her name is Rébecca Simonovitch; she is a nurse in a psychiatric hospital in Switzerland where one of the main characters, Paul Morel, spends a few weeks. She becomes his mistress, takes him back to Paris, then abandons him; he commits suicide, for various personal and political reasons.

After his death she joins forces with those who accuse (unjustly) the hero of the novel, Gilles, of having caused Paul's suicide. Actantially, then, Rébecca plays a doubly negative role: she is a false helper in relation to Paul, since in the guise of helping him she contributes to his death, and she is an opponent in relation to Gilles, since she joins forces with his enemies.

Now as her name already suggests, Rébecca's qualities are not at all neutral in the ideological system of the novel: she is Jewish, of Russian origin (i.e., a "foreigner"), a Communist, and an advocate of psychoanalysis. These are qualities defined along the semantic axes of religion, nationality, political ideas, and medico-philosophical allegiances. Every one of them carries a strong negative charge in the novel, and they are linked to each other by at least one redundant element: Jewishness. The character's full name establishes a redundancy between Jewishness and "foreign-ness" (to be Jewish is here a hyperbolic way of not being French), and Communism and psychoanalysis are metonymic substitutes for the names of Marx and Freud. The link between Jewishness and Marx and Freud is established by Gilles in one of his remarks as a "correct interpreter" later in the novel: "There must be, in the role of Jews, a biological necessity which makes us find their words in the saliva of every decadence."[34] Rébecca's predominant quality, then, is her Jewishness, a synonym for modern decadence. Through this single character, who is not even a main character, one can discover the whole ideological "line" of the novel: anti-Semitism, xenophobia, anti-Communism, an equation of modernity with cultural decay. These were precisely the ideological themes of French fascism during the 1930s.

But up to this point we have not yet encountered the phenomenon of the amalgam, for even though there is a strong redundancy between Rébecca's actantial functions and her qualities, and among her qualities themselves, all those I have mentioned until now belong to the ideological domain of fascism, not to the larger domain of general cultural values. Rébecca is not only Jewish, a foreigner, a Communist, and an adept of psychoanalysis, however; she is also ugly, envious, and promiscuous to the point of lubricity. It is in the linking of these two sets of qualities that the amalgam comes into play: attributes generally recognized as negative in our culture are amalgamated with attributes whose pertinence is specifically ideological, in such a way that the latter seem to be the "natural" consequence (or perhaps even the *cause*) of the former. It is as if Rébecca Simonovitch were ugly, envious, and lewd *because* she is Jewish, Communist, etc. My analysis rejoins here Roland Barthes' analysis of modern myth.[35] A myth is what presents itself as the "natural state of things," as what is unquestionably so—and which, in so doing, lies.

The technique of the amalgam is not, of course, exclusive to the *roman à thèse*. We have all seen westerns where the villain is dirty, shifty-eyed, and an Indian, or gangster films where he is a murderous Italian. We have also read novels by Balzac where the heartless usurer is Jewish. But despite these evident similarities, there is an important difference, both in nature and function, between these amalgams and those that characterize the *roman à thèse* (I should perhaps say the *roman à thèse* at its worst, for not all *romans à thèse* are as blatantly manipulative as *Gilles*). First, as the above examples suggest, in westerns, gangster movies, and Balzac novels the pertinent semantic axes are religion, race, or nationality, not political or philosophical allegiances. In the *roman à thèse*, on the other hand, it is the political and ideological allegiance of the character which is usually most important. Even in the case of *Gilles*, where the predominant axis seems to be that of religion, that axis is treated as *ideologically* pertinent: Jews are seen as representing Communism, psychoanalysis, and modern decadence. In the thriller where the gangster's name is Cavalieri or in the Balzac novel where the usurer is a Jew, those qualities are not there in order to *demonstrate* the criminality of Italians or the cupidity of Jews. To be sure, they transmit and reinforce racist and ethnic prejudices, but they transmit them innocently, as it were—as though the author were himself the unconscious victim of the racist myth rather than its manipulator. In the amalgams one finds in the *roman à thèse*, by contrast, the use of the myth is intentional and manipulative. It is what Barthes calls the "cynical" approach to myth.[36]

This difference explains yet another one—namely, that in the *roman à thèse* the amalgams repeat themselves and tend to constitute a highly coherent system. Rébecca is not the only "amalgamated" Jewish character in *Gilles*, far from it; similar characters occur throughout the novel, including the Epilogue.[37] There are non-Jewish characters, furthermore, who play an important role and who are similarly "amalgamated": one is a Communist and homosexual, another is a Freudian and a coward, a third is a Communist and very ugly, a fourth is an anti-fascist and a cuckold, and so on. It is therefore not the presence of the amalgam as such that functions as an indicator of genre; it is, rather, the demonstrative nature of the amalgams and their constitution into a coherent system congruent with a specific ideology.

Finally, we should note that in the case of the amalgam as in that of other types of redundancy, a wide range of variations exists even within the *roman thèse*. In *L'Etape*, for example, there is an important Jewish character (Crémieu-Dax) who, although he plays an actantially negative role and ideologically has the "wrong" beliefs (he is a Marxist), nevertheless is endowed with some culturally valorized qualities (honesty, intelligence, generosity, etc.). Similarly in Nizan's novels, many actantially negative characters (e.g., the "bad" fathers in *Antoine Bloyé* and *La Conspiration*) are not all of a piece as far as their negative qualities are concerned. Absolute generalizations are difficult to make in this domain. What does seem certain is that the semantic investment of the characters in the *roman à thèse* often carries (and always does so in the case of main characters) an ideologically pertinent component. Characters in a *roman à thèse* all potentially incarnate ideas—which does not mean that every novel in which ideas are discussed is a *roman à thèse*.

Redundancy and the Problem of Evaluation

I cannot end this chapter without confronting a problem that has surely not escaped the reader: although I have stated several times that my use of the term "redundancy" is nonpejorative, I have not refrained from strongly critical comments in my discussions of individual *romans à thèse*. Have I been less than honest? Do I consider redundancy in fiction a "bad" thing after all?

No. Redundancy is necessary, it is a condition of discursive and narrative coherence. Why, then, do I find the amalgam, which is based on redundancy, so condemnable in *Gilles*? And why do I suggest that Barrès' and Bourget's *romans à thèse* verge, by virtue of their redundancies, on the unreadable?

The reason, I think, is twofold. First, my own political and ideological sympathies are not in the direction of right-wing nationalism and fascism, and for that reason my tolerance of semantic redundancy in right-wing novels is particularly low. This is a subjective fact that may seem hardly pertinent to the kind of analytic discourse I have been practicing here. Yet it is a fact I must acknowledge, and that today's growing emphasis on "subjective criticism" would in any case not allow me to leave unacknowledged.

But there is another, more analytically respectable reason as well. In every case of a negative evaluation, what I was objecting to was *excessive* redundancy, not redundancy as such. This solution of sorts only raises more questions, however: How can one define "excessive" redundancy? Do some types of redundancy become more quickly "excessive" than others? Is it possible to establish objective criteria in this domain?

I have no certain answers to these questions, but I can offer a few tentative ones. First, excessive redundancy seems to exist when a text is so predictable that it no longer offers the encoded reader any area of uncertainty on which to exercise his imaginative or guess-making capacities. This predictability can occur on several levels (plot, character, style); the more levels it occurs on, the more excessively redundant the text. Christine Brooke-Rose, using her own terminology, suggests the same thing when she writes: "The text overdetermines certain codes, but must compensate either by underdetermining others . . . , or by over- and underdetermining within the same code but in such a way that the final result is underdetermined." Commenting on my own analysis of *Gilles,* Brooke-Rose continues: "Drieu's devices, which amount to an overdetermination of the semic code, are not only 'patent' (Suleiman), they are also uncounterbalanced by nondetermination in any other codes that open up areas of mystery and above all dialogize the characters." [38]

What Brooke-Rose calls an overdetermination in one code uncounterbalanced by nondetermination in the same code or in others, is what I call excessive redundancy. The excessively redundant text is one that allows for no surprises, that "follows the rules" of readability, of genre, of semantic or formal or discursive coherence *too* faithfully. This definition, I might add, allows us to see why most examples of "low-brow" genres like the thriller are considered unworthy of serious attention (as individual works). They are excessively redundant, for they follow the formula of the genre without innovation. They are all too familiar, and if that very fact constitutes their charm for their fans, it is also what prevents them from acceding to the status of serious literature.

Conversely, the notion of excessive redundancy allows us to see why some thrillers, or detective novels, or, for that matter, *romans à thèse,* are more interesting than others. They are so precisely to the extent that they go against the "rules" of the genre. *The Murder of Roger Ackroyd* breaks the elementary assumption that the narrator of a whodunit cannot be the killer. *L'Espoir* breaks the rule of the *roman à thèse* which forbids any ambiguity of values.

Despite this valiant attempt at an objective definition—made possible by recourse to the encoded reader who remains fixed, in opposition to actual readers who are variable—it must be admitted that excessive redundancy, like over- or underdetermination, is in the last analysis a relative, and therefore variable, concept. Even encoded readers are known only by actual readers, and the degree of predictability of a text or the degree of its overdetermination necessarily varies with the historical, cultural, and personal circumstances of its readers. Although recourse to the encoded reader and to pseudo-quantifiable notions such as overdetermination or excessive redundancy is indubitably appealing and useful in practice, the theoretical validity of the results obtained should not be overestimated.

Do some types of redundancy become more quickly excessive than others? The question refers to the perception of readers (actual readers this time, not encoded ones), for it is the reader who tires more or less quickly of a redundancy. Without denying the potentially infinite nuances of individual response, one may suppose that certain types of redundancy are felt by certain kinds of readers to be more objectionable, and are therefore perceived more quickly as excessive, than other types. A reader who reads chiefly for meaning may soon tire of a work which makes its meaning too patent; a reader who prefers experimental fiction may find realist novels intolerably redundant, not because of their meanings, which may be quite complex, but because of what she or he judges to be their excessive "readability" in the formal sense. One feels this kind of impatience with realistic fiction in the critical writings of Nathalie Sarraute, for example, and in that of avant-garde French theorists in general (Ricardou, Robbe-Grillet, Barthes). My own tendency being to read for meaning (or more exactly for meanings), I find an excess of semantic redundancy the most irritating. But occasionally an author's stylistic mannerisms can have the same effect (unless of course they have the opposite effect of making a reader love precisely those mannerisms). And even in the matter of semantic redundancy, other factors play a part. As Auden put it in one of his poems, we forgive an author much for "writing well." And, as I noted earlier, our degree of forgiveness varies with our degree of agreement with an author's views, as well as with our emotional and temporal distance from the subject treated.

All of this has of course already answered my last question. No, it is not possible to establish objective criteria in the domain of literary evaluation, whether as concerns redundancy or anything else. Structural and semiotic analyses provide a method and a tool, but they are no substitute for personal engagement with a text—fortunately for all of us, theorists and "ordinary readers" alike.

Chapter 5 Subversions, or the Play of Writing

> To be blessedly fallible, to have the capacity to subvert manifest senses, is the mark of good enough readers and good enough texts.
>
> Frank Kermode[1]

IN ONE of his early essays, Roland Barthes suggested that there are two kinds of writers: the *écrivain*, whose activity consists solely in "working at language," so that he "radically absorbs the *why* of the world into a *how to write?*"; and the *écrivant*, for whom writing is a "transitive verb": "what defines the *écrivant* is that his project of communication is *naïve:* he will not tolerate that his message should turn back on itself and close in on itself, nor that one should be able to read in it, diacritically, something other than what he means to say."[2]

The *écrivain* works with multiple meanings and ambiguities; his characteristic gesture is to question. The *écrivant* works with certainties; he makes affirmations.

But no sooner has Barthes distinguished these two types than he makes the gesture of conjoining them: "Today, each member of the intelligentsia harbors both roles in himself, one or the other of which he 'retracts' more or less well: *écrivains* have the impulses, the impatiences of *écrivants; écrivants* sometimes ascend to the theater of language. We want to *write something,* and at the same time we *write* (intransitively). In short, our age seems to have produced a bastard-type: the *écrivain-écrivant*."[3]

There is no doubt that Barthes' attitude toward the hybrid figure of the *écrivain-écrivant* was negative. Barthes' per-

sonal evolution as a critic and theorist tended toward the refusal of discourses of authority, whatever they might be—and
of course this refusal was problematic, since Barthes' own discourse was received by others as more and more authoritative,
whether he wished it or not. He was the first to recognize this
contradiction, and to accept its ironies; not for nothing did he
publish his inaugural lecture at the Collège de France under
the canonical title: *Leçon*. But if he could not escape from the
"authority of assertion," the service of power that characterizes all language "as soon as it is spoken," he could at least
have recourse to "that salutary trickery, that dodge, that magnificent lure which allows us to hear language outside power,
in the splendor of a permanent revolution of discourse [which]
I for one call: *literature*." [4]

By defining the practice of literature as the only means of
acceding, however incompletely, to a language outside power,
Barthes defined at the same time the project of contemporary
avant-garde writers: to rid themselves of the *écrivant*, of the
authoritarian voice they carried within them. There was a time,
in the early days of the *nouveau roman* and of its theory, when
this project seemed realizable. The writer had but to reject the
"dogma of expression-representation," to recognize that "It is
the very notion of a work created *for* the expression of a social,
political, economic, or moral content that constitutes a lie." [5]
But today we know that the notion of a work created for the
expression of nothing other than its own functioning as language is just as illusory. The *roman à thèse*, which "means to
say only what it means to say," and the postmodern text, which
above all does not wish to be imputed with "saying" anything
at all, are both utopian projects—and like all utopias, they contain elements of coercion.

This by way of introduction to a chapter I wish to situate
slightly off-center in relation to the preceding ones. Until now,
I have insisted almost exclusively on the "thesis" side (or the
"écrivant" side) of the *roman à thèse*. The thrust of my argument has been to show how this genre, at once novelistic and
demonstrative, narrative and doctrinaire, uses fiction in order

to impose (or attempt to impose) a "truth," and possibly a mode of being or an action, on the reader. The models I have proposed, which make no claim to being exhaustive, are based on a limited number of novels. But it would be both easy and tedious to demonstrate that these models can serve to elucidate other works, in French literature and in other national literatures. The application of the models would become all the easier as one descended from the plateau of "good" literature to a literature of pure propaganda.[6]

It is at this point, however, that the question of writing (or more precisely, of *écriture* in its contemporary sense) comes up, and with it a decentering of my own critical discourse. What constitutes, for me, the greatest interest of the *roman à thèse* lies in its hybrid character, generating tension between two opposing tendencies: the simplifying and schematizing tendency of the thesis, and the complicating and pluralizing tendency of novelistic writing broadly conceived (not only as a matter of style on the level of words and sentences, but as a matter of the putting into discourse of a story). In order to construct models that would allow us to distinguish the *roman à thèse* within the larger category of the realist novel, it was necessary to emphasize the first tendency at the expense of the second—to show that the *dominant* traits of the genre constitute it as a separate category, and that in the *roman à thèse* the *écrivain* is finally always subordinated to the *écrivant*. This method corresponds to what might be called the desire (or what Elizabeth Bruss has called the "Linnean lust")[7] of any analyst or theorist of genres: to order the literary field by categories, insisting on the similarities among works of one class and situating the differences *between* classes rather than *within* each one, or within individual works. Now the *roman à thèse* has the particularity (which both irritates and provokes) of facilitating this project even while rendering it problematic. It facilitates the project by its own tendency to simplify, to eliminate internal differences and ambiguities; but it renders it problematic too, for the more one insists on the "simplistic" and authoritarian character of the genre, the more one is

obliged to ask oneself whether this character is not *also* that of
the analyst, who leaves aside everything that does not enter
into her constructions.

There is only one way out of this impasse: to recognize
the suppressed elements that "didn't fit," to allow them a place
within the description of the genre and within the reading of
works that belong to the genre. I already noted, in discussing
the structure of apprenticeship, that there are few novels, no
matter how didactic, that do not complicate in unexpected ways
the elementary schemas derived by analysis. Similarly, I have
suggested that the absence of redundancy deserves as detailed
a study as does redundancy. There always exist elements that
tend to perturb or disorganize a system, whether it be the system of the genre (Jacques Derrida has gone so far as to claim
that "the law of genre" is "precisely a principle of contamina-
tion, a law of impurity"),[8] or of its description. Within the
genre, these "impure" elements introduce the possibility of
breaks, gaps, or inconsistencies between the story and its thesis, thus threatening to subvert the latter's assertive authority. Within the description, these elements threaten to subvert
the very notion of (the) genre.

The risk must be run, however. In a preceding chapter, I
spoke about the perturbations or subversions produced in the
narrative and thematic structures of the *roman à thèse* by the
constraints of the real. Here I shall speak about subversions
that come not from the outside, but that are the result of the
internal play of novelistic writing.

"Irrelevant Details"

We recall that in the *exemplum,* the story exists only in order
to lead to a predetermined interpretation. If there is to be a
seamless "fit" between the story and what it is designed to
demonstrate (its thesis), the following condition has to be met:
no element of the story must be felt as superfluous or irrelevant to the thesis. In other words, all the elements of the fic-

tion must have a clearly perceived illustrative function. If this condition can perhaps be satisfied by the *exemplum,* which is by definition a very short narrative, one can see right away that it becomes problematic in the case of longer "exemplary" narratives, and especially so in the case of narratives like the *roman à thèse,* which lay claim to realism. As Barthes has shown, realism is an effect produced by the multiplication of details, some of which have as their sole function to proclaim: *"We are the real."* [9] These "superfluous" details are impossible to integrate into any "meaning" of the narrative (and even more so into a thesis), for their only meaning is "the real." But even if we exclude such details and consider only those elements that have an integrated function and are the vehicles of narrative meaning (the physical aspect or the atmosphere of a place, the face or attitude or actions of a character, etc.), it is hardly conceivable that every one can be illustrative in terms of the novel's thesis. If every gesture or action, every place and every character down to the most minor, were "meaningful" in terms of the demonstration, the result would be such a degree of redundancy that the narrative would grind to a halt. Inevitably, every *roman à thèse* contains elements—ranging from a character trait or a setting to whole episodes—that are not explicable in terms of the bipolar supersystem required by the demonstration, but that are there to fill up fictional space and time.

As long as these elements do not contradict the thesis, they may be considered irrelevancies rather than subversions.[10] Even so, if there are a great many of them, they risk weakening the demonstrative force of the story by distracting the reader's attention or focusing it on things that have nothing to do with the demonstration. The reader may then find the demonstration—or a reading in terms of the demonstration— reductive and inadequate in comparison with the wealth of detail in the story.

It is in order to counter this threat that the *roman à thèse* multiplies its interpretive redundancies, one of whose functions is to endow elements that may appear at first glance irrelevant with a demonstrative meaning. In *L'Etape,* for example, there is an important episode immediately preceding Jean's conversion: the tumultuous meeting of *l'Union Tolstoi,* at which the most "fanatical" members prevent the socialist priest, Abbé Chanut, from giving his lecture. At one point, just before the negative vote, we find the following sentence:

> —"Votons . . ." répéta Jean, qui ne pouvait s'empêcher, même dans sa misère, de plaindre l'abbé Chanut, lequel, debout dans un coin de la salle, affectait de regarder attentivement une magnifique photographie représentant le portrait d'un homme lauré, par Antonello de Messine."[11]

> ["Let us vote . . ." Jean repeated. Even in his misery, he couldn't help feeling sorry for Abbé Chanut, who, standing in a corner of the room, was making a point of examining a magnificent photograph representing the portrait of a man crowned with laurel by Antonello di Messina.]

What is this portrait doing in the narrative? One might think that its sole function is to signal the feigned indifference of the priest, who is doing his best to appear calm in an embarrassing situation. Here then is one of those details that are irrelevant to the thesis of the novel, but that fulfill a "local" signifying function (in this case, signaling the attitude of the priest). This hypothesis proves insufficient, however, for the text continues:

> Ce chef-d'oeuvre de peinture qui se voit au Castello Sforzesco, à Milan, évoquait, sur ce pauve mur nu, l'âpre vigueur de l'Italie aristocratique du quinzième siècle. Le faire solide et impassible de l'artiste y proclamait une civilisation dure, mais ordonée, aussi bien que la forte expression du modèle. Cette image, contemporaine du *Prince,* n'était pas plus à sa place dans ce repaire de socialistes que ce prêtre lui-même, qui, d'ailleurs, ne la voyait même pas.

> [That masterpiece of painting, which can be seen at the Castello Sforzesco in Milan, evoked, on that poor naked wall, the harsh vigor of fifteenth-century aristocratic Italy. The solid and impassive art of the painter, as well as the strong expression of the model, proclaimed a civilization that was severe but ordered. That

image, from the same period as *The Prince*, was no more in its place in that den of socialists than was the priest himself, who in any case did not even see it.]

The accessory element becomes here charged with a meaning that reinforces and repeats, in its own way, the thesis of the novel: it creates an opposition between the ordered, strong, aristocratic past and the chaotic, weak, democratic present; between the "severe but strong" philosophy of Machiavelli (metonymically associated with the portrait) and the dangers of socialism ("den"). The priest does not even see the portrait; it is the omniscient narrator who sees it and immediately "moralizes" it to serve his argument.

If this example suggests that in its extreme form the *roman à thèse* tries to make *everything* relevant to its thesis without leaving anything to chance, the fact still remains that such an attempt is bound to fail. Even in this example, there are "free" elements, not linked to the thesis: Why the mention of the Castello Sforzesco in Milan? Why is the photograph of the portrait called "magnificent"? (To establish the opposition between past and present, it is the portrait that must be magnificent, not its reproduction.) The narrative always carries with it superfluous details that cannot be integrated into the demonstrative network: "His face, with its shining brown eyes in a pale Southern complexion, framed by hair that was once very black and now all white . . ." This is the description of a "positive" character in *L'Etape*, the kindly Catholic doctor, Graux (2:146). The facts that he has brown eyes and a pale complexion, that he is old, that he is a Southerner, are not relevant to the novel's thesis. The only facts relevant to the thesis are that he is Catholic and that he helps the hero along on his road to conversion. But it is the "irrelevant details" that make him into a fictional character. Whereas the thesis requires the impoverishment and the restriction of details to the "necessary minimum," the novel requires expansion and prodigality. Even if the latter brings no contradiction with it (Dr. Graux, for example does not have a "malicious glint in his greenish eyes," which would be a trait contradicting his Catholic kindness), it risks making us forget the "minimum," or buying it under its weight.[12]

"Saying Too Much"

Irrelevant details may attenuate the demonstrative force of the story, but they do not necessarily contradict it. What I call the "overflow effect" or "saying too much" does not merely attenuate the thesis, but subverts it: the narrative tells so much and so well that it ends up producing contradictory meanings that blur the limpidity of its own demonstration. The effect may be only local or momentary, so that on the whole the demonstration remains intact—we are still in the *roman à thèse*. Nevertheless, the tightly woven system of redundancies is perturbed and one has the impression, however fleeting it may be, of a "dangerous" opening.

The clearest manifestation of the overflow effect occurs when a character whose value in the ideological supersystem of the work is strongly negative succeeds in becoming *charming,* that is, in exercizing a certain seduction on the reader. The effect produced by a fictional character on an individual reader is, of course, variable; no matter what means are employed to limit or direct the reader's emotions, she or he is always free not to follow the directives of the text. The charm I am speaking of here, however, is other than a purely individual or personal effect; it is localizable in the text, in the way in which it presents the character and makes the latter "come alive" before our eyes. As we have seen, the *roman à thèse* tends to stack the cards against actantially negative characters, denying them any dignity or authenticity. The words of such a character, like his actions or his behavior generally, are necessarily false; his judgments or interpretations are erroneous, subtle poisons against which one must protect oneself. But there is a possible paradox here: in order to condemn the character's words, the narrative is obliged to report them; if it reports them, however, with sufficient detail and precision—through direct discourse, for example—those words can acquire an authentic tone that will counteract the condemnation they are supposed to provoke. There results an internal contradiction or blurring, since the reader is attracted by words he "should" be rejecting—and it is the text that provokes this attraction. The negative character acquires thereby an ambiguity that can in the long run subvert, or at least put into question, the very doctrine whose validity the work seeks to demonstrate.

Let us return for a moment to a character we have already encountered: Astiné Aravian, "la belle Asiatique" who is Sturel's first mistress in *Les Déracinés*. At the end of the novel, she is robbed and murdered by Sturel's one-time classmates, Racadot and Mouchefrin. Despite her role as victim, which necessarily invites sympathy, the value of this character within the novel's ideological supersystem is indubitably negative. Astiné is both a foreigner and a corrupter, more exactly a corrupter *because* she is a foreigner. In Sturel's story she plays a role of pseudo-donor similar to that of the "educator Bouteiller." The ominiscient narrator tells us that, through Astiné, Sturel undergoes no less than "l'invasion énervante de l'Asie."[13]

Astiné influences Sturel through words. The narrator's negative judgment about her "invasion" comes after the long first-person narrative in which she tells Sturel about her Armenian childhood and about the journey she made as an adolescent to Tiflis, in the Caucasus. Now this exotic narrative, which unfolds over several nights and in which Astiné occupies the position of "Scheherazade next to her sultan" (p. 111), exercises its seduction not only on Sturel, but also on the reader. Austiné's narrative is a whimsical, poetic evocation of *la vie orientale*, "smelling of death and roses" (p. 121), as it was lived by a dreamy young girl and as it is remembered by a woman who is a talented storyteller. Even though the subsequent comments of the narrator leave no doubt as to how we

"should" judge Astiné's narrative and the young woman herself, they do not succeed in *effacing* her narrative—and its seductive effect—from the novel.

But there is more, for Astineé's story has not only seduced the reader, it has also given a certain "roundness" to
the character (in E. M. Forster's terminology). It is impossible,
after that, to consider "la belle Asiatique" as nothing more than
the corrupter of Sturel's imagination. Astiné interests us, provokes our curiosity and sympathy. The omniscient commén-
tary following her narrative appears thus to be an attempt to
reduce the character in order to make her fit into the demonstrative schema. There is a contradiction between what we are
given to see and hear of Astiné, and what the ideological narrator (whose words are *not* meant to be taken ironically) attempts to make us think about her.

A similar contradiction occurs later, in the staging and description of Astiné's murder, which occupy a whole chapter
toward the end of the novel. In this instance, however, the
contradiction exists not between the words or actions of a
character and what the ominiscent narrator says about them,
but within the narrator's own discourse. On the one hand, the
narrator recounts the murder in a way that invites a strong
emotional reaction:

> Ce beau corps, cette gorge de vierge qu'elle avait gardée, et que
> baigne le fleuve d'un sang encore vivant, ces jambes adorables,
> tout cela qui eut tant de plaisir à éveiller les instincts de la vie, ils
> l'ont jeté sur le dur gazon des berges de Billancourt. (p. 422)

> [That beautiful body, that virgin-like breast she had kept, and
> which now bathes in a stream of still warm blood, those charming
> legs, all that took so much pleasure in awakening the instincts of
> life—they have thrown it on the stiff grass of the riverbanks of
> Billancourt.]

On the other hand, this same discourse attempts to distance
us from the character by invoking racial determinism and
adopting a pseudo-analytic tone (as if the narrator were an
anthropologist or a naturalist):

Cette fille d'Orient, originaire des pays où la moyenne de la vie
humaine est bien plus courte qu'à Paris, semble vraiment s'être
toujours appliquée à multiplier autour d'elle les mauvaises occa-
sions et à se créer autant de risques qu'en présente la vallée de
l'Euphrate où campa sa famille. Son gémissement dans les terrains
de Billancourt vaut sa mère expirant sur la rive d'Asie. Il est na-
turel qu'une Astiné Aravian meure assassinée. (p. 425)

[That daughter of the Orient, born in a region of the world where
the life expectancy is a great deal shorter than in Paris, seems
really to have always made an effort to place herself in as many
dangerous situations as possible, and to create as many risks for
herself as exist in the valley of the Euphrates where her family
pitched their tent. Her moans on the banks of Billancourt match
her mother's dying breath on the shores of Asia. It is natural that
an Astiné Aravian should die assassinated.]

Here again, then, we find a double movement: an attraction for the character followed by the attempt to reduce her
to her "just proportions." Astiné does not deserve to interest
us further—she was only a "daughter of the Orient" destined
to die a violent death. What is really important about this crime
is the fact that it was committed by two *déracinés*, whose action
demonstrates the nefariousness of their education at the hands
of Bouteiller and his cronies.

One might argue that a character like Astiné, who over-
flows the novel's demonstrative framework, does not subvert
the thesis but on the contrary serves it, since the novelist gives
us the impression that he has not stacked the cards and not
created characters who are all-of-a-piece, designed expressly
for the demonstration. But in Astiné's case, we see both the
overflow of the demonstrative framework *and* the attempt to
limit it. This puts into question, *from the inside,* the interpretive
authority of the ominiscient narrator and the status of the
"truths" he is seeking to communicate. It is as if the text itself
proclaimed that the story it tells is more complex than the reductive interpretation to which the authoritative narrator tries
to subject it.

We must not exaggerate, of course: Barrès' text does not

exactly proclaim its own duplicity, it merely murmurs it from time to time. Nevertheless, it seems to me significant that even in a novel as obviously oriented toward a thesis as *Les Déracinés,* there exist elements that allow one to "read in it, diacritically, something other than what it means to say." If narrative is a trap (to use Louis Marin's expression),[14] it can entrap the writer as well as the reader.

Another, more complex example of the overflow effect exists in Aragon's *Les Beaux Quartiers,* a novel that juxtaposes two exemplary apprenticeship stories, one negative and one positive. Aragon, giving his own gloss on the novel, said that he had "tried to show, in young men who were not yet adults, . . . the contradiction, in a provincial bourgeois family, between two brothers—that is, people totally comparable, in the same situation, the same social status—one of whom becomes a veritable parasite and the expression of his class . . . ; and the other, Armand, seeing this brother, the very image of parasitism, who separates himself from him and seeks in the working class his own destiny and the destiny of man."[15] This unambiguous interpretation corresponds, in effect, to the novel's demonstrative schema. According to the official Communist version of "Aragon's itinerary" as summed up by Roger Garaudy in 1961, *Les Beaux Quartiers* "was written by him as one of the tasks assigned by the Party."[16] The task was to show the readers of 1937 that the French Communist Party was not antipatriotic—on the contrary, that it was the France of the working class which, already before the First World War, represented the real France, in contrast to "that truly foreign fortress that dominates it, the fortress of the *beaux quartiers.*"[17] This thesis is demonstrated by the divergent trajectories of the two Barbentane brothers during the summer of 1913: Armand, the positive subject, having started out from a position where "he didn't grasp the system" (p. 181) and where he "understands nothing about the drama that is unfolding" (p. 339),[18] ends up by throwing off the "tutelage of darkness" [*la tutelle des ténèbres*] and understanding, with the aid of Jaurès, "what France really is" (p. 497); whereas Edmond, the "parasitic" brother, completing his initiation into the dark world of the Parisian upperclass, "abandons his studies and allows himself to be kept by a prostitute [*une fille*] whom he shares with his new boss."[19]

This last quotation is part of Garaudy's summary of Edmond's story. According to the novel's demonstrative schema, Edmond's story, as well as its settings, whether physical ("les beaux quartiers"), moral (gambling, prostitution) or political-economic (high finance and industry), are endowed with a heavy negative charge. This is indicated by the scornful tone of Garaudy's summary, which condemns in one sentence Edmond, the "fille" whom he allows himself to be kept by, and the boss, the powerful financier Quesnel, who keeps the "fille" and consents to share her with the young gigolo.

Now it is precisely around this "fille," the very seductive Carlotta, that the overflow effect is produced. Far from being simply a figure who illustrates Edmond's degradation (that function would have been sufficient for the thesis), Carlotta gradually becomes one of the central characters in the novel. Although she makes her first appearance relatively late (chapter 17 of Part 2), once she is on the scene she becomes a magnet not only for Edmond but also for other characters, both male and female (Richard Grésandage, Jeanne Cartuywels, the police inspector Colombin), who until then appeared somewhat peripheral. The plot gets more complicated, with murder, theft, blackmail, and international conspiracies. Carlotta is threatened, together with Edmond and indirectly Quesnel, by a gang of criminals linked to the police and to the financial underworld; she solicits the aid of Grésandage, a man of great integrity who is madly in love with her; but in the end all is well: the threats are eliminated, she will have Edmond, the friendship of Grésandage, the protection of Quesnel.

In other words, Carlotta's problems, intimately linked to Edmond's and Quesnel's, not only take up considerable space in the novel, but are recounted in such a way that they elicit a great deal of involvement with and sympathy for the character. Whereas Carlotta could have played a role of "vamp" or

perhaps the role of a destroyer like Nana, her role is rather
that of an irresistible but positive female object. This means
that it is difficult to read her simply as a "prostitute" or a "kept
woman." More exactly, the way she fills out the paradigm of
the "kept woman" is too appealing for that label to carry only
a negative charge.

Is the Communist thesis of the novel subverted thereby?
On the whole I think not, for the framework of the two apprenticeship stories is very firm, and there is no doubt as to
their examplary function. Nevertheless, Carlotta blurs the clear
line of the demonstration—all the more so since it turns out
that she is originally from the same provincial town as the two
brothers, but unlike them from the wrong side of the tracks.
Her trajectory is thus the exact opposite of Armand's: she
"climbs" from the poor neighborhoods of Sérianne to the "fine
neighborhoods" of Paris, while he "descends" the other way.
Now if Armand's *déclassement* must be read, according to the
Communist grid of the novel, as an ascent to authenticity, just
as Edmond's climb (from provincial bourgeoisie to Parisian "big
time") must be read as a degradation, Carlotta's itinerary does
not lend itself to such a simple reading. To be wholly consistent with the line of the thesis, Carlotta's ascent would have to
be read in one of three ways: either she is a traitor to her class,
or she is a victim of the bourgeoisie (who "buy" working class
girls if they are beautiful enough), or yet again she is an enemy of the bourgeoisie who takes her revenge by depraving
its powerful men. But in fact, none of these readings corresponds to the presentation of the character: Carlotta is presented as too candid and childlike to be a traitor, too strong
to be a victim, and too happy with her situation to be the enemy of those who make it possible (she states several times that
she *loves* Quesnel, "in her own way"). If Carlotta fits into some
familiar stereotypes (the childlike woman, the Parisian cour-
tesan, the great-hearted prostitute, etc.), these stereotypes are
outside the demonstrative line of the novel.

It is possible that I am exaggerating, for the purpose of
my own demonstration, the subversive aspect of this character,
as well as her importance in the novel. After all, as Garaudy's

summary indicates, one can read Carlotta far more simply, as the degraded and inauthentic object of Edmond's quest. What I have been suggesting is that such a reading is inadequate, because it impoverishes a character over whom the text lingers too lovingly to allow for this kind of impoverishment.

One could take up the argument by objecting that Carlotta is "irresistible" only to the men of the bourgeoisie, and that that is precisely one of the lessons of the novel. The reader who feels attracted to Carlotta would then be the victim of bourgeois myths that reduce women to sex objects, to "being beautiful and keeping still" (as Baudelaire put it), and so on. But if there is mystification here, the text is not exempt from it either. It is the way the novel presents Carlotta that encourages the reader to play his or her role of mystified admirer. Here, for example, is Carlotta as she appears the first time we see her:

> Une grande fille blonde, c'est tout d'abord ce qu'Edmond en avait pu voir. Elle avait une espèce de charme animal fait de mobilité. Le teint mat comme une brune, et les yeux noirs, peut-être pas très droits, sous le casque d'or des cheveux, aux confins de la rousseur. Elle se coiffait comme toutes les femmes alors, les cheveux tirés en arrière, et la masse portée au-dessus de la tête avec une frange sur le front. Quand elle penchait ce cou flexible, et plus fort qu'on ne l'attendait, le soleil jouait dans les frisettes des petits cheveux sur la nuque. Un mélange incroyable de violence et de douceur: très enfantine, avec une petite bouche cruelle, qu'un rien pinçait méchamment, et des dents claires comme le rire; sur son visage aux traits petits passaient des vagues de sentiments qu'on craignait qui ne fussent point de caprices. Elle s'allumait ou s'éteignait d'un coup, sur une phrase, ou quelque idée dans cette tête folle; et c'était une transformation comme chez les autres femmes il n'en vient que pendant l'amour. L'oeil s'embuait, toute la peau se mettait à vivre, le désir, le désir fou rougissait jusqu'au lobe minuscule de l'oreille qui s'échappait sous une mèche roulée. Les hommes autour d'elle en avaient la respiration coupée . . .
> (p. 217)

[A tall blond girl, that's all Edmond had been able to see at first. She had a kind of animal charm composed of movement. An olive complexion like a brunette, and black eyes, maybe not too straight, beneath the golden helmet of her hair—a blond verging on red. She wore her hair like all the women at that time, pulled back, piled on top of her head with bangs in the front. When she bent her supple neck, which was stronger than one expected, the sun played with the little curls at her nape. An unbelievable mixture of violence and sweetness: very childlike, with a small cruel mouth that would curl up at the slightest thing, and teeth as bright as her laughter; waves of feeling, which one feared were not mere whims, passed over her face with its small features. She would light up or become extinguished all of a sudden, on a sentence, or on some crazy idea in her head; and it was a transformation that, in other women, occurs only while they are making love. Her eyes became misty, her whole body came alive, and desire, mad desire, made her blush right up to the tiny earlobe peeking out from under a curl. The men around her, seeing it, became breathless.]

This vision is, of course, Edmond's; he is fascinated and already half in love with this sensuous "doll" (as he calls her later). Now we know that Edmond, like all the other men around Carlotta, is a center of consciousness (or more precisely a "focalizer")[20] whose vision the novel rejects. But there is nothing to be done: by detailing so attentively, and with such desire, the face, the body, and the clothing (further on in the paragraph) of this provocative woman, the text enters into the game of provocation. If Carlotta is a degraded object that we "must" refuse in the name of more authentic values, this obligation is, to say the least, compromised by the fascination she exercises on us—a fascination that the novel invites us to feel.

Once again, then, the text says more—and consequently something other—than "it means to say." The overflow effect produced by Carlotta extends, furthermore, to other ideologically negative characters—Edmond and Joseph Quesnel in particular. Edmond, as we know, is the brother who turns out badly; as for Quesnel, one of J. P. Morgan's great admirers and one of the most powerful bankers in Paris, he is among those who are responsible for the rearmament that will lead to war: not only is he part of the "forteresse des beaux quartiers," he is one of its lords. And yet, when he proposes his deal of sharing Carlotta to Edmond, a deal that will definitely mark the young man's degradation, the text lends him accents of pathos that make him exceed his status as a capitalist pseudo-donor:

> "Abandonnez," dit-il, "votre médecine. Je vous trouverai dans mes affaires une situation qui vous fera l'égal de cette Carlotta, riche, adulée, fantasque, auprès de laquelle je garderai ma place de bar-bon trompé. Nous aurons nos jours, nos heures. Le monde n'en saura rien, car il nous stigmatiserait tous les deux, vous et moi, pour un tel accord. Le monde n'en saura rien, comme il ne sait jamais rien de ce qui est affaire du désespoir, de l'amour et de la faiblesse. Il ne comprendrait pas que sans moi vous ne pourriez garder Carlotta, comme je la perdrais irrémédiablement sans vous." (p. 482)

> ["Give up your medical studies," he said. "I'll find a place for you in one of my businesses, which will make you the equal of our wealthy, adored, whimsical Carlotta; as for me, I'll keep my place as the cuckolded oldster. We'll each have our days, our times. The world will know nothing about it, for it would condemn both of us, you and me, for such an agreement. The world will know nothing about it, just as it knows nothing, ever, about things that have to do with despair, love, and weakness. It wouldn't under-stand that without me you couldn't keep Carlotta, just as I would lose her forever without you."]

Is erotic love a bourgeois lure? Perhaps. Is the love that Ques-nel contents himself with a poor, degraded thing? Without a doubt. And yet, however fleetingly, I feel myself drawn by the bitterly poetic quality of his words. Might Quesnel be an ad-mirable man? Might Edmond be right in accepting his offer?

But no. The end of the novel approaches, and soon we shall see Quesnel and Carlotta at the military parade at Longchamp—nothing but a *cocotte* and a banker after all, mil-itaristic and mystified. We shall also see Armand, discovering that "the real France" is not on their side. The thesis remains intact, triumphant; we know who is right, who is wrong, and why. But one is still not unhappy to have heard a few dissonant notes before the final dominant chord; and perhaps, in some hidden corner, one even shares with Edmond "a secret sympathy for this man [Quesnel] who was ready to throw all human dignity overboard for a woman, for Carlotta" (p. 482). Is it not the novel itself that provoked these subversive feelings?

The overflow effect is not linked only to the representation of characters. It may also be produced by events. In such cases it appears that the meaning of an event is not exhausted by the "right" interpretation according to the thesis of the novel. The event reveals itself more fraught with meaning, and this surplus of meaning can even contradict the "right" interpretation.

That is how I read the culminating event of *Antoine Bloyé*— the protagonist's confrontation with his own death. *Antoine Bloyé,* we recall, realizes the structure of a negative exemplary apprenticeship: it is the biography of a character who, from his childhood to his old age, bears the action of the "social machine" without understanding it, and consequently without understanding himself. Born into the class of "humble folk" [*petites gens*], Antoine becomes a railroad engineer, a gentleman—a bourgeois. This social advancement is presented in a wholly negative perspective: what the omniscient narrator never ceases proclaiming, and what Antoine himself realizes at the end of the novel, is that by abandoning his working-class ties and the collective struggles they implied, he entered into a world of irremediable solitude, a "life that was not life."[21] By becoming a gentleman, Antoine had become a "man who lived badly" [*un mauvais vivant*] (p. 284).

Now this realization occurs too late, when Antoine is already close to death. It is the physical awareness of his inevitable death (chest pains that eventually lead to a fatal heart attack) that gives Antoine the ability to interpret his life correctly. As Sartre put it (speaking about Nizan's own father, whom he considered as the model for Antoine), "he realized what he was, too late, and became horrified with his life; that means that he saw his death and hated it."[22] Antoine's interpretation, as reported and shared by the omniscient narrator, goes something like this: death horrifies me, it is an absolute negation; but there are other men for whom death does not represent such negation and such horror; they are men who have lived a full and active life; if death frightens me so much, it's because I haven't really lived—"my life is empty, it deserves only death" (p. 284).

In other words, it is bourgeois life that produces the anguish before death. At the time of the book's publication, Nizan explained in an interview that "Bloyé is a man constantly gnawed by death, because he does not accomplish the actions that negate it. He accomplishes nothing: he exists like all the men of the bourgeoisie, he lives in an imaginary way in a world of phantoms. His life has no meaning . . ."[23]

What life does have meaning, then? What life is not made absurd by the confrontation with death? The novel's narrator replies:

> Il faut beaucoup de force et de création pour échapper au néant. Antoine n'avait rien créé, il avait laissé se dissiper sa force, il n'avait rien inventé, il n'avait pas frayé avec les hommes; il comprenait enfin vaguement qu'il n'aurait pu être sauvé que par des créations qu'il aurait faites, par des exercices de sa puissance. (pp. 286–287)

> [One needs a great deal of strength and a great many creations to escape nothingness. Antoine had created nothing, he had allowed his strength to ebb, he had invented nothing, he had not associated with other men; he finally understood, obscurely, that he could have only been saved by his creations, by the exercize of his power.]

And a few pages later, more explicitly:

> Antoine avait su d'une manière obscure toute sa vie que l'union véritable, l'union qui défiait déjà la solitude, qui balayait déjà la poussière de la vie bourgeoise était l'union des ouvriers (p. 293).

[Antoine had known obscurely all his life that genuine union, a union that already defied solitude, already swept away the dust of bourgeois life, was the union of workers.]

So much for the "right" interpretation, which implies a very powerful injunction: if you do not wish to hate your death, do not live a bourgeois life; be a revolutionary. But if we look at the text more closely, we find that it says something else as well. Antoine's confrontation with death and his reflections about it are *written* in such a way that it is difficult not to draw less rousing conclusions from them. What happens to the injunction if revolutionaries too can be subject to the sentiment of the absurd in the face of death?

One would have to quote almost a whole chapter (Part 3, ch. 20) to answer this question. I shall limit myself to two rather long passages; the italicized words (my emphasis) are those I consider problematic—because they "say too much"—in relation to the thesis. Here is the first:

Antoine ne cessa plus de penser à sa mort. Il se demandait ce qui se passerait le jour où le verdict atteindrait son corps. Comment prendrait-il sa perte? Se révolterait-il? Comment apparaîtraient les choses lorsqu'il serait mort? *On ne peut penser ces événements, on ne peut être réellement mort et se voir mort, étendu dans la mort, il n'y a que le vertige:* sa propre mort n'était pas imaginable, à peine pouvait-il se voir flottant au-dessus de son corps, comme une ombre, mais ce dédoublement n'était pas la mort. Il s'irritait comme devant un problème de saisir que son néant n'était pas représentable. *L'homme joue trop souvent avec les idées, les images, pour s'accommoder d'une angoisse dédaigneuse de toutes les formes.*

Tous les autres hommes, les amis rencontrés, les femmes aperçues étaient des complices de la vie, *ils vivaient dans un autre monde, ils jouaient un tout autre jeu, ils allaient, ils aimaient, ils avaient encore de l'ambition, ils formaient des plans, ils tiraient des espèces de traites sur le temps, assurés que l'avenir les accepterait,—ces sales vivants, ces égoïstes vivants qui n'étaient pas vides, qui avaient l'espoir devant eux—,* Antoine les prenait en haine, il prenait en haine son fils même qui disait: Quand je serai grand . . . (pp. 277–278).

[Henceforth Antoine never ceased thinking about death. He would ask himself what would happen the day the verdict reached his body. How would he react to his loss? Would he rebel? How would things appear to him when he was dead? *One cannot conceive these events, one cannot be truly dead and see oneself dead, stretched out in death; there is only dizziness:* his own death was not imaginable; he could see himself vaguely hovering above his own body like a shadow, but this division was not death. It irked him like a problem to realize that his nothingness was not representable. *Men play too often with ideas and images to be able to come to terms with an anxiety that scorns all palpable forms.*

All other men, the friends he met, the women he glimpsed, were accomplices of life; *they lived in another world, were playing another game; they came and went, they loved, they still had ambition, they made plans, they wrote promissory notes on time, certain that the future would accept them—those filthy living beings, those selfish living beings who were not empty, who had hope before them.* Antoine began to hate them, he even hated his son who would say: "When I grow up . . ."]

What one remarks here above all, aside from the rhythmic and lyrical density of the writing, is the precision of details in the reporting of Antoine's thoughts and the constant tendency to generalize from his individual case—a tendency that belongs to the narrator in his guise as an authoritative interpreter, as much as to the character. In the first paragraph, it is the narrator who formulates the generalizations in the present tense; in the second paragraph the source of generalization is Antoine—he is the focalizer—but his thoughts are reported by the narrator without any ironic distance. Nothing here indicates that Antoine's anguish is due solely to his having lived a "bourgeois life": on the contrary, the generalizations suggest that in the face of death all men are alike. By a curious effect that one might call a "retrospective echo," this passage evokes the protagonist of Sartre's "Le Mur," written five years after *Antoine Bloyé*. Pablo Ibbieta, unlike Antoine, was a man of action, a worker, even a revolutionary; and yet, as soon as he sees his own death, he too separates himself from his past, from the "sales vivants" who are unaware of death; and he too uses the metaphor of "writing promissory notes on eternity" [*tirer des traites sur l'éternité*] [24] to describe the blind optimism of the living.

It would appear, then, that anxiety in the face of death, the feeling that one's life has become emptied of meaning, is not exclusively a class phenomenon. The fundamental opposition suggested by the text is not, as the "right" interpretation would have it, an opposition between the bourgeoisie and the revolutionary workers, but between those who have a visceral awareness of death and those who do not.[25] Whereas the interpretive strategy of the novel tries to particularize Antoine's despair and make it appear as the consequence of his *embourgeoisement* (if he had chosen another life, death would not appear to him so horrifying), the writing subverts this strategy by suggesting that "the anxiety that scorns all palpable forms" is potentially universal.

In one of his critical essays, Nizan wrote about Dostoevsky: "The essential problem in Dostoevsky is probably that of degradation. And the secret he dissimulates is perhaps this: to transform social degradation into an essential degradation of man, to make social humiliations and decline into permanent characteristics of human destiny." According to Nizan, this transformation on Dostoevsky's part is a profoundly antirevolutionary gesture; for the revolutionary writer, "Degradation would not be a characteristic of human destiny, but a *social evil.*"[26] One might see in *Antoine Bloyé* Nizan's attempt to show that not only degradation, but even the fear of death, is in the last analysis a "social evil." The problem is that the written version of this demonstration suggests the opposite. Instead of circumscribing and particularizing Antoine's anguish, the text generalizes it: Antoine becomes not an example of *bourgeois* man confronting death, but an example of *man* in the face of death.

The tension between the particularizing demonstration and the generalizing play of writing is especially apparent in the following passage. Antoine's wife, Anne, sometimes asks him in a "philosophical" tone whether he would like to start his life over:

Mais Antoine répondait mal à cette question, elle l'entraînait trop loin, elle l'entrainaît à dire à Anne des choses qu'elle ne lui pardonnerait plus, qui gâcheraient ses dernières années. C'était une question dont il sentait que l'étude véritable l'aurait conduit loin, l'aurait fait rougir, fuir, pleurer! Même dans la philosophie de tout le monde, il y a des pièges. Quelle question! Recommencer une vie où la menace de la mort ne viendrait pas—trop tôt! Si seulement on pensait qu'on a peu de temps avant la mort, si seulement on ne vivait pas légèrement, comme si les erreurs ne comptaient pas, n'étaient toujours que des erreurs, des mauvais chemins qui ramènent après tout aux grandes routes . . . *Mais tout défend aux hommes de faire attention à leur future mort. Ce n'est pas une connaissance qu'ils ont en eux,*—ce n'était pas une connaissance qu'Antoine avait eue, avant le jour de juin sur la petite place,—*rien ne les incline à cette contemplation, ils ne savent pas qu'ils perdent leur temps, ils ne savent même pas que le temps peut se perdre au milieu de toutes ces choses vivantes qui peuplent le monde. Les hommes, les femmes sortent et circulent au milieu des rues, ces lâches ont des travaux, des enfants, des compagnons de table et de lit, ils se laissent entraîner par le mouvement irrésistible des chaînes de leur vie; des êtres de l'autre sexe dorment dans leur lit, marchent à leur côté, leur donnent des apparences de bonheur, conjurent pour eux des ombres de malheur; ils sont entourés des barrières, des remparts que l'espèce édifie avec son obstination, sa patience de corail pour cacher à tous les yeux ouverts les abîmes et la profonde aspiration de la mort. Les falaises bien crépites des maisons, les jeux des enfants,* l'orgueil, la misère, *les courses des chiens errants au printemps, la floraison des arbres, les transformations des nuages,* les usines, les casernes, les prisons, *les façades des théâtres, les tables blanches des cafés, les lettres imprimées,* les drapeaux, les écrans, les familles, les devoirs, les profits, les Etats, les dieux, tous les assurent sans relâche de la stabilité, des motifs inébranlables de la vie. Mais il y a une pauvreté humaine derrière ces écrans qui empêchent les hommes de se dire que le temps presse et qu'il faut vraiment vivre. (pp. 280–281)

[But Antoine answered this question badly. It involved too much, it would involve his telling Anne things for which she would never forgive him, things that would spoil her last years. He felt that a really close study of that question would have led him too far, would have made him blush, flee, cry! Even in the most banal philosophy there are traps. What a question! To start over on a life in which the threat of death would not present itself—too early! If one realized that one has little time before death, if only one didn't live lightly, as if errors didn't count, as if they were only errors, only wrong tracks that would soon lead back to the main roads . . . *But everything forbids men to pay attention to their future death. It is not an awareness they possess*—it was not an awareness that Antoine had possessed before that day in June on the little square; *nothing inclines them to such contemplation. They are unaware that they are losing their time, unaware even that time can be lost in the midst of all the living things that inhabit the world. Men and women go out and walk in the streets; those cowards have their work, their children, their companions at table and in bed; they allow themselves to be dragged along by the irresistible movement of the chains of their lives; beings of the opposite sex sleep in their bed, walk next to them, give them the appearance of happiness, keep away from them the shadows of misfortune; they are surrounded by barriers, by ramparts that the species erects with coral-like obstinacy and patience in order to hide from all eyes the abysses and the profound suction of death. The stuccoed walls of houses, children's games,* pride, poverty, *dogs running about in springtime, the flowering of trees, changing clouds,* factories, barracks, prisons, *the façades of theatres, white tables in cafés, printed words,* flags, screens, families, duties, profits, Nations, gods—all unceasingly assure them of the stability, the unshakable motive of life. But there is human poverty behind those screens which prevent men from telling themselves that time is short and that they must really live.]

At the beginning of the paragraph as in the last sentence, we are close to the demonstration: Antoine's bitterness comes from his initial error, from having chosen as a young man the "wrong tracks" that have forever kept him away from the "main roads," from a life really lived. This conclusion reinforces, in a repetitive manner, the demonstrative line of the novel: we know what the "right" track would have been, with its "full" life and so on. However, an overflow effect becomes apparent with the generalizing sentence in the present tense which begins after the suspension points (the latter are in the text). Here we are no longer dealing with men who, like Antoine, made the wrong choice in life, nor with a certain kind of life in opposition to other sorts; the text speaks, rather, of the ramparts the *species* erects against the "profound suction of death." In the movement of the very long next-to-the-last sentence, there is a gradual return, like a musical modulation, to the demonstration: the sentence begins by speaking about everyday activities or objects like the walls of houses, children's games, clouds, trees—universal phenomena; then it evokes things closer to the ideological preoccupations of the novel (factories, barracks, prisons), then returns to the general (theaters, cafés), and finally builds up to a series of expressly "bourgeois" phenomena (duties, profits, Nations, gods). There it rejoins the line of the beginning. But that line has been irremediably shaken by what has preceded. The "lesson" one carries away after reading this text on the blindness of human beings in the face of death is not quite as simple, nor as optimistic, as the revolutionary thesis would require it to be.

No surprise, then, if the Communist reviewers of *Antoine Bloyé* were quick to smell a fault. Jean Fréville, the critic of the party paper *L'Humanité*, reproached Nizan for having lingered too long over the "sterile anxieties" of the novel's bourgeois protagonist: "We would have been pleased if, in contrast to this life of failure, our comrade Nizan had presented a revolutionary worker, happy to fight for his class."[27] To really nail down the demonstration, the revolutionary worker would undoubtedly have had to die a happy man.

"Not Saying Enough"

To the Communist critic of *Antoine Bloyé*, what I call the overflow effect (the text says more, and consequently something other, than what it "means to say") appeared as a lack: there was lacking, according to him, the positive character who would have cleared up any ambiguity as far as the novel's thesis was concerned. This view was consonant with what had by then become the official literary doctrine of Soviet literature: socialist realism, which demanded a "positive hero."[28] From our point of view, however, the interest of Fréville's critique lies not so much in its dogmatic orthodoxy as in the question it implicitly raises: does not the *roman à thèse* (at least if it is freely practiced, not ordered and enforced by an official State apparatus, as was the case with socialist realism in the Soviet Union) always run the risk of not being "clear" enough, of missing its aim in the very process of moving toward it? Unless one calls things exactly by their name and only by their name, one always runs the risk of being misunderstood. But the novel, like any writing that goes beyond the level of the simplest kind of communication (one might even say *"including* the simplest kind of communication," which would reinforce my argument) is by its essence an indirect way of naming. It advances not straight toward its aim, but by means of detours and resting places, sending out signals along the way; if it affirms "absolute" truths, these are immediately relativized by the fiction, for even if it is an omniscient narrator who affirms those truths, he himself is a fictional being; and if the novel makes no explicit affirmations but is content to let its truths "speak for themselves," it leaves the door open to every kind of misunderstanding.

Saying too much, not saying enough: two sides of the same coin. If the text can subvert itself by exceeding its demonstrative frame, it can produce the same effect through understatement, indirection, the suspension or withholding of meaning. Two novels in our corpus seem to me particularly interesting in this respect: Mauriac's *Le Noeud de vipères* and Nizan's *La Conspiration.*

Le Noeud de vipères has been considered, both by Mauriac and by his Catholic and non-Catholic commentators, as one of the most fully realized achievements of the Catholic novel. According to Charles Du Bos, this "great Catholic novel" is "the story of a gradual and progressive internal illumination, told by the very person in whom it takes place."[29] According to J. E. Flower, "the religious element forms an integral part of the action and structure" of this novel, which demonstrates "the forces of Grace."[30] In a preceding chapter, I mentioned *Le Noeud de vipères* as a specifically Catholic realization of the structure of apprenticeship. It would appear, then, that the demonstrative thrust of the novel is clear: a man whose life is drawing to a close, who has lived until his old age in a state of alienation from Christian charity, discovers before he dies the love of Christ and the "power of divine grace." He discovers that it is never too late to change, that one can be reborn at the moment of death; he also discovers that the practicing Catholics of his own family, for whom he has had nothing but scorn, do not represent what a genuinely Christian life might be; on the contrary, their life is a "coarse caricature" of the real thing: "I had pretended to see in it an authentic representation in order to have the right to hate it."[31]

Le Noeud de vipères evokes two opposing kinds of Christian life: an authentic one, founded on charity and love, and an inauthentic one, founded on a merely formal practice of religion unaccompanied by any genuine religious sentiment. The authentic Christian life is the one gradually discovered by the protagonist. It is incarnated by Christ, but is also represented within the novel by a few characters who function as helpers (adjuvants) in the story of Louis' conversion: his daughter Marie, who died while still a child; his young nephew—or perhaps his illegitimate son[32]—Luc, killed in the First World War; the young priest, Abbé Ardouin, who lived with Louis' family one summer. The inauthentic Christian life is represented by Louis' heirs: his son Hubert and his daughter Geneviève, in whom the love of money and of social appearances takes precedence over any religious feeling. In the conversion story these "mediocre" Christians play the role of opponents, since they prevent the sinner from seeing the truth. Mauriac, in his preface to the novel, emphasizes their negative role:

Au long de sa morne vie, [Louis' life], de tristes passions lui cachent la lumière toute proche, dont un rayon, parfois, le touche, va le brûler; ses passions . . . mais d'abord les chrétiens médiocres qui l'épient et que lui-même tourmente. Combien d'entre nous rebutent ainsi le pécheur, le détournent d'une vérité qui, à travers eux, ne rayonne plus!

[Throughout his joyless life, his unfortunate passions hide from him the presence of the light, whose ray occasionally touches him, will burn him; his passions, yes . . . but first of all the mediocre Christians who spy on him and whom he himself torments. How many of us thus repel the sinner, turn him away from a truth that no longer shines through them!]

In global terms, then, this story of a conversion is anything but ambiguous, especially since the preface gives us one authoritative clue as to how to read it. And yet, the story turns out to be problematic as soon as one looks at it closely.

In the first place, there is no omniscient narrator. All the events are recounted, in the form of a memoir or in that of a journal, by the protagonist himself. Part 1 (chapters 1–11) is addressed to Louis' wife, who will presumably read it after his death; this memoir, written in Louis' sickbed in their country house near Bordeaux, is a recall of the past, and especially of Louis' growing alienation from his wife; an apology *pro vita sua;* and an indictment of his whole family, including his grown children and grandchildren. Starting with Part 2 (which also introduces a change of setting: chapter 12 is headed "Paris, rue Bréa"), Louis gives up his narratee and begins to write a journal for himself. But soon another change occurs (once again indicated by a change in setting: chapter 15 is headed "Calèse"—Louis is back in his country house), and the narrative is again destined for someone other than Louis. He does not identify the narratee this time—he merely remarks, at one point, that he will have to shorten it, since a complete reading will be "too much for them" ("au-dessus de leurs forces"—p. 168). He envisages the narratee, then, as more than one person; since we know that his wife has died, this plural narratee can only be his two children, on whom he has now settled his huge fortune (he had previously tormented them by threatening to disinherit them) and toward whom he feels, for the first time, a kind of disenchanted love. The way his children read this narrative will therefore be important.

Louis' narrative is fragmented in several ways: by the alternation between past and present (especially in Part 1, where the evocations of his past life alternate with frequent allusions to the present of writing); by gaps in the story that are filled

in only retrospectively (the death of his wife and his divest-
ment of his fortune occur between the end of chapter 14 and
the beginning of chapter 15; they take place in Bordeaux but
are reported only when Louis is already back in Calèse, alone);
and finally by the change in narratees. Despite these discontinuities, however, one can easily reconstruct the principal stages
through which the narrator-protagonist passes on his way to
his final "illumination": the fugitive moment, in his youth,
when he had "the almost physical certitude that another world
existed" ("la certitude presque physique qu'il existait un autre
monde"—p. 39); his recognition, after a conversation with
Abbé Ardouin, that the priest was "a man who lived in the
spirit of Christ" ("un homme qui vivait selon l'esprit du
Christ"—p. 95); his sentiment of his "own deformity" in the
presence of Marie and Luc (pp. 85, 120); his feeling, on the
night of a hailstorm, that a "blind force," "perhaps a love," was
carrying him along, detaching him from what until then had
been his only love—his money (p. 131); his feeling of inner
peace after he has divested himself of his fortune, and his discovery that it "no longer interested" him, "no longer concerned" him (p. 200); the recognition of his own past crimes:
his hatred of his children, his desire for vengeance, his love of
money (p. 212); his impression that, despite his physical weakness, he had before him "a whole existence, as if this peace
which possessed me were someone" ("toute une existence,
comme si cette paix, qui me possédait, eût été quelqu'un" (p.
228); and the recognition, finally, that Marie had died for him,
and that he had all his life tried to forget it—tried to "lose that
key which a mysterious hand has always returned to me"
("perdre cette clef qu'une main mystérieuse m'a toujours ren-
due"—p. 233).

It is because of these stages that Du Bos could speak of a
"gradual and progressive inner illumination." Despite the absence of an omniscient narrator who would have functioned
as guarantor and authoritative interpreter of the events recounted, and despite the formal discontinuities of the narrative, its "line" is evident to all those who wish to follow it.[33]

But herein lies the crux: *it is evident only to them.* Louis' narrative is so reticent, so allusive and so elliptical that those who do not wish to "follow the line" can see in it something quite different—and this possibility is itself incorporated into the novel.

Although it is evident, if one considers the stages I have just mentioned, that Louis is gradually transformed into a different man and that as soon as he gives up his fortune he is touched by grace, this is nowhere stated explicitly. In speaking of what is happening to him, especially toward the end when his "recognitions" become more frequent, Louis never pronounces the word "conversion," or even the name of Christ. All is said indirectly, by allusion or metaphor: he speaks of the "key returned by a mysterious hand," of the cruelty of those who, like himself, "are not on the side of the Lamb" ("ne sont pas du parti de l'Agneau—p. 175), of his appeal to "someone who would bear witness to me, who would have relieved me of my foul burden, who would have taken it on" ("quelqu'un qui porterait témoignage pour moi, qui m'aurait déchargé de mon fardeau immonde, qui l'aurait assumé"—p. 217). All this signals his awareness of a divine presence and points to his conversion without actually naming it. It is emblematic of the novel's reticence that Louis' narrative breaks off in the middle of a word:

> Ce qui m'étouffe ce soir, en même temps que j'écris ces lignes, ce qui fait mal à mon coeur comme s'il allait se rompre, cet amour dont je connais enfin le nom ador . . . (p. 234)

> [What is stifling me this evening while I write these words, what is making my heart ache as if it were about to break, this love . . . I finally know its name, its ador . . .]

The narrator dies before being able to name the name or to describe the crucial discovery. The end of his narrative is indicated in the text by three lines of suspension points: a gap filled in by signs without a referent.[34]

The novel does not end there, however. After the suspension points, there follows a letter from Hubert to his sister

Geneviève. Hubert, who has read his father's narrative, has
understood nothing:

> D'ailleurs, qui de nous n'est pas maltraité, dans ces pages fiel-
> leuses? Elles ne nous révèlent rien, hélas! que nous ne sachions de
> longue date. (p. 235)

> [Besides, which of us is not maligned in these venomous pages?
> Alas, they reveal nothing to us that we hadn't known for a long
> time.]

In his son's eyes, Louis remained totally unchanged: still "ven-
omous," still a miser; he gave away his fortune not through
generosity or charitable feelings, but because he felt himself
vanquished—and to top it all off, his last days were spent in a
state of "intermittent madness":

> Eh bien, ma chère Geneviève, ce cahier, surtout dans les dernières
> pages, apporte avec évidence la preuve du délire intermittent dont
> le pauvre homme était atteint. Son cas me paraît même assez in-
> téressant pour que cette confession fût soumise à un psychiatre.
> (p. 238)

> [Well, my dear Geneviève, this notebook, especially in its last pages,
> brings irrefutable proof of the intermittent madness with which
> the poor man was afflicted. I even find his case sufficiently inter-
> esting to show his confession to a psychiatrist.]

Hubert is wrong, of course; his interpretation is that of the
mediocre Christian who cannot envisage a religious sentiment
unlike his own, outside the well-worn path of "reasonable and
moderate" practice (p. 240). Nor does Hubert have the last
word: his niece Janine, Louis' granddaughter, writes in turn
to Hubert. Her own letter offers an interpretation that "repeats" both the author's preface and some of the interpretations formulated in Louis' own narrative. According to her,
her grandfather would have been a different man if he hadn't
taken the practicing Catholics in his family for representative
Christians:

> Nos pensées, nos désirs, nos actes ne plongaient aucune racine
> dans cette foi à laquelle nous adhérions des lèvres. De toutes nos

forces, nous étions tournés vers les biens matériels, tandis que
grand-père . . . Me comprendrez-vous si je vous affirme que là
où était son trésor, là n'était pas son coeur? (p. 245).

[Our thoughts, our desires, our actions were not rooted in the
faith to which we paid service with our lips. All of our energies
were turned toward material goods, whereas grandfather . . . Will
you understand me if I tell you that his heart was not where his
treasure lay?]

Janine also furnishes independent testimony about the last days
of her grandfather: he had had three meetings with the parish
priest, was going to take communion, and was only waiting for
Christmas to do so; doubtless he would have mentioned these
facts in his journal if death had not cut him off "in the middle
of a word" (p. 243).

Janine addresses her remarks to Hubert, but it is safe to
suppose that they will not have a great influence on him. First
of all, and paradoxically, Janine offers her interpretations
without having read Louis' narrative; it is in order to request
his permission to read it that she writes to Hubert. She therefore possesses less information than he, which would allow him
to question her competence as an interpreter. But even if Janine had read the journal, Hubert would no doubt claim the
right to contest her interpretation. The reticence of Louis'
narrative, or its fatal interruption, has left a text from which
the last word will always be missing.

J. E. Flower, in his book on Mauriac, reproaches the author for the letters that conclude the novel. According to
Flower, these letters contain an "explanation or message," and
are part of the "unsuccessful method of a writer who is
preaching."[35] What I am suggesting is the opposite. Far from
providing an unambiguous explanation, or confirming the
"correct" interpretation of Louis' narrative, these letters emphasize the altogether relative status of the "right" interpretation. In order to be convinced of Louis' conversion and of the
power of divine grace that it manifests, one must (like Janine)
believe in it already.

Was Mauriac aware of this paradox? That is not the important question. If we are to believe his preface, he himself thought that the meaning of his protagonist's story would be obvious, would speak for itself:

> Non, ce n'était pas l'argent que cet avare chérissait, ce n'était pas de vengeance que ce furieux avait faim. L'objet véritable de son amour, vous le connaîtrez si vous avez la force et le courage d'entendre cet homme jusqu'au dernier aveu que la mort interrompt . . .

> [No, it was not money that this miser held dear, not vengeance for which this furious man thirsted. You will understand the veritable object of his love if you have the force and the courage to hear this man out until his final confession, interrupted by death.]

Every reader who reads Louis' story to the end will understand what must be understood, interruption or no. Such is the hope of the author, and the faith he places in his readers. But it does not escape the reader that the author himself leaves his sentence suspended and speaks only by allusion. Nor does it escape one that the author's hope is shown to be vain *in the novel itself:* Hubert has read Louis' confession to the end, and he does not understand; he needs proof, but the proof is missing.

Naturally, as I suggested above, one can see in Hubert the incarnation of the failed (or ill-willed?) interpreter, who "has ears but hears not." In that case, we can say that author and reader are united in their right understanding and in their ironic condemnation of the failed interpreter. This is perhaps what Flower had in mind in stating that the concluding letters "preach" a message—Janine's telling us how we are to read Louis' narrative, Hubert's showing us the opposite. *But Janine has not read Louis' narrative.* Is there any better indication of the vulnerability—not to say the arbitrariness and the nonpertinence—of the "right" interpretation? If *Le Noeud de vipères* is a novel that preaches, it does so in a remarkably evasive way.

There is one thing, however, that is certain. Despite the

conflict of interpretation that it dramatizes, *Le Noeud de vipères* is situated in a mental and discursive universe that is exclusively Christian. The conflict in Hubert's and Janine's interpretations turns around two different kinds of Christian practice, and two different ways of conceiving conversion and the manifestation of divine grace. The reality of grace or conversion as phenomena is never doubted; only their existence in Louis' story is placed into question. *Le Noeud de vipères* is thus very precisely a Catholic novel; the problems it raises are inconceivable outside a Christian framework.

In *La Conspiration*, we are not only dealing with a different doctrine; it is the pertinence of any doctrinal interpretation at all that is finally put into question by the novel's indirections and understatements.

La Conspiration tells three apprenticeship stories, antithetically juxtaposed to each other. The protagonists are three young men engaged in a common politico-literary project—a "revolutionary" journal they call *La Guerre Civile,* financed by the capitalist father of one of the young men. Aside from this common project, the three are linked by the fact that they are students with no serious responsibilities, who have not yet had to confront adulthood. The action takes place in 1928, on the eve of the economic and political upheavals that put an end to what Sartre later called the "vacation atmosphere" of the post-World War I decade in Europe. Nizan's young men are a little like all Frenchmen before 1930, according to Sartre: they have not yet "discovered, with stupor, their historicity."[36] Rosenthal, the leader of the group and a brilliant *normalien,* confuses revolution with adolescent rebellion against the family, and ends up committing suicide over a love affair with his sister-in-law. Pluvinage, a young man full of existential resentment, joins the Communist Party, but for the wrong reasons; he too confuses an Oedipal conflict with the class struggle, and ends up committing a symbolic suicide: he betrays his comrades and becomes a police informer.[37] Only Laforgue, who becomes the "reader" of his friends' negative apprenticeships (he is given Rosenthal's papers after the latter's suicide, and it is to him that Pluvinage addresses his confession), emerges at the end of the novel ready to live a "new life" as a responsible adult.

Laforgue's positive apprenticeship is accomplished through his experience as witness of his friends' failure and through a serious illness that functions in his story as a rite of initiation. Having been close to death, he recovers with the feeling that he is "existing for the first time":

> —Fallait-il donc risquer la mort pour être un homme? Tout commençait, il n'avait plus une seconde à perdre pour exister rageusement; le grand jeu des tentatives avortées avait pris fin, puisqu'on peut réellement mourir.—Il va falloir choisir. Les songes sur l'étendue de la vie ont fait leur temps . . . Il va falloir chercher l'intensité . . . Sacrifier ce quit compte peu.[38]

> [Did one have to risk death, then, in order to be a man? Everything was beginning, he had not a moment to lose to begin existing furiously; the great game of abortive attempts had come to an end, since one can really die.
> "Choices will have to be made. Dreams about the expanse of life have had their time . . . The imperative is to seek intensity . . . Sacrifice what's unimportant."]

This is the conclusion Laforgue arrives at—but this conclusion is so inconclusive that it leaves the door open for any number of interpretations.

There are, to be sure, indications elsewhere in the novel that limit the scope of interpretations and suggest that the only authentic way of "being a man" is to join in the struggles of the Communists. Even the traitor Pluvinage recognizes that "the Communists were right," and that in betraying them he betrayed "truth and hope" (p. 242). Furthermore, in order to establish a contrast both with Pluvinage and with the other young men, Nizan made a place in the novel for the mature Communist militant Carré, whose function is to state explicitly the values according to which the young men's stories are to be judged. Carré is a man in the prime of life, an intellectual who acts and reflects on his actions. Only a few pages are devoted to him, but they are crucial: in his conversations with

the non-Communist intellectual Régnier, to whom he is linked
by their common experiences during the war, Carré explains
that Communism is not only a political movement, but also,
and above all, a "way of life." He has been a Communist since
the *Congrès de Tours* (1920, when the Communists split off from
the French Socialist Party), because it is with the Communists
that he is able to live: "Even if only awkwardly, even if only
gropingly, even if he falls back now and then, a Communist
has the ambition of being absolutely a man. A Communist has
nothing. But he wants to be and to do" (p. 173).

Carré's words can be read as an explicit anticipation of
Laforgue's conclusions at the end of the novel; inversely, one
can see in Laforgue's conclusions an implicit echo of Carré's
words.[39] When Régnier insists on the difficulty of being an
intellectual in the Party, asking Carré how he can bring himself to accept "a discipline that extends to thought itself," Carré
replies that for him, true greatness consists not in critical negativity but in affirmation and loyalty:

> Il est vrai que tel jour, telle nuit, j'ai pu me dire: le parti a tort,
> son appréciation n'est pas juste. Je l'ai dit tout haut. On m'a ré-
> pondu que j'avais tort, et j'avais peut-être raison. Allais-je me
> dresser au nom de la liberté de la critique contre moi-même? La
> fidélité m'a toujours paru d'une importance plus pressante que le
> triomphe, aux prix même d'une rupture, d'une de mes inflexions
> politiques d'un jour. (p. 173)

> [It's true that in some specific instances I've told myself: "the Party
> is wrong, its assessment of the situation is not the right one." I
> spoke my thought out loud. They told me I was wrong, even
> though I was perhaps right. Was I, in the name of critical liberty,
> going to turn against myself? Fidelity has always seemed to me
> more important than the triumph of one of my political whims, if
> the price of that triumph was a break.]

Carré is speaking here only about minor political disagree-
ments, where the choice of fidelity does not pose much of a
problem; he does not envisage a situation that Nizan himself
was to confront less than two years after the publication of *La*

Conspiration: a situation where the disagreement is so fundamental that choosing loyalty to the Party would be equivalent
to an irremediable personal betrayal.[40] At the time when Nizan was writing *La Conspiration,* things seemed infinitely simpler. By placing Carré at the center of the novel, he was affirming its thesis without the shadow of a doubt.

Why, then, did he not show Laforgue arriving at a less
allusive, more explicitly Communist conclusion? Why, furthermore, did he not allow for any contact between the young protagonists and Carré, so that Carré might have played the role
of "positive role model" (in our earlier terms, of a beneficent
donor) for the young men, or at the very least for Laforgue?
Carré's apology for the Communist Party does not go beyond
the restricted space of his conversations with Régnier, who
is in any case not convinced. Although Carré possesses all the
necessary characteristics of a beneficent donor, his words exist
in a void—or rather, they are aimed directly at the reader
without the mediation of a hero who would listen and be
swayed by them. Doubtless Nizan had confidence in the reader,
who would fill in the space between Carré and Laforgue in
the "right" way without being explicitly incited to do so.
Doubtless he also had confidence in the future, for *La Conspiration* was to be only the prologue to a novel devoted to the
first years of the Spanish Civil War, in which Laforgue was to
reappear as a Communist journalist.[41] The fact remains, however, that in the novel as it exists for us, Laforgue's story (the
only positive apprenticeship story in the novel) is left suspended: its doctrinal "meaning" is not stated anywhere.

This incompletion corresponds to the interrupted narrative of *Le Noeud de vipères,* but goes even further. Whereas *Le
Noeud de vipères* proposes two opposing but nevertheless Christian interpretations of Louis' story (even if one is the interpretation of a "mediocre Christian"), *La Conspiration* abstains from
all commentary, and consequently from any explicitly doctrinal interpretation, as far as Laforgue's evolution is concerned. Since the hero's own concluding injunctions to himself
are expressed in extremely vague and allusive terms, we have

no way of knowing whether they refer to a doctrinal "illumination."

The simplest and least ambiguous way to insert the "right" doctrine into a novel is, we recall, to show its discovery by a positive exemplary protagonist; the hero who discovers the "right" doctrine and states it, like Jean Monneron in *L'Etape,* Armand Barbentane in *Les Beaux Quartiers,* or the eponymous hero of *Gilles,* is one of the surest (but also one of the most transparent) means of communicating that doctrine to the reader. In *La Conspiration,* the doctrine is, in fact, proclaimed, but not by the hero and not as the result of a quest. Although it is stated several times in the novel that "the Communists are right," that indicates nothing about the nature of Laforgue's final discovery. The fact that he now wants to "be a man" and to "exist furiously" implies a successful *rite de passage* or initiation, but the exact nature of the new life that the hero projects for himself is not stated. (If we compare the end of *La Conspiration* with the concluding chapter of *Aden Arabie,* we can see very clearly the difference between a positive apprenticeship in which the doctrine is stated and one where, as in Laforgue's case, it is left unsaid.)

Of course one could claim that this understatement is not very important as far as the reader is concerned. Since the novel's Communist thesis is clear, it hardly matters whether Laforgue becomes a Communist or not; it is sufficient if the reader understands, from the novel's indirections, that the hero "should" become a Communist in order to really be a man. Nevertheless, there is a considerable difference between explicit statement and mere implication. By abstaining from repeating, through the hero's evolution, "truths" formulated elsewhere in the novel, *La Conspiration* gives up an important interpretive redundancy—which is perhaps an advantage for the novel, but a risk for its thesis.

It is time now to suspend these readings and look back at the ground we have covered. I have tried to show that even in novels whose demonstrative impulse and whose orientation toward a "single meaning" are obvious and predominant, there exist elements that act against the simple readability of the demonstration. The irrelevant detail, the overflow effect, the suspension of meaning—these are so many ways of designating the process by which the novel complicates its own thesis and subverts it from the inside.

I could have shaped my argument differently: showing that despite the presence of internal perturbations, the novel's "single meaning" is clearly marked. Either argument, however, would have led to the same question: is not the *roman à thèse* as much a phenomenon of reading as of writing? Corresponding to the novelist's desire to communicate a "total" truth that admits no opposition, there may exist a desire on the reader's part to be subjugated by fiction, to draw a "lesson" or a univocal interpretation from every novel. The psychoanalytic foundations of such a desire have been suggested by J.-B. Pontalis, who asks: "Does there not exist, more powerful than any drive [*pulsion*], a 'compulsion for synthesis' which impels us to find in the figure of another, whether person or work, the 'total object' without whose guarantee we would ourselves be threatened by fragmentation, by the explosion of the death instinct?"[42] It seems to me that the hallmark of modernist and postmodernist texts is that they *frustrate* the reader's compulsion for synthesis and *invite* the fragmentation against which the reader seeks protection in a total object, or in a single meaning—whence the threatening or "terroristic" quality of such works, to which many readers react with veritable fear and loathing.[43] The *roman à thèse,* by contrast, fulfills the reader's desire for unity; but it too risks becoming a threat, since the single reading it tries to impose is also a form of terrorism.

Fortunately for the reader, neither the postmodernist text nor the *roman à thèse* is totally successful in realizing its aims: despite its yearning for a kind of total "unreadability," the postmodernist text becomes, willy-nilly, readable—and even, on occasion, conventionalized;[44] despite its yearning for a repressive readability, the *roman à thèse* gets caught up in the play of writing and finally designates the arbitrariness of its own authority. By evoking, however indirectly or unwittingly, the possibility of "other readings" and the relative status of all interpretation (and consequently of all "absolute" truths), the *roman à thèse* allows the reader to become aware of his or her own freedom. The play of writing is perhaps none other than the coming of age of the reader.

Chapter 6 Conclusion

> To read, one must be innocent. . . . Because literature
> is so persuasive, we naturally assume that it should
> perform the duties of a teacher and have the authority
> of a preacher.
>
> Boris Tomashevsky[1]

> We have entered the age of suspicion.
>
> Nathalie Sarraute[2]

Reading for What?

HOW SHOULD one read? Why should one read? These questions, although rarely formulated explicitly, are inscribed in every novel, and perhaps in every work of literature. The theoretical interest of the *roman à thèse* resides in the simple answers it proposes. One reads in order to find meaning, submitting oneself to the authority of a voice, or of several voices that do not contradict one another and that all make manifest the meaning the reader seeks and that the novel has already found. Fiction proposes models of thought and action; the reader has but to follow his or her natural inclination, identifying with those who are right, rejecting those who are wrong, and through these judgments adapting his or her life to the truths that fiction offers.

Of course, this description is itself a fiction. One would have to go far to find a reader as "obedient," as innocent as the description presupposes. Even a three-year-old child who listens avidly to tales of punishment and reward ("good" children are happy and rewarded, "bad" children learn their lesson the hard way, as in the tales of the Comtesse de Ségur, which generations of French children have loved), even a three-year-old tempers his enthusiasm with the knowledge that these are made-up stories—lovely to listen to, but not to be confused with his own life.

And yet, the theoretical fiction of innocent reading is a powerful one, as Tomashevsky's remark quoted in my epigraph indicates. It is certainly a fiction that founds the *roman à thèse*, and that defines its ideal functioning. As Michel Beaujour has noted, the *roman à thèse* is paternal, it infantilizes the reader.[3] However, since he is acting in good faith and is sustained by his certainties, the author of a *roman à thèse* feels no need to apologize for his authoritarianism. The truths he teaches being "good" ones, his reader's subjection to them cannot be harmful.

According to some critics, the authoritarianism that characterizes the *roman à thèse* is endemic to all novels. "*Novel means exemplification.* The novel proves. It constitutes a parabolic, illustrative discourse, it invites assent to a meaning. To tell a story supposes the desire to teach, implies the intention of imparting a lesson and of making it obvious. The narrative, by means of the individual case recounted, offers (tacitly or otherwise) a model: it shows positively the code at work and makes one draw the necessary conclusion of assent from the spectacle."[4] This is one of Charles Grivel's conclusions, in his study based on an examination of two hundred French novels published between 1870 and 1880. According to Grivel, the novel as a genre is without exception an instrument of bourgeois domination. He claims to have shown "that the meaning of the novel is precisely the ideological demonstration of a class order and that a novel whose aim is not the authoritarian imposition of its archetypal closure is inconceivable (the meaning of this closure being none other than bourgeois order)." Whence it follows that "one can 'change the novel' only by 'making the novel cease' (the 'socialist novel' is a theoretical contradiction in terms)" (p. 342).

If what Grivel says about "*the* novel" were true of all novels, then all novels would be *romans à thèse*. And indeed, this is precisely what he suggests at the end of his book: "Novels of every level (whether they are received as 'literary' or not, and whatever their degree of innovation) are, from the point of view of ideological practice, *equivalent or identical*" (p. 362).

The argument may have a certain appeal, but I think it is basically wrong. Or rather, it is circular, for Grivel starts out with the idea that the novel is *in its essence* an instrument of bourgeois domination. With that premise as a starting point, it is not difficult to show (provided one chooses one's corpus well) that the novel is necessarily closed, authoritarian, and condemnable. Furthermore, the argument is based on an unproven proposition—namely, that verisimilitude and representation, the cornerstones of the novel as a genre, are in and of themselves, in their very essence, "reactionary." But one must question the "necessary" nature of the link that is thus established between a certain form of discourse and a repressive ideology. As Fredric Jameson has remarked, "Nothing is . . . more idealistic than the notion that a given thought-form (representationality, for instance, or the belief in the subject or in the referent) is always and under all circumstances 'bourgeois' and ideological, for such a position . . . tends precisely to isolate the form of thought (or its equivalent, the form of discourse) from that practical context in which alone its results can be measured."[5]

In fact, Grivel's argument in *Production de l'intérêt romanesque* corresponds to the political and aesthetic "line" that characterized a certain French intellectual discourse (roughly speaking, that of the *Tel Quel* group) in the early 1970s. The realist novel, defined as an instrument of class domination and a form of bourgeois ideological practice, was denounced in the name of the "text," constituted by *"signifying practices* whose plural series remains without origin and without end."[6]

Today, this denunciation appears somewhat dated. More exactly, the denunciation of *le vraisemblable* has become a "vraisemblable" of its own, has taken its place among a number of other familiar (or as Grivel might say, "coded") discourses.

Tzvetan Todorov noted some years ago: "If I speak, my utterance will obey a certain law and will be inscribed in a *vraisemblance* which I cannot make explicit and reject except by means of another utterance whose law will be implicit. Through enunciation, my discourse will always belong to some form of verisimilitude."[7] In other words, the "materialist" and "textual" critique of the novel as an ideological practice becomes itself, willy-nilly, the manifestation of an ideology. This ineluctable (and in some sense tragic) process may have been what Roland Barthes had in mind when he stated, in an interview published shortly before his death: "A good many of these works [the doctoral theses he was directing] consist in denouncing the ideological character of certain [kinds of] discourse, or of certain works. It's often very accurate, very soundly developed, analyzed, but one is obliged to denounce the ideology of others with a discourse that is, finally, also ideological. This produces a kind of impasse, in which we all find ourselves. We are very much aware of the ideology of others, but we don't manage to find a language free of all ideology, for such a language does not exist."[8]

There is no way out of the impasse, which belongs to all of us. And yet (or perhaps because of that very impossibility), it seems to me more useful to analyze than to denounce, more useful to establish and maintain distinctions than to do away with all distinctions, the better to reject the whole. If the analytic enterprise is itself part of an ideology (and it indubitably is), so be it. I shall continue to maintain, even while acknowledging the ideological baggage carried by my words, that all novels are not "equivalent and identical," and that even among works founded on verisimilitude and representation there exist non-negligible differences. One of these differences is precisely between the *roman à thèse*, which offers certainties and offers itself as a nonproblematic purveyor of truths, and novels which, even though they may share certain characteristics with the *roman à thèse*, are nevertheless more open, more uncertain, less categorical in their affirmations. These novels position the reader differently from the *roman à thèse*. Instead of pointing to the "right road" or the wrong one, they allow the reader to glimpse multiple, partial, relative solutions; they are invitations to "quests without a conclusion";[9] in short, they propose not definitive answers but questions.

Representation and verisimilitude are not, by their very nature, repressive and authoritarian; neither is the novel. It all depends on the use to which they are put, by writers and by readers. Nor is there any guaranteed correspondence between the use intended by the writer and the use practiced by a reader, just as there is no necessary correspondence between the writer's meaning and the meanings inscribed in his work. The most authoritarian *roman à thèse*, if it is questioned a certain way, ends up contesting its own authority.

But if that is true, does not the category itself of the *roman à thèse* become problematic? For either the *roman à thèse* exists in fact, and in that case it has specific traits that characterize it: authoritarianism, nonambiguity, redundancy. Or else everything depends on the way one reads, and in that case . . .

I shall nevertheless stick to my distinctions. The fact that I may read a *roman à thèse* by insisting on its problematic or ambiguous aspects does not negate its existence as a *roman à thèse*, nor does it invalidate the analytic attempt to define the characteristic traits of the genre. A genre is a system of dominant traits, not a scientific formula. In the *roman à thèse*, the trait that determines all the rest is the manifest intention to communicate an unambiguous, virtually exhortative message. The fact that this manifest intention is perhaps inevitably subverted by the play of writing does not change the basic given. On the contrary, the effect of autosubversion becomes perceptible only because of the manifest intention that is being subverted. The work's autosubversion functions as a "slip-of-the-text," and as such can be appreciated only in the context of a discourse that "means to say" something else.

There is one point, however, on which I am in agreement with analyses like Grivel's, even if I do not share their basic theoretical assumptions; it is the notion that the "innocent" or naive reading of novels (but I would add: of any genre or work that is linked, however indirectly, to communication or persuasion) consists in letting oneself be blinded by (to) the devices that found it, and that this sort of reading is potentially alienating and dangerous. This was already the guiding idea behind Barthes' analyses in his *Mythologies*. The analytic description of rhetorical devices, whether in novels or in other texts, reveals as artifice or as an attempt at manipulation what an "innocent" reading might be tempted to consider as natural, as itself an innocent depiction of an already constituted world. If my descriptions of the devices of the *roman à thèse* have some usefulness, it is in having suggested that lucidity and a certain suspicion are the right, and perhaps even the obligation, of any reader. "Philosophy," Wittgenstein once remarked, "is a battle against the bewitchment of our intelligence by means of language."[10] If that is true, then the only salutary way to read is not innocently, not altogether trustingly, but "philosophically."

Authority and Imitation: Sartre's *L'Enfance d'un chef*

Was the above a conclusion? Undoubtedly. But I wish to conclude for good on a note celebrating (after all) literature, that discourse infinitely richer and more paradoxical than what can be said *about* it. Here, then, is a final commentary, on a work that sums up, in my eyes, the whole problematic of the *roman à thèse* and of its reading: Sartre's novella *L'Enfance d'un chef*.

L'Enfance d'un chef is the story, set in France in the 1920s, of a young man in search of an identity, and who eventually finds one. Lucien Fleurier, the only son of a provincial industrialist, wants to escape from the uncertainties of adolescence—he wants "a character and a destiny."[11] Discovering and rejecting in turn the self-definitions offered him by surrealism and psychoanalysis, he finally finds his "truc self" as an anti-Semite and as a militant member of the Action Française. Armed with his convictions, he acquires the solidity of a rock.

He becomes a "leader of men," a "chef parmi les Français" (p. 252).

The story is, of course, ironic, even parodistic. Geneviève Idt has characterized it as a "parody of the *Bildungsroman* [*roman d'apprentissage*]."[12] In terms of my own categories, it is a parody of the *roman à thèse* with a positive exemplary apprenticeship structure. Parody is a slippery and paradoxical genre, however: its impulse is critical, since a parody means to ridicule—or at least put into question—the work it parodies, its antecedent. But in order to accomplish its critical project, parody must also *repeat* what it parodies, in such a way as to lay bare the devices of the antecedent and thereby to contest them. In the most successful parodies, there is a margin of ambiguity: the parody lends itself to two kinds of reading—on the one hand as a "naive" repetition of the antecedent, on the other as a critical commentary on it.

L'Enfance d'un chef is in this sense an extremely successful parody—perhaps even too successful. Since everything is presented from the point of view of the protagonist—with the narrator effacing himself behind the character and formally adopting the latter's perspective, according to a strictly maintained internal focalization—an overly "innocent" or overhasty reader might read Lucien's story as a straightforward positive exemplary tale. I once had a student who, after a first reading of the story (admittedly he read it in English, in a less than ideal translation), saw in Lucien a veritable hero.[13] Nor is such a misunderstanding entirely fortuitous. Since no narrative voice (or any other voice within the story) intervenes to contradict the protagonist's conclusions or put them into a different perspective, it is easy to follow one's bent, or the convention according to which, in the absence of contradictory elements, the "truth" formulated by the hero at the end of his quest is the "right" one: " 'Première maxime,' se dit Lucien, 'ne pas chercher à voir en soi; il n'y a pas d'erreur plus dangereuse.' Le vrai Lucien—il le savait à présent—, il fallait le chercher dans les yeux des autres" [" 'The first principle,' Lucien said to himself, 'is to avoid introspection; no error is more dangerous.' The real Lucien—he knew that now—had to be sought in the eyes of others."] (p. 250). We saw in an earlier chapter that the *roman à thèse* has a predilection for sentences of the type: "He (now) knew that *p*," where the proposition *p* is logically presupposed as true. In such a sentence, as Oswald Ducrot has remarked, "one has the impression that it is impossible to separate, where knowledge is concerned, the subjective mode of belief and its objective value . . . ; knowledge is a belief that acts as proof, a belief that demonstrates its own truth."[14] The *roman à thèse* tries to slip in the presupposition in such a way that the reader will not contest it. The formal pressure of the fiction (it is the hero, or in any case a positively valorized character, who "knows") reinforces the logical pressure of the discourse in order to bewitch the intelligence of the reader, to prevent the reader from examining the presupposition critically.

Now it is precisely this kind of passive obedience on the reader's part that the parody of *L'Enfance d'un chef* lays bare and contests. The "maxim" formulated by Lucien is a trap: to read it obediently is to misread it. The "right" reading here consists in rejecting the presupposition, in "undertaking a refutation that may explicitly question the very legitimacy of the speech act involved."[15] The reader must conclude that Lucien's discoveries are not right, that to be a man is not to be an anti-Semite, is not to feel oneself "hard and heavy like a stone" (p. 236), is not to have "nothing more to learn" (p. 233), is not to "refuse engaging in argument" (p. 235). But this imperative itself leads to a paradox: if there is a correct reading that consists in rejecting certain ideas as false, is not *L'Enfance d'un chef* a *roman à thèse* after all, albeit of a rather curious kind—a negative exemplary apprenticeship that is presented, ironically, as a positive one?

Yes and no. One can, in effect, read (and many commentators have read) Lucien Fleurier's story as a political and existentialist *exemplum:* by adopting once and for all the "being" of an anti-Semite, by believing in his "rights as a chief," by yearning for an unchanging essence and by seeking the definition of himself exclusively in the eyes of others, Lucien fulfills the role of a negative exemplary protagonist.[16] But a veritable *roman à thèse* must also present, however indirectly, a positive counterpart to the false convictions of the protagonist; and nothing of the sort exists in *L'Enfance d'un chef*. We do not know what would have been the "right road" to follow. The work offers no solutions, nor even explanations.

Obviously, one can look for explanations in Sartre's philosophical works, which function as an intertextual context for *L'Enfance d'un chef*. (The existentialist reading is possible only if one is familiar with the concepts and the vocabulary of *L'Etre et le néant*, which was impossible for readers in 1939). But if one brings the intertextual context to bear, one also understands why *L'Enfance d'un chef* is a critique of the *roman à thèse*.

Here is a passage from *Réflexions sur la question juive*, which can be read as an indirect commentary on Lucien Fleurier:

> But how can one choose to reason falsely? It's because one has the nostalgia for impermeability. The reasonable man seeks in fear and trembling, he knows that his reasoning is only probable, that other considerations will arise to put it in doubt; he never knows exactly where he is going; he is "open," he may appear hesitant. But there are people who are drawn to the permanence of stone. They want to be massive and impenetrable, they don't want to change: where would change lead them? They have a fundamental fear of themselves, and a fear of truth. And what frightens them is not the content of truth, which they don't even suspect, but the very form of truth, that object of indefinite approximation. It is as though their own existence were in a perpetual state of reprieve. But they want to exist all at once and immediately. They don't want acquired opinions, but wish their opinions to be innate; since they are afraid of reasoning, they want to adopt a way of life in which reasoning and seeking have only a subordinate role, where one never seeks anything but what one has already found, where one never becomes anything but what one already was.[17]

The nostalgia for impermeability, the desire for a rock-like permanence which characterize Lucien, and which are not explained in *L'Enfance d'un chef,* are here analyzed and put into perspective. We understand why Lucien tells himself, when he looks at his friend Lemordant: "That is how I should be: a rock" (p. 224). Lemordant is a member of the Camelots du Roy (the youth wing of the Action Française), he possesses a doctrine; he is weak in mathematics, but that weakness is a strength: what need has he for reasoning when his convictions support him?

If the above passage is a commentary on Lucien, it is also a commentary on—and a critique of—the *roman à thèse* and of its naive reading. To define truth as "that object of indefinite approximation" is already to criticize the *roman à thèse:* the fear of openings, of change, of hesitation, the search for truth in which one never seeks anything but what one has already found—what are these if not the characteristic traits of the genre at their most extreme?

Admittedly, the first readers of *L'Enfance d'un chef* did not have recourse to such intertextual glosses. Nor had they read what Sartre wrote in *Qu'est-ce que la littérature?* about "accusatory portraits" [*portraits-contestions*]: "Certain portraits are already accusations; that is because they are drawn from the outside, dispassionately, by a painter who refuses all complicity with his model."[18] We could claim that the portrait of an anti-Semite as a young man that Sartre paints in *L'Enfance d'un chef* is just such a portrait—with the interesting exception that Lucien is painted from the inside, not from the outside. Despite the element of ambiguity introduced by the internal focalization, however, Sartre's first readers seem to have realized full well that the work was ironic. What is striking is that they did not always understand (or wish to understand) exactly who, or what, the target of Sartre's irony was. The fascist writer Robert Brasillach is a good case in point. In his review of *Le Mur* (the volume in which *L'Enfance d'un chef* appeared), published in *L'Action Française,* Brasillach wrote: "The longest of these narratives, *L'Enfance d'un chef,* is almost a novel, not devoid of satiric observations, especially on the *années folles* of the after-war period. And it is an interesting idea to show us a timid individual ready to be seduced by every kind of error and ending up thinking of himself as a leader of men. But Mr. Sartre has accumulated around this foolish character so many disgusting details that we must consider this novella like the others, which deal with madwomen and madmen."[19] The chief interest of this commentary is that it shows what Brasillach did *not* read, or did not want to read, in the story. He sees Lucien as a "foolish character" who thinks he becomes a leader of men but is in fact a "timid individual ready to be seduced by every kind of error"—by which Brasillach no doubt refers to Lucien's flirtations with surrealism and psychoanalysis, those two discoveries of the twenties. What Brasillach seems not to have seen is that Lucien's chief error is his faithful, if somewhat naive, espousal of Brasillach's own doctrine. Writing in the newspaper of L'Action Française, he ignores the fact that the heaviest satire is directed against the Camelots du Roy, as well as against the very notion of being a "leader of men." What he also ignores is that Lucien's final incarnation is that of a reader and echo of one of the French Right's favorite novels: Barrès' *Les Déracinés*.

With the appearance of *Les Déracinés* in the text of *L'Enfance d'un chef*, Sartre's parody of the *roman à thèse* (or, if one wishes, his laying bare of the latter's characteristic devices) becomes almost explicit; he does not cover his tracks, on the contrary, he points to them. How, after all, does Lucien become a Camelot du Roy? Through the influence of his friend, the "rock" Lemordant. And Lemordant in turn acts through Barrès:

> "Where are you from?" asked Lemordant. "From Férolles. My father has a factory there." "How long did you live there?" "Until my next-to-last year of *lycée*." "I see," said Lemordant, "well, it's simple, you're a *déraciné*. Have you read Barrès?" "I've read *Colette Baudoche*." "That's not it," said Lemordant impatiently. "I'll bring you *Les Déracinés*, this afternoon: it's your story. You'll find in it the sickness and the remedy." (p. 230)

Lucien begins to read the novel with some suspicion—he has been disappointed in books before. "But, from the very first pages, he was charmed [*séduit*] . . . Lucien found that Sturel resembled him. 'It's true after all,' he said to himself, 'I am a *déraciné*' " (p. 231). Here is that mechanism of self-recognition in another, and of repetition/imitation that the *roman à thèse* solicits from its reader. By submitting himself to the novel's voice of truth ("he was charmed"), Lucien finds "a method to define and understand himself" (p. 231). Unlike Freud, whom he has also read (and I'll come back to that), Barrès offers him an "unconscious full of country odors . . . To capture it, Lucien had but to turn away from a sterile and dangerous contemplation of himself: he had to study the ground and the underground of Férolles, decipher the meaning of its gently rolling hills . . . Or else, quite simply, he had to return to Férolles to live there: he would find it at his feet, harmless and fertile . . . , like a nourishing soil in which Lucien would finally find the strength to become a chief" (p. 232). Twenty pages and some initiation rites later, what does Lucien discover? " 'The first principle is to avoid introspection; no error is more dangerous.' The real Lucien . . . had to be sought in the eyes of others, in the hopeful expectations of all those beings who were growing and ripening for him . . . , those big and little Ferrolians whose mayor he would one day be" (p. 250). At the very moment when Lucien believes he has at last found his true self as a leader of men, he is merely adapting to a mold fashioned for him by another, going so far as to repeat the very words and metaphors of the master text.

René Girard has pointed out, in discussing what he calls triangular desire, that "the process of mediation gives us a very strong impression of autonomy and spontaneity, at the very moment when we cease being autonomous and spontaneous."[20] And Sartre, in *Les Mots*, wrote something that can be read as another commentary on this process: "I am not a chief, nor aspire to become one. Commanding, obeying, it's all one. The most authoritarian figure commands in the name of another, of a sacred parasite—his father."[21] Barrès, in his novel, which Sartre parodies, acts as a symbolic father, reinforcing the lessons of Lucien's real father and doubtless those

that Lucien will repeat to his son. We can see here the full
pertinence of Michel Beaujour's remark, which I quoted in
my introduction: "[In the *roman à thèse*], an authority in the
text—echoing outside authority—interprets the meaning of all
that gives libidinal satisfaction in the text."[22]

By considering *L'Enfance d'un chef* only as the par-
ody/critique of the *roman à thèse* and of its naive reader, however, we are placing ourselves in a rather comfortable position. After all, everyone knows that, as Maurice Blanchot put
it, the *roman à thèse* "has a bad reputation." In the same way,
it costs us nothing to condemn or ridicule Lucien, for all nice
people believe, or at least claim to believe, that to be an anti-
Semite is not an admirable thing. But what if Sartre were par-
odying not only the *roman à thèse* and its naive reader? What
would happen if we discovered that Lucien is not only a condemnable "other," but that within his very otherness there lies
a profound resemblance to us?

Geneviève Idt has pointed out that in his early years Lucien bears a striking resemblance to young Poulou, the child
of *Les Mots*.[23] One thing he most certainly has in common with
Poulou is that he reads a lot—and that he puts his reading to
interesting uses: "he got in the habit of playing at being an
orphan . . . 'I'll be an orphan, my name will be Louis. I won't
have eaten for six days.' The maid Germaine called him to
lunch, and at the table he continued to play; . . . He ate and
drank very little; he had read in *L'Auberge de l'Ange Gardien*
that a starving man's first meal had to be a light one" (*Enfance*,
pp. 159–160). Later, Lucien reads in a book that some people
get up at night and walk around while sleeping: "Some people
get up at night, and speak, and walk around in their sleep;
Lucien had read about it in *Le Petit Explorateur* and he had
thought there must be a real Lucien who walked, talked and
loved his parents for real during the night; only, once morning came, he forgot everything and he started all over pre-
tending to be Lucien" (p. 166). One day, when he and his
cousin Riri pull down their pants to see who has the bigger
"pipi," Riri says: " 'Mine is bigger.' 'Yes, but I'm a sleepwalker,'

Lucien said calmly. Riri didn't know what a sleepwalker was, and Lucien had to explain it to him. When he had finished, he thought: 'So it's true, I really am a sleepwalker,' and he very much felt like crying" (p. 166). Still later, as an adolescent contemplating suicide, Lucien becomes more ambitious: rather than imitating a single action (eating and drinking very little), or adopting a simple identity that frightens him (sleepwalker), he envisages repeating a whole narrative sequence under a more positive label: "he thought that all the great leaders had known the temptation of suicide. Napoleon, for example. Lucien did not hide from himself that *he was in the depths of despair, but he hoped to emerge from this crisis with a stronger mettle* and he read with interest the *Mémorial de Sainte Hélène* (p. 183, my emphasis).

Unfortunately, the *Mémorial* does not solve his problem: "And yet, when he had accepted to go on living, he felt sharp pangs of disappointment" (p. 184). Soon enough, he finds another authority to rely on—inspired by his new-found friend Berliac: "he read a work by Freud on dreams at the Sainte-Geneviève library. It was a revelation. 'So that's it,' Lucien repeated to himself as he wandered around in the streets, 'so that's it!' He then bought the *Introductory Lectures on Psychoanalysis* and *The Psychopathology of Everyday Life,* and all became clear to him. 'By God, he thought, 'I have a complex' . . . Lucien thought all day long about his complexes and he imagined with a certain pride the dark, cruel, and violent world teeming beneath the vapors of his consciousness" (pp. 187–188). He even writes a poem to celebrate his new discovery—a poem whose chief metaphor is not without recalling Poulou, or, for that matter, Sartre: "Les grands crabes tapis sous le manteau de brume" ["The great crabs lurking beneath the blanket of mist"—p. 189]. After Freud, it's Rimbaud's turn. Lucien's new mentor, the surrealist Bergère, asks him (just as Lemordant would ask him later about Barrès): " 'Have you read Rimbaud?' 'N-n-n-o,' said Lucien. 'I'll lend you the *Illuminations.'.* . . . He lent him *Les Illuminations, Les Chants de Maldoror,* and the works of the Marquis de Sade" (p. 195). " 'You are Rimbaud,' [Bergère] told him, 'he had your big hands when he came to Paris to see Verlaine' . . . 'I am Rimbaud,' Lucien would think to himself at night, while taking off his clothes with gentle movements . . ." (pp. 199–200).

Barrès, then, is simply the last in a long line of mediators, all of whom function as both authors and authorities for Lucien. It so happens that the image of the self that Barrès offers is the one Lucien feels most at home with: "the young men that Barrès talked about were not abstract individuals, *déclassés* like Rimbaud and Verlaine, nor neurotics like all those idle Viennese women who had themselves psychoanalyzed by Freud" (p. 231). The question, for Lucien, is not whether to follow a model, but simply *which* model to follow. And indeed, after Barrès, Lucien does no more reading. Like the Camelots du Roy whom he admires, it appears that he has "nothing more to learn"—at least not from books.

It might be tempting to see in Lucien's chain of reading and repetition, of authority and imitation, one more example of his ridiculousness, and one more proof of his "otherness." He is, quite simply, a bad reader—not like us. But then, when we look around, we notice that Lucien is not alone: Berliac, who imitates Freud's neurotics; Bergère, who takes himself for Verlaine; Lemordant, who is a follower of Barrès; Lucien's father, who quotes Bourget; his philosophy professor, who lispingly parrots Descartes ("Goghito, ergo çoum")—no one speaks with an authentic voice; each one is an echo of other voices, other texts. Can we ourselves, then, be sure that we are free of imitation? Can we even be sure that we possess, to begin with, a genuine self from which bad reading—or bad representational fiction, to come back to Grivel—alienates us? Lucien, when he thinks he is a sleepwalker, imagines that his real self is the one that walks at night—the daytime self, the Lucien he actually experiences, is one he pretends at being. *L'Enfance d'un chef* suddenly begins to read like that story by Borges in which the hero discovers that he is being dreamt by someone else.

On the other hand, perhaps the problem lies in reading

itself—not just in "naive" reading or the reading of realist fiction, but in all reading. Perhaps if Lucien were not a reader but a writer, things would be different. Geneviève Idt suggests as much when she states that Lucien is Poulou-Sartre's negative alter ego: "Lucien has a father, landed property, and sexual experiences; consequently, he is not afraid of death and he does not write; Poulou is his negative."[24] But the notion that writing might be a way out of imitation and a way into authenticity is also corroded by *L'Enfance d'un chef.* Lucien, we recall, writes a poem after reading Freud. During his suicidal period, he thinks about writing a philosophical treatise to demonstrate that no one exists—a *Treatise on Nothingness* (yet another resemblance to Sartre). But then he decides that that kind of writing won't convince anyone: what is needed is something more immediate, more exemplary—a writing so authentic that it could not fail to be heeded. He fantasizes killing himself:

> A gunshot, a young body bleeding on a carpet, a few words scrawled on a sheet of paper: "I am killing myself because I do not exist. And you too, my brothers, you are nothing!" People would read their morning paper; they would see: "An adolescent has dared!" And they would all feel terribly shaken and would ask themselves: "And I? Do I exist?" There were historical precedents, for example after the publication of *Werther,* for such epidemics of suicide. (p. 183).

Admittedly, there is not much actual writing going on in this fantasy—but the structure of the fantasy is such that it places Lucien in the position of a writer acting on readers, rather than in his more usual position of a reader who is acted on. As the allusion to *Werther* makes clear, however, even in this phantasmic version of himself as writer, Lucien ends up imitating the gesture of another. Goethe was there before him. And as for *The Sorrows of Young Werther,* when Werther lies dying in a pool of blood ("a young body bleeding on a carpet"), there is an open copy of Lessing's *Emilia Galotti* on his desk. Emilia, the young woman who has her father kill her to save her virtue (imitating thereby a Roman model), was there before Werther (who borrows his suicide pistol from the father-figure Albert). Lessing was there before Goethe, and the Roman legend was there before Lessing.

But what about Sartre, and Sartre's readers? Are they not, at least, free from the circle of imitation and repetition? Yes and no. Yes, because although *L'Enfance d'un chef* is itself the repetition of previous texts, it is an ironic and self-conscious repetition. Paraphrasing what Sartre wrote in another context, we could say that "This possibility of taking off from a text in order to see it in perspective . . . is precisely what we call liberty." But also no, at least as far as the reader is concerned, because despite Sartre's well-known insistence that literature should be an "appeal to the reader's freedom," if one looks closely at what he actually says about the process of reading, one notices that the reader is called upon to tread a path where another has been before: "However far he might go, the author has gone further. Whatever correspondences he [the reader] might establish between the different parts of the book . . . , he possesses a guarantee: it's that they were expressly intended . . . Reading is induction, interpolation, extrapolation, and the basis of these activities lies in the will of the author, just as it was thought for a long time that the basis of scientific induction lay in the divine will. A gentle force accompanies us and supports us from the first page to the last."[25]

So much for the reader's freedom: instead of being subjugated by an open show of authority, he has won the right to be led around by a "gentle force." It would appear, then, that Sartre alone is saved—is he not the author, who unmasks imitation and lays bare the mechanisms of our self-deceptions? Does not his will, independent of others, resemble "divine will"? Indeed. But twenty-five years after the fact, the author of *Les Mots* unmasked the author of *L'Enfance d'un chef*: "impossible myself, I differed from others only by the mandate to manifest that impossibility, which suddenly became transformed, became my innermost possibility, the object of my mission, my springboard to glory . . . A fake through and through and mystified, I wrote joyously about our unfortunate condition. Dogmatically, I doubted everything except that I was the one chosen to doubt."[26]

Perhaps one can never wholly escape from mystification, nor from imitation. Whatever I say, my word is an echo. A free, autonomous, innocent discourse does not exist. But that does not mean that all words are identical, nor all novels. If *L'Enfance d'un chef* is a *roman à thèse,* the truth it teaches is that there is no such thing as incontestable authority. Whence one must conclude that one will never have said the last word about the paradoxes of fiction that claims to "teach the truth"—nor about the questions posed by literature, of the "authoritarian" kind or not.

Notes

Introduction

1. See Raymond Williams, *Marxism and Literature*, pp. 55–71; the last quotation is on p. 64.
2. Nadine Dormoy Savage, "Rencontre avec Roland Barthes," p. 435.
3. Williams, pp. 55–56.
4. Alain Robbe-Grillet, "Sur quelques notions périmées," in *Pour un nouveau roman*, p. 33.
5. Maurice Blanchot, "Les Romans de Sartre," p. 121. In *La Part du feu*, p. 195.
6. Quoted in Charles Brun, *Le Roman social en France au XIXᵉ siècle*, pp. 59, 60.
7. *Discours de réception* at the Académie Française, December 17, 1907; quoted in Brun, p. 63.
8. Brun, p. 59.
9. See in particular Bourget's Preface to Henry Bordeaux's *Les Pierres du foyer*, pp. 3–9. It is in that preface that he cites Sand's novels and *Les Misérables* as *romans à thèse*.
10. Bourget's preface to his *La Terre promise*, p. vii.
11. Victor Brombert, *The Intellectual Hero. Studies in the French Novel, 1880–1955*; Micheline Tison-Braun, *La Crise de l'humanisme. Le conflit de l'individu et de la société dans la littérature française moderne*. See also Maurice Rieuneau's study on the themes of war and revolution in the French novel between the wars: *Guerre et révolution dans le roman français, 1919–1939*.
12. Symptomatic of this interest is the number of biographical studies that have been published in recent years, mostly by intellectual historians, on Barrès, Drieu, and Nizan. See, for example, Zeev Sternhell, *Maurice Barrès et le nationalisme français*; Robert Soucy, *Fascism in France: The Case of Maurice Barrès*, and *Fascist Intellectual: Drieu La Rochelle*; Dominique Desanti, *Drieu La Rochelle ou la séduction mystifiée*; Frédéric Grover and Pierre Andrieu, *Drieu La Rochelle*; W. D. Redfern, *Paul Nizan. Committed Literature in a Conspiratorial World*; Annie Cohen-Solal and Henriette Nizan, *Paul Nizan, communiste impossible*; Pascal Ory, *Nizan. Destin d'un révolté* (Paris: Ramsay, 1980). One could add to this a long list of historical studies on the question of the engagement of intellectuals in politics: e.g., David Caute, *Communism and the French Intellectuals*; Max Beloff, *The Intellectual in Politics*; David L. Schalk, *The Spectrum of Political Engagement: Mounier, Benda, Nizan, Brasillach, Sartre*; Frank Field, *Three French Writers and the Great War. Studies in the Rise of Communism and Fascism*; Walter Laqueur and George L. Mosse, eds., *The Left-Wing Intellectuals Between the Wars, 1919–1939*. And so on.

13. See, for example, Irving Howe, *Politics and the Novel;* M. Adereth, *Commitment in Modern French Literature. A Brief Study of "Littérature Engagée" in the Works of Péguy, Aragon, and Sartre;* John Mander, *The Writer and Commitment;* Catherine Savage, *Malraux, Sartre, and Aragon as Political Novelists.*

14. See, for example, Sartre's scornful remark about the work of his immediate predecessors as *"littérature à thèse,* since these authors, although they virulently claim the contrary, all defend ideologies." ("Qu'est-ce que la littérature?," p. 238). Interestingly enough, Iris Murdoch has criticized Sartre's novels in terms that are similar to the traditional criticisms addressed at the *roman à thèse:* according to her, Sartre's "rhetorical anxiety to persuade" robs his novels of genuine novelistic interest, for Sartre "has an impatience, which is fatal to a novelist proper, with the *stuff* of human life." Iris Murdoch, *Sartre: Romantic Rationalist,* pp. ix and 112. Significantly, Maurice Blanchot devoted a large part of his 1945 article on Sartre's novels to showing why they are *not romans à thèse.* For my discussion of Sartre's fiction and its relation to the *roman à thèse,* see my reading of *L'Enfance d'un chef* in chapter 6 below.

15. The distinction I make here between form and content may appear naive, since we have known for some time that the two are not really dissociable. But in this particular context, I believe the distinction is justified; as we shall see, one of the characteristics of the *roman à thèse* is that it "says" explicitly what one should do or think—in other words, it openly expresses a doctrinaire or ideological conviction. By "ideological content," I refer here to the ideological statements explicitly formulated by an authorized voice in the text. By "narrative content," I mean either the subject matter treated in the fiction (for example, the Spanish Civil War), or, more specifically, the thematic and narrative structures of the story.

16. Tzvetan Todorov, *Introduction à la littérature fantastique,* p. 26.

17. *Ibid.,* p. 12.

18. Michael Riffaterre, "Système d'un genre descriptif," p. 16, n. 3.

19. Todorov, *Introduction à la littérature fantastique,* p. 10.

20. Riffaterre, "Système d'un genre descriptif," p. 16. n. 3.

21. Monroe Beardsley, *Aesthetics: Problems in the Philosophy of Criticism,* p. 403.

22. Livia Polanyi, "So What's The Point?"

23. See A. Kibédi-Varga, "L'Invention de la fable," pp. 110–111.

24. See, for example, Stephen Heath, *The Nouveau Roman: A Study in the Practice of Writing,* and Linda Hutcheon, *Narcissistic Narrative: The Metafictional Paradox;* both works argue for the broader philosophical and epistemological implications of avant-garde fiction.

25. Michel Beaujour, "Exemplary Pornography: Barrès, Loyola, and the Novel," in Susan R. Suleiman and Inge Crosman, eds., *The Reader in the Text: Essays on Audience and Interpretation,* pp. 344–345.

26. Following upon the pioneering work of T. W. Adorno and his colleagues on the "authoritarian personality," which was devoted almost exclusively to right-wing authoritarianism, some sociologists and political theorists have insisted on the fundamental similarities between right-wing and left-wing "brands" of authoritarianism. See in particular Edward A. Shils, "Authoritarianism: 'Right' and 'Left,' " in Richard Christie and Marie Jahoda, eds., *Studies in the Scope and Method of "The Authoritarian Personality,"* pp. 24–49. Even more interesting, from my standpoint, is Richard Sennett's recent work on the psychological dimensions of the relation to authority. As Sennett points out, authority both provokes fear and exerts an immense seduction; part of its seduc-

tiveness is that it offers images that are "clear and simple." I find Sennett's analysis of the ambivalence toward authority very suggestive, as I do his argument that the only way to become truly free of repressive authority is to know it "from the inside." See R. Sennett, *Authority,* especially chs. 1, 2, and 5.

27. Gérard Genette, "Genres, 'types,' modes," p. 418.

28. At least two North American critics have proposed categories that correspond, in part, to the *roman à thèse.* Northrop Frye's category of the anatomy, or Menippean satire, might be considered a "pre-novelistic" version of the *roman à thèse*—as Frye puts it, "the anatomy . . . eventually begins to merge with the novel, producing various hybrids including the *roman à thèse* and novels in which the characters are symbols of social or other ideas, like the proletarian novels of the thirties of this century." *The Anatomy of Criticism,* p. 312. Sheldon Sacks proposed the term "apologue" to designate a very broad category of narratives which he opposed to what he called "represented actions" (corresponding roughly to the realist novel). Sacks' definition of the apologue has several points in common with my definition of the *roman à thèse,* but also some important differences. According to Sacks, apologues are "designed to alter our attitudes toward or opinions of the world we live in. . . . In an apologue all elements of the work are synthesized as a fictional example that causes us to feel, to experience as true, some formulable statement or statements about the universe. The statement itself can be so simple as 'there is no happiness on earth' or 'it is absurd to identify goodness with greatness,' or it may be so complex as to require a book-length treatise, a *Myth of Sysiphus,* for its explication" ("Golden Birds and Dying Generations," p. 277). According to this definition, didactic narratives like *Pilgrim's Progress* are apologues, but so are Camus' *The Stranger,* Kafka's novels and stories, and just about any work that solicits symbolic or allegorical interpretations. My definition of the *roman à thèse* is a great deal more restrictive—thus, according to my definition, Kafka's novels are at the antipodes of the *roman à thèse,* for they constantly suggest allegorical interpretation but just as constantly withhold interpretation, thus inviting any number of readings without validating any one of them. However, Sacks' notion that in the apologue the story functions as a fictional "example" is very close to my own ideas concerning "exemplary" narratives (see chapter 1 below).

29. Among the more interesting collective works on realism to have appeared in France in the last fifteen years, one can cite the special issue of *Poétique* (no. 16, 1973), devoted to "le discours réaliste," and the special issue of *Communications* (no. 11, 1968), devoted to "le vraisemblable." Among individual works published during the same period, the most influential one has perhaps been Barthes' *S/Z.* Two recent works of interest are Henri Mitterand's *Le Discours du roman* and Jean Decottignies' *L'Ecriture de la fiction.*

30. As is evident, this definition does not attempt to distinguish between the traditional categories of realism and naturalism, nor between the various "realisms" of individual authors (Balzacian realism *versus* Flaubertian realism, for example),which Henri Mitterand has emphasized in *Le Discours du roman.* It places the emphasis on a single general trait of the realist novel: the virtual correspondence between the everyday world of the reader and the world of the fiction. As Claude Duchet has put it: "the 'realities' that the novel writes about, whether they be words, gestures, objects, places, events, or characters, are credible realities, in the sense that they have an *analogon* in extralinguistic reality, and the textual matter is not a purely fictive being. If the novel says 'chair,' it is of course a paper chair that only the characters can use,

but it is also a piece of furniture having a real existence in the world where people sit. . . . To say this is merely to recognize, in a perfectly banal way, that the sign cannot be the thing itself; but it can become the verisimilar representation of the thing only by being founded on our experience and usage of the world." ("Une Écriture de la socialité," p. 450.) The one qualification I think must be introduced is that the reader to whose experience the novel "corresponds" is a contemporary of the author, and by extension a contemporary (more or less) of the world represented by the fiction. This does not mean that a modern reader cannot recognize the "realities" of a nineteenth-century novel: hansom cabs, Victorian drawing rooms, and so on; but such a reader does so only by imaginatively "relocating" him or herself in the world represented in the novel.

31. Some radical critics of the realist novel have claimed that there is no appreciable difference between the *roman à thèse* and the novel as such. Charles Grivel, for example, in his *Production de l'intérêt romanesque,* makes statements about "the novel" (*le roman*) that are very close to my own views on the *roman à thèse.* For my critique of Grivel's position, see chapter 6.

32. Todorov, *Introduction à la littérature fantastique,* p. 25; see also pp. 18–20.

33. Todorov, "The Origin of Genres," p. 162.

34. Genette, "Genres, 'types,' modes," p. 419.

35. See, in this regard, Christine Brooke-Rose's closely argued defense of theoretical genres: "Historical Genres/Theoretical Genres: A Discussion of Todorov on the Fantastic," esp. pp. 152–154.

36. I have not been able to determine the exact date when the term "roman à thèse" or "littérature à thèse" entered the critical vocabulary; it seems to have been at the end of the nineteenth century. It is interesting to note that the *Larousse du XIXe Siècle* (1866), in its long article devoted to the novel, mentions neither the didactic novel nor the *roman à thèse,* despite the author's predilection for classification by "types." (From the "roman chevaleresque" to the "roman psychologique," the article cites close to twenty "types," including the "exotic," the "military," "the scientific," the "fantastic," the "naval" and the "pathological"—the last designating the works of the Goncourt brothers!) The absence of a mention of the didactic novel would seem to indiate that, around 1860, this category was not perceived as a distinct type, since all novels could possess a more or less strongly pronounced didactic element. It also indicates that the typology was based above all on narrative content. The absence of the pejorative label "roman à thèse" suggests that a novel with strong ideological preoccupations was not considered as part of an "inferior" category.

37. Todorov, *Introduction à la littérature fantastique,* p. 11.

38. Claude Lévi-Strauss, "La Notion de structure en ethnologie," in *Anthropologie structurale,* p. 317; English trans., "Social Structure," in *Structural Anthropology,* p. 288.

39. Jean Ricardou, *Problèmes du nouveau roman,* p. 202.

40. Jean-Paul Sartre, "Qu'est-ce que la littérature?" p. 71.

41. Julia Kristeva, *Le Texte du roman,* pp. 21–22.

42. Georges May, *Le Dilemme du roman au dix-huitième siècle.*

43. Roman Jakobson, "Closing Statement: Linguistics and Poetics," pp. 350–377.

44. *Ibid.,* p. 357.

45. Jan Mukařovsky, *Aesthetic Function, Norm and Value as Social Facts,* p. 5.

46. *Ibid.,* pp. 8–10.

47. Gérard Genette, "Structuralisme et critique littéraire," p. 146.

48. *Ibid.*, p. 147.

49. Ricardou, *Problèmes du nouveau roman*, p. 178.

1. "Exemplary" Narratives

1. See especially Tzvetan Todorov, "The Origin of Genres," and Elizabeth W. Bruss, "L'Autobiographie considérée comme acte littéraire." The discussion of illocutionary speech acts in what follows is based on John R. Searle, *Speech Acts: An Essay in the Philosophy of Language.*

2. *Speech Acts*, p. 69.

3. *Ibid.*, p. 71.

4. For a discussion of the difference between systematic texts and narrative texts, and how the former can be transformed into the latter, see K. Stierle, "L'Histoire comme Exemple, l'Exemple comme Histoire."

5. Cf. Aristotle, *Rhetoric*, Book II, ch. 20; see also Roland Barthes, "L'Ancienne Rhétorique," pp. 200–201.

6. Barthes cites the following *exemplum,* given by Quintilian: "Flute players who had left were called back by a decree of the Senate; all the more should the Senate recall great citizens who had earned the respect of the Republic and whom the misfortunes of the time had forced into exile" ("L'Ancienne Rhétorique," p. 200). The effect of the *exemplum* resides in the analogy it establishes between the flute players (past) and the "great exiled citizens" (present). This analogy is established by means of an implicit generalization: "Rome needs all citizens who are useful to the Republic."

7. The widespread use of the *exemplum* is shown by the great number of collections of *exempla* that were circulating as early as the thirteenth century: the *Exempla of Jacques de Vitry,* the *Alphabetum Narrationum* (which groups *exempla* alphabetically by title, the title usually containing the "moral" of the story), and so on. Here preachers short of inspiration could find the matter, as well as the manner, of their sermons. It is significant, however, that the use of *exempla* was condemned by the Church in the fourteenth century, and was officially forbidden during the Counter-Reformation. The reason is that *exempla* tended increasingly to become ends in themselves, told for entertainment rather than in order to transmit a religious message. *Exempla* were becoming like secular tales; but the influence no doubt went in both directions, since secular tales often assimilated the didactic vocation of the *exemplum*—whence a possible link to the didactic novel. For a brief history of the medieval *exemplum,* see J. Mosher, *The Exemplum in the Early Religious and Didactic Literature of England,* ch. 1. For an exhaustive study, see J.-Th. Welter, *L'Exemplum dans la littérature religieuse et didactique du Moyen-Age;* Paul Zumthor discusses the *exemplum* in a modern perspective in *Essai de poétique médiévale,* pp. 391–404.

8. Cited by Mosher, p. 11.

9. *Ibid.*, p. 13, n. 46.

10. *New English Bible.* I should say a word about the criteria I have used in delimiting the text of the parables. As Louis Marin has remarked, the first problem one must resolve in the analysis of any narrative is the problem of the "closure of the text." In his own study of the parable of the sower, Marin, who is interested primarily in the Gospel narratives as a whole, rather than in the parables proper, chooses as his textual unit verses 1–23 of Matthew 13. These verses include not only the parable told by Jesus, but also an introduction by the narrator of Matthew (vv. 1–3a: "That day Jesus went out . . ."), a continuation of the narrative after Jesus stops speaking

(vv. 10–17: "The disciples went up to him and asked: 'Why do you speak to them in parables?' . . .), and finally Jesus' explanation of the parable addressed to the disciples (vv. 18–23: "You, then, may hear . . ."). Since I am interested in the parable proper, as if it were autonomous in relation to the larger narrative, I have defined the textual unit differently: according to my definition, the parable begins when Jesus starts to speak and ends with the return of the first narrator, Matthew. Thus the phrase "He said," which is uttered by Matthew, is not part of the parable; but verse 9 ("If you have ears, then hear!"), even though it constitutes a break in the narrative discourse, is still part of the parable, since Jesus is still the speaker. The first narrator returns only in verse 10. For Marin's analysis, see L. Marin, *Le Récit évangélique,* pp. 95–98.

11. I use the terms "sequence" and "narrative unit" ("kernel") in the sense proposed by Roland Barthes in a famous article, originally published in 1966; see "Introduction to the Structural Analysis of Narratives."

12. This definition of a story was formally stated by Arthur C. Danto in his *Analytical Philosophy of History,* p. 236:

1) x is F at t_1
2) H happens to x at t_2
3) x is G at t_3

The story (H) is thus what brings about a transformation (F→G) in a subject (x) over time (t_1→t_2→t_3). This schema suggests that any narrative with more than one character may be analyzed as the combination of at least two stories, since every character can be considered the subject of his or her own story. (This insight lies behind Tom Stoppard's *Rosencrantz and Guildenstern Are Dead,* which "rewrites" *Hamlet* by taking two minor characters as the subject.)

13. Such explicit designation is a characteristic device in *The Divine Comedy.* See, for example, *Inferno* 9. 61–63, where Dante suddenly interrupts his story and tells the reader to "look carefully at the doctrine hidden beneath" his verses.

14. Curiously, Jesus does not interpret the phrase "it bore fruit"; he merely repeats it in his interpretation as a *metaphor,* whereas in the parable it was a literal statement.

15. In the traditional commentaries on the New Testament parables, one often sees a distinction made between "allegorical" parables like the parable of the sower, and more extended narratives (similar to fables) like the parable of the Good Samaritan or the Prodigal Son. This distinction corresponds to a more general one, recently elucidated by Tzvetan Todorov in *Symbolisme et interprétation:* the distinction between *lexical symbolism,* where a single word or phrase is interpreted metaphorically (e.g., seed equals Christ's Word), abolishing the literal meaning of the sentence that contains it; and *propositional symbolism,* where a whole sentence or proposition is interpreted in such a way that to its literal meaning (which is not abolished) there is added another, "second" meaning (e.g., the Samaritan helped the traveler; one must always help those in need). One could argue that only this second type of parable, founded on propositional symbolism, is genuinely "exemplary"—that is, functioning by means of analogy. But in our present perspective this distinction is not pertinent, for two reasons: first, even in the parable of the sower, where every element has an allegorical meaning, the literal meaning of the narrative propositions is not necessarily "abolished" by allegorical interpretation: the statement that the sower went out to sow can be considered "true" (the way all fictive statements are "true"), and can at the same time be interpreted as meaning "something else." Second, from the point of view of

their didactic and pragmatic function, "allegorical" and "exemplary" parables are identical: they both realize the triadic structure of *story → interpretation → injunction.*

16. Starobinski, "Le Démoniaque de Gérasa: analyse littéraire de Marc 5:1–20," in R. Barthes, F. Bovon et al., *Analyse structurale et exégèse biblique,* p. 86.

17. The question has a philological source: what is the meaning of the conjunction *hina* in the Greek text of Mark (4:11–12), where Jesus explains why he speaks in parables? If *hina* means "so that," then the parables are designed to *exclude* those who "have ears but hear not." But *hina* can also be interpreted to mean "in such a way that," or even "because." In Matthew, for example, we find *hoti* ("because") in place of *hina,* suggesting perhaps that Jesus speaks in parables because his audience would not otherwise understand his message. Even here, however, there remains a certain ambiguity, for with "because" the sentence can still be interpreted in two ways. For a discussion of the grammatical problem and its implications (which are obviously more than grammatical), see Frank Kermode, *The Genesis of Secrecy: On the Interpretation of Narrative,* pp. 29–34.

18. Kermode, *The Genesis of Secrecy,* pp. 33–34.

19. If it is to produce a rule of action, the interpretation must be univocal, that is, unambiguous and containing no internal contradiction.

20. Barthes, "L'Ancienne Rhétorique," p. 201.

21. "Narrative" is here opposed to "interpretive" and "pragmatic," not to "mimetic," "dramatic," or some other term. In terms of the traditional distinction between "narration" and "dialogue," or *diegesis* and *mimesis,* this text would have to be considered as not exclusively narrative, since it contains direct discourse by the characters. For our present purposes, however, the distinction between "pure" narrative (containing only narrator's discourse) and "impure" narrative (containing narrator's discourse and characters' discourse) is not pertinent. What is pertinent, on the other hand, is the distinction proposed by Emile Benveniste between *récit historique,* or impersonal narration, and *discours,* where the narration bears the subjective marks of the narrator as a person (see Benveniste, "Les Relations de temps dans le verbe français," in *Problèmes de linguistique générale*). In the present instance we can consider the whole text as *récit historique* (despite the "quoted" discourse of the characters), because signs indicating the subjectivity of the narrator are almost totally absent. Dialogue by the characters can be integrated into a *récit* without suggesting the presence or the subjectivity of the narrator.

22. One might, however, consider the clause "where he squandered it in reckless living" as containing an implicit interpretation or judgment, given the negative connotations of the words "squandered" and "reckless." This is an example (a fairly discreet one) of tendentious narration, which judges even as it "tells." As Gérard Genette has shown, absolutely "pure" *récit,* devoid of all signs of subjectivity on the part of the narrator, is just about nonexistent. See his "Frontières du récit."

23. We recall that these two parables, like that of the prodigal son, are provoked by the complaint of the Pharisees and the Scribes: "This fellow . . . welcomes sinners and eats with them" (Luke 15:2). Jesus replies to these accusations by the short parable of the lost sheep, which ends with the following interpretation: "In the same way, I tell you, there will be greater joy in heaven over one sinner who repents than over ninety-nine righteous people who do not need to repent." This parable is immediately followed by that of the lost coin, also very short and telling a story (albeit a minimal one) with the same narrative structure: *object lost—search for the object by its owner—object*

found—general rejoicing. The parable of the lost coin also ends with an interpretation: "In the same way, I tell you, there is joy among the angels of God over one sinner who repents." Now these two explicitly interpreted parables create a specific competence (in addition to the general competence created by the reading of other New Testament parables), which allows the reader to supply the interpretation of the final parable in the series. Once the reader has recognized, in the story of the prodigal son, a longer and more complex variant of the narrative structure realized by the two preceding ones, he or she will inevitably arrive at the interpretation stated by Jesus in the first two parables but "omitted" in this one.

24. The role of the father or one of his substitutes (master of the house, lord of the land, etc.) as the ultimate interpreter—or as the absolute guarantor of Truth—is invariable in the whole corpus of New Testament parables; it is one sign that would allow for a detailed analysis of the ideology of this corpus—and indeed, the ideology of patriarchal culture, which is both lampooned and terrifyingly presented in Barthelme's *The Dead Father.* We shall have further occasion to discuss the role of the father in our analyses of the *roman à thèse.*

25. Barthes, "Rhétorique de l'image," p. 40.

26. The term "intertextuality" was first proposed by Julia Kristeva, but it is already implicit in Mikhail Bakhtin's notion of dialogism. See Bakhtin, *Problems of Dostoevsky's Poetics* and *The Dialogical Imagination;* Kristeva, *Séméiotiké: recherches pour une sémanalyse,* pp. 133–137, 143–173, 191–196, and *passim.* For more recent uses of this increasingly popular term, see *Poétique* (1976), no. 27, special issue on "Intertextualités"; Suleiman, "Reading Robbe-Grillet: Sadism and Text in *Projet pour une révolution à New York";* and Michael Riffaterre's forthcoming book *Typology and Intertextuality.*

27. Julia Kristeva gives examples of such "misquotations" of Pascal and La Rochefoucauld by Lautréamont in *Séméiotiké,* pp. 255–257.

28. In Gide's version, as we might expect, the prodigal son is shown to be regrettably weak for having returned to the fold. See Gide, *Le Retour de l'Enfant Prodigue* (1907), in *Romans, Récits et Soties.*

29. Verses 13–27, which are not mentioned in the above schema, constitute an ancillary episode with the bassa as subject. This episode does not form an essential element of H_1; its function is chiefly to motivate B's decision not to take vengeance on M but to try acting on him by persuasion.

30. Here we should no doubt introduce another variable in the relation between narrator and narratee. Between the bassa and the merchant, there exists a relation of power: the bassa could eventually do real harm to the merchant. The story he tells him is thus backed by the possibility of veritable coercion and could even be understood as a veiled threat (cf. vv. 34–35: "sans tant de dialogue et de raisons qui pourraient t'ennuyer"—if the merchant is not persuaded by the story, the bassa has other, more "annoying" means at his disposal to make him change his mind). Between the extradiegetic narrator and *his* narratee, however, such potential coercion does not exist (usually). Whence a less utopian, more cynical conclusion: in order to act on someone by means of words, it helps to have material power on one's side.

31. That brevity is a characteristic trait of the *exemplum* has been mentioned by all those who studied it (see n. 7). As for its "simplicity," it is manifested not only on the level of narrative structure (necessarily simple in a very short tale), but also, and above all, on the level of norms. Any universe founded on unambiguous values is simple, and the *exemplum* is the domain par excellence of unambiguous values.

32. Barthes, *S/Z*, p. 85.

33. See the article "Redondance," in J. Dubois et al., *Dictionnaire de Linguistique*.

34. See, in this regard, *S/Z* and also Philippe Hamon, "Un Discours contraint." I shall come back to this in detail in chapter 4.

35. Barthes, *S/Z*, p. 26.

36. The relation between the religious *exemplum* and a doctrine is even clearer in the case of medieval *exempla*, which were all in one way or another illustrations of Church doctrine. In the case of the New Testament parables this relation is more tenuous, since the Gospels date from a period when the doctrine was not yet fully elaborated and since they *speak* of a period (Jesus' lifetime) when the doctrine did not even, strictly speaking, exist. But if we consider the Sermon on the Mount as a kind of primitive doctrinal text, we can say that Jesus' parables are all more or less directly related to it as illustrations.

37. The notion of "family resemblances" to speak of certain categories or concepts was proposed by Wittgenstein for the category "games." According to Wittgenstein, it would be useless to look for necessary and sufficient properties to define a "family"; thus, in comparing different kinds of games, we would find not a set of properties they all had in common, but rather a complicated network of resemblances (*Philosophical Investigations*, pars. 66, 67). It seems to me, however, that this conclusion does not necessarily follow from Wittgenstein's analysis; he himself admits that one can, if one wishes, draw *boundaries* to circumscribe "concepts with blurred edges" like the concept "game" (pars. 69, 70). On a certain level of generality, it is possible to find properties that all games have in common and that are sufficient to distinguish them from objects or activities that are *not* games. Conversely, if one considers certain "families" of games (board games, card games, sports games, etc.), one can establish criteria to distinguish them from each other and to distinguish one game from others within a given "family." As Todorov has remarked, "every class of objects can be converted into a series of properties by a passage from extension to comprehension" ("The Origin of Genres," p. 162). One merely has to be careful to define the level of generaliy on which one is working.

38. See Goldmann, *Pour une sociologie du roman;* Pierre Macherey, *Pour une théorie de la production littéraire;* as concerns in particular Balzac and *Le Père Goriot*, see Pierre Barbéris, *Le Père Goriot de Balzac*.

2. *The Structure of Apprenticeship*

1. Fredric Jameson, "Magical Narratives: Romance as Genre;" a substantially revised version of this essay appeared in Jameson, *The Political Unconscious*. In this revised version, Jameson no longer speaks of finding the "fixed form" to which a given mode may "correspond."

2. See Lukács, *The Theory of the Novel*, p. 80.

3. The term *Bildungsroman*, designating a type of story that emphasizes the formation (*Bildung*) or the "self-education" of the hero, was first proposed in 1810, by the literary critic Karl von Morgenstern; it became generally used after 1870, due to the influence of Dilthey's *Life of Schleiermacher*. See François Jost, "La Tradition du *Bildungsroman*," pp. 101–102. Some specialists distinguish the *Bildungsroman* from a neighboring genre, the *Erziehungsroman*, in which the emphasis is not on the hero's self-education, but on the influence of an outside agent. This distinction (maintained

by Jost, for example, in the above-mentioned article) does not seem to me essential, given that in any *Bildungsroman* one finds outside agents as well as internal factors that determine the hero's evolution.

4. Lukács, *The Theory of the Novel*, p. 89.

5. I say "young man" and not young woman, for the model that Lukács has in mind—and that corresponds to the major examples of the genre in nineteenth-century European fiction—is a masculine model. "Going into the world to test and find oneself" was (perhaps still is?) a program evisaged chiefly for—and by—men. In any case, the possibilities exploited by stories of *Bildung* with feminine protagonists are "different." The question of female *Bildung* has come to the fore only recently, in the work of American feminist critics. See, for example, Nancy K. Miller, *The Heroine's Text*, which studies the destiny of female protagonists in eighteenth-century novels by male authors; and Sandra Gilbert and Susan Gubar, *The Madwoman in the Attic*, which deals occasionally with the nineteenth-century female *Bildungsroman* by women writers.

6. For the first, and clearest, version of Greimas' theory of actants (somewhat modified later, but not in essential ways), see his *Sémantique structurale*, pp. 172–191. Actants are general syntactic categories that can account for the large-scale structures of a story. In Greimas' schema, elaborated to account for myths and folktales, but useful for other genres as well, there are six actants who define the principal spheres of action of any story: the subject or protagonist; the object, or what is desired, valued, sought by the subject; the receiver (*destinataire*), who is to benefit from the object; the donor (*destinateur*), who facilitates the communication of (or who simply gives or bequeaths) the object to the receiver; the helper (*adjuvant*), who helps the subject in his action for obtaining the object; and the opponent (*opposant*), who hinders or tries to hinder the subject's action. One needn't accept as definitive all of Greimas' categories, nor consider them as exhausting all of the possibilities of fiction; they are abstractions, extremely reductive—but that is precisely their usefulness. What they allow one to see is that the number of *actants*, or syntactic categories, in any story (even in a very long and complex one) is limited; the number of *actors*, however, can be very large, since every actantial category may be occupied by more than one actor. The latter is defined as any agent, animate or inanimate, who fulfills a particular actantial function; actors may range from living persons (what we usually call "characters") to abstract entities like "Truth." Conversely, a single actor may participate in more than one actantial category.

7. For the preceding, see Lukács, *The Theory of the Novel*, pp. 97–143.

8. Albert Feuillerat, *Paul Bourget. Histoire d'un esprit sous la Troisième République*, p. 229.

9. Goguel, *La Politique des Partis sous la Troisième République*.

10. In this paragraph, all of the expressions between quotation marks are employed by the omniscient narrator of *L'Etape*. The edition is the two-volume one published by the Editions Plon (1902).

11. See "Les Jeux des contraintes sémiotiques," in A. J. Greimas, *Du Sens*.

12. Mikhail Bakhtin, *Problems of Dostoevsky's Poetics*, pp. 64–68 and *passim*.

13. François Rastier, "Les Niveaux d'ambiguïté des structures narratives." Rastier seems to think that the dialogism of *Dom Juan* is due to the fact that it consists literally in "dialogues," i.e., that it is a dramatic, not a narrative, work. According to Rastier,

the novel is a "monological genre," since "the unity of the narrator assures a homogeneous framing of the utterances [*énoncés*]" (p. 291). But the presence of a single narrator does not necessarily make a novel monological (not even if the narrator is of the "omniscient" variety), just as the absence of a narrator does not make all dramatic works dialogical. A "socialist realist" play is just as monological as a "socialist realist" novel. What makes a play *or* a novel monological is not the presence of a narrator, but the presence of an ideological supersystem that dubs one way of seeing things "correct" and discredits all others.

14. *Ibid.*, p. 341. Shlomith Rimmon has proposed an elegantly simple formula to define ambiguity: A ∧ b, where *a* and *b* are propositions and ∧ is a "hybrid" sign indicating both logical disjunction (if *a* is true, *b* is false) *and* the actual coexistence of the two propositions. As a result, there is "equal evidence for the truth and falsity of both *a* and *b*. We cannot decide whether *a* or *b* is the true proposition and, consequently, which of the two is the false one. Both possibilities thus remain equitenable and copresent" (*The Concept of Ambiguity: The Example of James*, pp. 8–9). If one considers *a* and *b* as the two possible readings of *Dom Juan*, then Rimmon's formula sums up Rastier's argument: the two readings are contradictory, but both are "in" the play with equal presence. This also makes clear what is unambiguous about the *roman à thèse*: only one reading is proposed as necessary (or valid) by the text.

15. I have analyzed this kind of conflict in my essay on Drieu's *Gilles*, using my own reactions as a basis (Suleiman, "Ideological Dissent from Works of Fiction: Toward a Rhetoric of the *roman à thèse*"). Obviously, the reactions of even a single reader to a single text can vary from occasion to occasion; this does not invalidate my argument, however. The study of individual reactions to literary works has come to the fore in recent years in "subjective" and psychoanalytic criticism, as practiced by David Bleich (*Subjective Criticism*) and Norman Holland (*Five Readers Reading*); it has also been studied in certain sociological surveys (see in particular Jacques Leenhardt and Pierre Józsa, *Lire la lecture. Essai de sociologie de la lecture*). For an overview of reader-oriented criticism, see my "Introduction: Varieties of Audience-Oriented Criticism," in S. Suleiman and I. Crosman, eds., *The Reader in the Text: Essays on Audience and Interpretation*.

16. Bourget, *L'Etape*, 2:235–236. Further references, to volume and page, will be given in parentheses in the text.

17. Oswald Ducrot, "La Description sémantique des énoncés français et la notion de présupposition," p. 40.

18. Ducrot, *Dire et ne pas dire*, p. 268.

19. Simone Vierne has done interesting studies on the role of this scenario in fiction. See her *Rite Roman Initiation* and *Jules Verne et le roman initiatique*.

20. Vierne, *Jules Verne et le roman initiatique*, pp. 13–15.

21. The distinction between a character's syntagmatic and semantic functions corresponds to the distinction—generally recognized by structural analysts of narrative—between what a character "does" and what he "is" ("faire" vs. "être"), or between actions and qualifications. For a detailed discussion of redundancy, see chapter 4.

22. Paul Nizan, *Aden Arabie*, p. 129.

23. The principal "malevolent fathers" in *Aden Arabie* are the idealist philosophers who were the hero's teachers at the university (and whom Nizan in his next book called the "watchdogs of the bourgeoisie"), on the one hand; on the other hand,

businessmen like "Monsieur C . . . ," his employer at Aden, who tries to enroll him as one of his permanent collaborators.

24. From here on I shall reserve the term "hero" to designate the subject of a positive exemplary apprenticeship.

25. See A. Jolles, *Formes simples*, pp. 46–49.

26. Joseph Salvador (1796–1873) was the author of numerous works on Jewish history and philosophy. James Darmesteter (1849–1894), a philologian of Semitic languages and professor at the Collège de France from 1885 on, was the author of *Prophètes d'Israel* (1892). I had to look these names up in a biographical dictionary, but I suppose that Bourget's first readers (or at least a great many of them) had no such difficulties. The function of historical names in fiction is a fascinating and little-explored subject.

27. Paul Nizan, *Antoine Bloyé*, p. 281.

28. *Ibid.*, p. 293. This sentence is an excellent illustration of the way the presupposition functions in "X knows that *p*."

29. Nizan, *La Conspiration*, p. 242.

30. The metaphor of uprootment (*déracinement*) was for a long time one of the favorite metaphors of the extreme Right in France, especially after the publication of Barrès' *Les Déracinés* (1897). I shall discuss *Les Déracinés* in the next chapter.

31. Bourget's ideas about the "guilt of the teacher" for his disciple's crimes have been perceptively analyzed by Victor Brombert, in *The Intellectual Hero*. Brombert points out the similarities between Joseph Monneron and the "guilty teacher" of *Le Disciple*, Adrien Sixte. In Monneron's case, the guilt is compounded by the fact that he is the father as well as the educator of his "criminal" children.

32. This is all the more remarkable considering that in an earlier chapter the narrator did not hesitate to condemn Crémieu-Dax for a similar type of reasoning: "this terminology of a scientific type in which certain demagogues excel today and which reveals the least precise bent of mind, the one most contrary to direct observation: the habit of reasoning by analogy" (2:123). A curious admission by the "voice of Truth!" It is almost as if the narrator were here subverting, in advance and without wishing to (at least we must suppose that he does not wish to) the very "proof" on which the thesis of the novel rests.

33. The theme of the "foreigner harmful to France," like that of the "continuation of the race" (the two are in fact closely linked), were privileged themes of the French Right up to the Second World War, and doubtless beyond. Although the literary sources of this theme go back at least as far as Gobineau, it was only in the late nineteenth-century that the theme became fully developed in literature. Barrès, with his extolment of "la terre et les morts," was perhaps the best known exponent of the "continuation of the race" theme. But we also find the "harmful foreigner" in his novels, especially in *Leurs Figures*, where the Panama scandal and the decadence of France of which it is a symptom are blamed on "cosmopolitan bankers"—to be read as "German Jews." This same thematic is found practically unchanged forty years later in Drieu La Rochelle's *Gilles* (1939), which also lays the blame for the decadence of France on the "Jewish influence." For a more detailed discussion, see the analysis of Barrès' trilogy in chapter 3.

34. For those who enjoy this kind of thing, here is a table summarizing all the possible combinations of our three variables:

Neg. valorization: only contextual (+) vs. contextual and cultural (−)	Doctrinal awareness (+) vs. indifference (−)	Recognition of own negativity (+) vs. non-recognition (−)	Example
−	−	−	Antoine Monneron
−	−	+	?
−	+	−	Julie Monneron
−	+	+	Pluvinage (*La Conspiration*)
+	−	−	?
+	+	−	Joseph Monneron
+	−	+	Antoine Bloyé
+	+	+	Louis (*Le Noeud de vipères*)

Grosso modo, one can say that the protagonist's "negativity" increases as one moves from bottom to top. For a more precise evaluation, one would have to take a number of other variables relative to the character into account (moral and intellectual qualities, physical aspect, relations with other characters, ways of speaking, etc.), which are not easily transposable from one work to another. This means that a precise study of the valorization of a character must be based on a detailed analysis of a single work, and is valid only for that work. For an interesting attempt to define various criteria on the basis of which such an analysis might be undertaken, see Philippe Hamon, "Pour un statut sémiologique du personnage."

3. The Structure of Confrontation

1. Serres, "Connaissez-vous René Girard?" Review of Girard, *Des choses cachées depuis la fondation du monde,* p. 72.

2. Prince Rodolphe is the hero of Eugène Sue's *Les Mystères de Paris.* Like the Lone Ranger, he is a "masked" figure (he visits the poor neighborhoods of Paris *incognito*) who helps the weak and the innocent.

3. John Huizinga, *Homo Ludens. A Study of the Play Element in Culture,* p. 89.

4. *Ibid.,* p. 210.

5. Henri Dubief, *Le Déclin de la IIIe République, 1929–1938,* p. 77.

6. *Ibid.,* p. 78.

7. Robert Brasillach, *Notre Avant-Guerre,* p. 152; quoted (with wrong page number) in David L. Schalk, *The Spectrum of Political Engagement,* p. 146, n. 29.

8. See Dubief, pp. 154–163.

9. One might well ask why Nizan chose such an allusive title, so evocative of a certain bourgeois culture, for a novel that celebrated the union of workers. In fact, the first title of the novel, as announced in a letter to his wife a few months before publication, was simpler: *Le Jour de la colère (Day of Wrath).* It is not known why he changed the title, but the question is perhaps not very important. Although he was a Communist militant, Nizan never adopted the posture of a "proletarian writer," either in his style of dress or in his prose style. As he wrote ironically in *Aden Arabie,* he had not "gotten his classical education for nothing."

10. Paul Nizan, *Le Cheval de Troie,* pp. 80–81; other page references will be given in parentheses in the text. Clearly, the relation between individual and group is here

one of integration rather than of opposition. This is in marked contrast to the nineteenth century, specifically Romantic, paradigm, which one still finds in Zola's novels (including the "revolutionary" novel *Germinal*)—the individual hero being characterized by his "difference" from (and ultimately rejection by) both organized and spontaneously formed groups. For an interesting analysis, see Naomi Schor, *Zola's Crowds*, ch. 2.

11. I should note that in speaking about conformity to the model, I do not mean that a generic narrative model exists outside and independently of the works that realize it. It is not a matter of explicit "rules" to which the novelist conforms or against which he rebels. The model is a construction of the analyst. After constructing the model on the basis of a number of works, however, one can examine other works and speak of their more or less complete realization of—or conformity to—the model. If every structure implies constraints (which are not necessarily felt as such by those who confor to them), there nevertheless remains a fairly wide leeway for individual variations.

12. Until the Epilogue, *Gilles* is a positive exemplary apprenticeship story, although of a somewhat special kind. Gilles evolves gradually toward fascism, after making a number of false starts and being sidetracked by women, money, and his own vacillations as a "decadent" intellectual of the 1920s. On February 6, 1934, he is passionately in favor of a *coup d'état*—but he finds no one, on the Right or the Left, to join him. His story therefore is that of a positive exemplary apprenticeship that stops short because of the isolation of the hero (cf. the narrative cliché of "the prophet who preaches in the desert"). In fact, the chapter immediately preceding the Epilogue shows Gilles leaving Paris, alone and having lost all hope. The main function of the Epilogue seems to be to emphasize the *positive* value of his apprenticeship, despite his apparent failure (his "new life" as a militant is authentic)—or perhaps to furnish a "happy ending" to a story that otherwise would have ended on too somber a note.

13. [Pierre] Drieu La Rochelle, *Gilles*, p. 475. The sentence about "living an idea" is on p. 476.

14. This does not mean that Manuel's evolution plays no role in the story of confrontation. On the contrary, it is *because* he becomes an effective leader that he can contribute to the victory of Guadalajara, with which the novel ends. But this kind of added motivation, although it makes the story more complex, is not an essential element of the confrontation model. Thus, the other characters in the novel who function as confrontational heroes (Garcia, Magnin, etc.) undergo no changes in their convictions or in their inner being in the course of the war. See the more detailed discussion of *L'Espoir*, later in this chapter.

15. The only exception one can imagine to this would be a narative of the Last Judgment and of the end of time—or, in a different code, of the "final struggle" and the end of history as we know it. But since the end of time would signal not only the end of all conflict but also the end of narrative, narratives of the Apocalypse (whether of the Christian variety or others) are fairly rare—and always set in the future.

16. For a detailed and authoritative, if altogether hostile discussion of socialist-realist fiction, and in particular of the "positive hero," see Rufus W. Mathewson, Jr., *The Positive Hero in Russian Literature*.

17. It is in this perspective that one must read, I think, one of the better known (because extremely eloquent) chapters in the novel: the one describing the death of Catherine, wife of one of the Communist workers, after an illegal abortion (pp. 164–

174). Catherine's death has nothing to do with the confrontation between fascists and antifascists, but it functions as a significant element in the long-term struggle: in the "new world" of the future, this kind of death will no longer occur.

18. *Le Cheval de Troie*, pp. 237–238. In this context, it is fascinating to note the change wrought in Nizan's confrontational schema by a recent theatrical adaptation of *Le Cheval de Troie*. Merely by altering a few minor details, Philippe Madral's play, *La Manifestation* (presented at the Théâtre de l'Odéon in April 1978) changed the whole meaning of the work. In the play, the murder of the Communist demonstrator is attributed to Lange, not to the National Guard. From the point of view of the authorities, the death of the Communist is a regrettable accident. The Prefect himself reprimands the Chief of Police and then expresses his regrets to Bloyé and his freinds when the latter go to the hospital to identify the body. These few details totally alter Nizan's meaning, since the authorities are seen in an entirely non-confrontational perspective. In the novel, the murder of the Communist is expressly attributed to the National Guard (pp. 202, 209); the Prefect never meets any of the Communists, much less apologizes to them. He is the one who is responsible, at a distance, for the activity of the National Guard. The Communist's death is interpreted by his friends as one more reason for continuing the struggle: "L'adversaire reprenait toute sa taille, . . . la haine sa vertu" (p. 224). This antagonistic schema is entirely effaced in Madral's play, which, although set in 1934, has a 1978 perspective.

19. Lévi-Strauss, "La Structure des mythes," in *Anthropologie structurale*, p. 21. Curiously, this sentence is not translated in *Structural Anthropology*, the English version of this essay.

20. Zeev Sternhell, *Maurice Barrès et le nationalisme français*, p. 113. The mention of the Dreyfus Affair in the trilogy occurs in *Leurs Figures*, p. 72. In *Leurs Figures*, the narrator identifies himself several times as "the author of this book," which contributes to "defictionalizing" this last volume of the trilogy.

21. Sternhell, p. 110. Sternhell speaks about the "new Right," nationalistic and anti-Semitic, which was being formed during the 1890s and one of whose first representatives was Barrès. Sternhell also quotes an article by Barrès published in 1901, in which he stated that "nationalism crystallized around the Dreyfus Affair" (Sternhell, pp. 248–249). See also Sternhell's subsequent study on "the revolutionary Right" in France, which he sees as the forerunner of the fascist movements of this century: Sternhell, *La Droite révolutionnaire*.

22. Philippe Barrès, Introduction to *Les Déracinés*, in *L'Oeuvre de Maurice Barrès*, 3:4. According to Philippe Barrès (Barrès' son), "*Le Roman de l'énergie nationale* never had, in Barrès' mind, the form of a trilogy. Barrès conceived it, wrote it, and wanted to publish it in a single block." One may nevertheless doubt that Barrès *wrote* it "in a single block," if for no other reason than the length of the trilogy (more than a thousand pages in the Club de l'Honnête Homme edition). Or if so, then the "single block" occupied several years which is in fact what is indicated by Barrès' published notebooks for the years 1896–1902 (*Mes Cahiers*, vols. 1 and 2).

23. *Ibid.*, p. 4.

24. *Les Déracinés*, p. 28. Further page references to the trilogy will be given in parentheses in the text, using the following abbreviations: D—*Les Déracinés*; AS—*L'Appel au soldat;* LF—*Leurs Figures*. All page numbers refer to the Livre de Poche editions.

25. Cf. the narrator's commentary, D, 252: "For this situation [that of the young *déracinés*], the *bureaux* are responsible. The Bureau of Education has inspired them

with distaste for their little homeland, has trained them through emulation and without instilling in them a religious thought—whether revealed religion or scientific ideal—that would provide them with a social bond." Since, according to this analysis, Bouteiller's role is but that of an agent of the State, the real corruptor of the young men is the Republic itself. We should note, however, that Barrès was not a monarchist. He rejected the parliamentary republic not in the name of the *ancien régime* but in that of the "revolutionary Right."

26. It should be recalled that the Radicals were neither Socialists nor Marxists; in the political spectrum of the Third Republic, they occupied the left-Republican position. During the early years of the Republic, their opponents were the monarchists, the Bonapartists (those that remained after the death of Napoleon III), and various right-wing nationalists. See Gordon Wright, *France in Modern Times*, pp. 271–342.

27. The narrator's interpretations occur throughout the trilogy. Saint-Phlin's is summed up in his "Lettre sur une 'nourriture' lorraine," addressed to Sturel (*LF*, 276–289). Saint-Phlin's letter contains an obvious allusion (and response) to Gide's *Les Nourritures terrestres* (1897). Gide had written his own response to Barrès in December 1897, after the publication of *Les Déracinés;* as one might expect, he criticized rather severely, albeit with a good dose of irony, Barrès's metaphor of *déracinement*. See A. Gide, "A propos des *Déracinés*," pp. 51–60.

28. Albert Thibaudet, *La Vie de Maurice Barrès*, p. 171 and *passim*. Cf. Pierre Bourdieu and Jean-Claude Passeron, *Les Héritiers* (Paris: Minuit, 1964).

29. It is interesting to note that Barrès, like Bourget and Drieu, uses organic metaphors (uprootment, disease) to support his thesis. Risking a rather broad generalization, one might suggest that this preference is characteristic of right-wing writers; Marxists like Nizan and Aragon, on the other hand, favor theatrical and mechanical metaphors (unmasking, exposing the workings of a machine, being caught in the "cogs" of the system, etc.). The metaphor of illness or decadence to characterize French society seems to be a *leitmotif* of the French Right up to our own day—which might explain both the title and the best-selling success of a book like Alain Peyrefitte's *Le Mal français*. In a similar vein, we know that Hitler considered Jews as "germs" that had to be exterminated to make Germany "healthy" again.

30. One may wonder why Paris figures, in the context of the trilogy, as a "foreign" element. First of all, it is obviously in opposition to Lorraine. What seems more important, however, is that Barrès, like other theorists of the "revolutionary Right," saw Paris as a *cosmopolis* without its own traditions, dominated by the egotistic drive to money and power. Paris as a symbol of the capitalist "jungle" became a cliché of the political novels of the 1930s, on the Right as on the Left (cf. *Les Beaux Quartiers, Gilles*, Céline's *Bagatelles pour un massacre*, among others). Furthermore, Barrès thought of the centers of power in Paris as dominated by the secret activities of Jewish financiers, "born in Frankfurt"—men like Joseph Reinach or Cornelius Herz, fiercely attacked by Barrès in *Leurs Figures*. Without going so far as to theorize an "international Zionist conspiracy," Barrès shared with Drumont and Maurras (and later with Céline) the vision of a France totally at the mercy of foreigners, first of all of Jews. The background presence of the Dreyfus Affair in the trilogy is here altogether palpable, even if it is true that the anti-Semitism of Drumont—and of Barrès—was manifest several years before the Affair. (Drumont's *La France juive* was published in 1886; Barrès' first anti-Semitic articles appeared in *Le Courrier de L'Est* in 1889).

31. Cf. *D*, 416: "Wasn't that foreign woman [*cette étrangère*] linked to all his

thoughts, coloring them all . . . , truly *it was Astiné's poison acting in his blood.* Wherever he goes, he carries her with him;" *D*, 469: *"The Asian woman continued to live in him;" LF*, 225; "Sturel experienced [in 1893] some of the same feelings that had been stirred in him from 1882 to 1885 by *Astiné the Asian [Astiné l'Asiatique]*" [my emphases].

32. For a succinct account of the Boulanger affair, see Wright, *France in Modern Times*, pp. 312–316; see also Jean-Marie Mayeur, *Les Débuts de la IIIe République*, pp. 165–180.

33. Mayeur, p. 205.

34. *Ibid.*, pp. 206–207.

35. Fanfournot is a young anarchist who first appears as a child in *Les Déracinés;* Sturel counts on his support after the publication of his list. Fanfournot too is a "spiritual son" of Bouteiller, since his father was the *concierge* at the lycée in Nancy where Bouteiller taught. Fanfournot, who, at the end of *Leurs Figures*, throws a bomb on the street and is torn apart by the crowd, realizes the narrative cliché of the sorcerer's apprentice; by pushing Bouteiller's teachings to their logical conclusion, he demonstrates their dangerous implications.

36. "Allocution de Maurice Barrès au second dîner de *L'Appel au Soldat*, 7 février 1901," in *Scènes et doctrines du nationalisme* (Paris, 1902) and in *L'Oeuvre de Maurice Barrès*, 5:123.

37. Mikhail Bakhtin, *Problems of Dostoevsky's Poetics*, p. 64.

38. Malraux, *L'Espoir*, pp. 91 and 273. Further page references will be given in parentheses in the text.

39. One possible actantial schema is the following:

Subject: Spanish Republicans (or perhaps all those who fight on Republican side)
Object: Brotherhood, social justice
Donor: History
Receiver: Spanish people
Helper: Foreigners fighting on Republican side (if not included in subject); all those who sympathize with Republican cause.
Anti-subject: Spanish fascists (or all those who fight on their side).
Anti-helper: Foreigners fighting on Franco's side (if not included in anti-subject); all those who sympathize with them (Mussolini, etc.)

40. See Lucien Goldmann, "Introduction à une étude structurale des romans de Malraux," in *Pour une sociologie du roman*, pp. 216–239, and W. M. Frohock, *André Malraux and the Tragic Imagination*, pp. 104–125.

41. For a detailed history of the war, see Hugh Thomas, *The Spanish Civil War.* For a first-person account emphasizing the internal strife in the Republican ranks, see George Orwell, *Homage to Catalonia.*

42. In the battle for the defense of Madrid, for example, Malraux has the anarchist "le Négus" say: "You understand, the Communists work well. I can work with them, but as for liking them, no matter how hard I try, there's not a chance" (p. 364)—the point being that for the sake of the common cause, ideological and personal differences can be overlooked (if not forgotten). A similar thought is expressed by the communist Ramos during the bombardment of Madrid: "In front of the disemboweled houses, Ramos passed twenty or so corpses, stretched out, parallel and in a heap, all alike before the ruins. [. . .] Anarchists, Communists, socialists, republicans—how the inexhaustible roaring of those planes joined into one stream the blood

of men who had thought themselves adversaries, in the fraternal depths of death" (p. 306).

43. Goldmann, pp. 232–233.

44. Goldmann, p. 217. We are not told in the novel what party Garcia belongs to—only that he is a highly respected anthropologist who before the war spent several years in Peru. Garcia's lack of affiliation with a political party makes him a more trustworthy—because more disinterested—spokesman for the pro-Communist argument.

45. Frohock, p. 121. In general, I am sympathetic to most of Frohock's readings. His book remains one of the best studies of Malraux's novels; the same can be said, incidentally, of Goldmann's long essay.

46. Goldmann, p. 236.

47. Frohock cites the scene with Alvear as one example of the conflict between art and propaganda (Frohock, p. 116). I see it as an example of the way a *roman à thèse* can transcend or relativize its own certainties.

48. Goldmann cites the ending of the novel, but does not seem fully to realize what it does to the model of confrontation. He suggests that Malraux included the "brief concluding paragraphs" because he realized that the main argument of the novel—in favor of sacrificing ethics for discipline—would risk appearing unjustified and "dérisoire" if, "far from being effective, it led not to victory but to defeat" (Goldmann, p. 236). The suggestion that Malraux ended the novel the way he did simply in order to hedge his bet about the outcomes of the war seems to me unsatisfactory.

49. Here again, I find Goldmann's reading a bit too categorical. Acording to Goldmann, *L'Espoir* is "wholly oriented toward the valorization of command and of the leader, the main story line consisting in the transformation of Manuel from an enthusiastic and spontaneous revolutionary into a political chief." Goldmann sees this perspective as being diametrically opposed to that of Sartre in *L'Enfance d'un chef*, which "treats the same problem" (Goldmann, p. 223). But it is not at all the same problem: for the protagonist of *L'Enfance d'un chef*, "becoming a chief" means assuming a class identity that will define him once and for all, whereas for Manuel it means assuming a necessary role in the midst of a war. Manuel is not valorized in the novel as a "permanent" chief (a chief in his very essence, as it were), nor as a political leader, but as a military commander in a specific and limited situation. After the war, he will become "un autre homme." Sartre's protagonist, on the other hand, becomes a "chief" in order to close off other possibilities and to flee from his own freedom, which is an altogether different thing. (For a more detailed discussion of *L'Enfance d'un chef*, see below, chapter 6.)

50. For a detailed theoretical study of the narratee, see Gerald Prince, "Introduction à l'étude du narrataire" (English translation in Jane P. Tompkins, ed., *Reader-Response Criticism*, Baltimore: Johns Hopkins University Press, 1980, pp. 7–25). The extradiegetic narratee is the counterpart of the extradiegetic narrator, and, like the latter, may be more or less precisely defined or characterized in a given text. In every case, however, the extradiegetic narratee functions as a means of communication with the actual reader—in other words, as the inscribed reader of the text. For a discussion of this notion, see my "Introduction" to *The Reader in the Text: Essays on Audience and Interpretation,* Susan R. Suleiman and Inge Crosman, eds., pp. 13–15.

51. It is possible, even, that the real function of the *roman à thèse* is to confirm already accepted truths rather than to persuade or to convert. The great majority of

the actual readers of a *roman à thèse* already espouse, perhaps, the values and the doctrine to which the novel is supposed to lead them. Since all reading takes place in a specific cultural and ideological context, we may suppose that contemporary readers "know what to expect," as far as ideology is concerned, before they open the book. If they do not share the author's ideology or if they are hostile to it, they will either not read the novel or read it with suspicion, knowing that he has a particular position to defend and illustrate; if they share his ideology, then reading the novel will confirm or satisfy their previous expectations. The secret of persuasion through fiction is no doubt to find readers who are ready to let themselves be persuaded. The "ideal" reader of a *roman à thèse* is someone who is not yet convinced but is very close to it.

52. In order not to complicate the discussion overmuch, I shall limit myself here to stories with a confrontation structure; but *mutatis mutandis*, the observations apply equally to stories of apprenticeship. There too, the inscribed reader occupies a role of pseudo-helper, since he must wish for the hero to evolve in the "right" direction. If the doctrine discovered by the hero has contemporary relevance for the reader, the latter can become a pseudo-intradiegetic helper, and so on.

53. Linda Hutcheon, *Narcissistic Narrative. The Metafictional Paradox*, pp. 93–94.

54. *Ibid.*, pp. 155 ff.

55. Sartre, "Qu'est-ce que la littérature?," p. 123.

56. We should note that the link between *Vérité* and the Dreyfus Affair is not the same as that between *L'Espoir* and the Spanish Civil War. The story told in *Vérité*, although it is closely modeled on the Dreyfus Affair (it concerns a miscarriage of justice) is nevertheless not the story *of* the Dreyfus Affair; it is a fictional story, which its readers in 1903 could recognize as an obvious transposition of the historical event. *Vérité* thus occupies an intermediary position between a political allegory (i.e., nonrealist in mode) like France's *L'Ile des Pingouins* or Orwell's *Animal Farm*, and a "documentary" novel like *L'Espoir*. This difference does not affect my present argument, however.

4. Redundancy and the "Readable" Text

1. Roland Barthes, *S/Z*, pp. 11–12.

2. The most radical (in the etymological sense of the word) critique of structuralism was formulated by Jacques Derrida, especially in the opening section of *De la grammatologie* (Paris: Minuit, 1967) and in *Positions* (Paris: Minuit, 1972). The attack on representational fiction in the name of the "plural" text was led primarily by Jean Ricardou and Julia Kristeva, as well as by Barthes, and was until recently the "official" position of the *Tel Quel* group. For perceptive critiques of this position, from a basically sympathetic perspective, see Jonathan Culler, *Structuralist Poetics*, ch. 10, and Fredric Jameson, "The Ideology of the Text." Jameson remarks, about the opposition between "realist" and "modern" texts, that "like so many oppositions of this kind, to the negative or straw term has been attributed everything which is error, illusion, and the like" (p. 234). In other words, this opposition is itself ideological. See also my comments in "The Place of Linguistics in Contemporary Literary Theory."

3. Dubois, *Grammaire structurale du français: nom et pronom*, p. 9.

4. Dubois et al., article on "Redondance," in *Dictionnaire de linguistique*, pp. 411 and 413. The classic formulation of the role of redundancy in communications theory can be found in Claude E. Shannon and Warren Weaver, *The Mathematical Theory of Communication* (Urbana: University of Illinois Press, 1949).

5. Dubois et al., *Dictionnaire de linguistique,* p. 411; my emphasis.

6. Greimas defines isotopy as "a set of redundant semantic categories which makes a uniform reading possible" (*Du Sens,* p. 188). For a useful discussion of this concept, see J. M. Klinkenberg, "Le Concept d'isotopie en sémantique et en sémiotique littéraire."

7. An obvious exception would be the lexeme "mortes" ("dead"), which contains the seme "inanimate." But in order for something to be dead, it must once have been alive; the lexeme therefore contains a seme one might call "animated in the past," rather than simply "inanimate."

8. Dubois et al., *Dictionnaire de linguistique,* p. 412.

9. See in particular Roman Jakobson, "Closing Statement: Linguistics and Poetics," in Thomas A. Sebeok, ed., *Style in Language,* pp. 350–377.

10. Barthes, *S/Z,* pp. 85–86.

11. In a very suggestive recent essay, Shlomith Rimmon-Kenan points out some of the paradoxes of repetition, both as a phenomenon and as a concept: "The Paradoxical Status of Repetition."

12. See especially Hamon, "Pour un statut sémiologique du personnage," *Littérature* (1972), vol. 6, revised and reprinted in Barthes et al., *Poétique du récit,* pp. 115–180; "Qu'est-ce qu'une description?" "Un Discours contraint."

13. Hamon, "Un Discours contraint," p. 423.

14. I want to emphasize that this definition does not imply the priority, either temporal or ontological, of the story over the discourse. No story (and certainly no fictional story) can be said to exist except as it is recounted; the reader's—and even the writer's—knowledge of the story develops simultaneously with its putting into discourse. The analyst, however, is one who already "knows" the story, since the work of analysis comes only after a complete reading of the text; the definition is, therefore, a purely analytic one. As Barthes pointed out in *S/Z,* all critical reading is and must be a *re-*reading.

15. See Barthes, "Introduction à l'analyse structurale des récits;" reprinted in Barthes et al., *Poétique du récit* pp. 7–58.

16. "Character," as I use the term here, designates any individual agent or potential agent of an action, whether human or nonhuman. In realist narrative most agents are human, whence my preference for the commonly-used term here and in the classification that follows. But the extended meaning of the term should be kept in mind. Characters possess qualities ("being") and perform actions or functions ("doing"). Since events are constituted by the actions of characters (in the broad sense), I have drawn a dotted line in the schema from Events to Functions to indicate it.

17. See Greimas, *Sémantique structurale, Du Sens,* and *Maupassant: La Sémiotique du texte;* Claude Bremond, *Logique du récit;* Vladimir Propp, *Morphologie du conte.*

18. Seymour Chatman, in his *Story and Discourse,* uses "event," but instead of "context" he uses the more specific term "setting." It is at times like this that one wishes for a comparative dictionary of terms in modern poetics!

19. Genette, "Discours du récit," pp. 262–263.

20. Some of the reactions when I presented a version of this chapter at a recent conference on the poetics of narrative (Tel-Aviv, June 1979) oblige me to insist on what I thought was evident: in saying that one element of a story is redundant with another, I do not mean that one of the two is superfluous or nonfunctional in the work as a whole. In a fully realized work, every element can be considered functional

on some level; yet, redundancies exist in every work. *A forteiriori*, I do not consider the redundancies classified here as necessarily "negative" features. I call two elements of a work redundant with each other when they both convey the same information, or more exactly when there is *some* information that is identical in both, and no information that is contradictory. Redundancy between two complex elements can be, and usually is, only partial (see Remarks on categories A.2.1. and A.5.2). This obviously raises the question of non-redundancy or difference as well, since the notion of sameness is indissociable from that of difference. Right now, however, it is the former I am dealing with.

21. Genette, "Discours du récit," p. 262.

22. See Bal, "Narration et focalisation."

23. Booth, *The Rhetoric of Fiction*.

24. Bourget, *L'Etape*, 2:9–10. Other references, to volume and page, will be given in parentheses in the text.

25. A two-dimensional schema is quite inadequate here. One would need to represent the chains three-dimensionally in order to show all the possible links.

26. Such total closure is actually impossible, especially in a written artistic text. I shall develop this point in the next chapter.

27. Gide, "A propos des *Déracinés*," p. 54.

28. The six characters who formulate the thesis of discipline (with more or less explicitness or development) are the following; the page numbers refer to the Gallimard edition, 1937: C1: Ramos (p. 82); C2: Garcia (pp. 105 ff., 113, 191, 349, 439); C3: Enrique (p. 140 ff.); C4: Manuel (p. 186); C5: Heinrich (pp. 217, 360); C6: Ximénès (p. 150). Ramos, Enrique, Manuel, and Heinrich are Communists, the other two are not. It is worth noting that the leader of the aviators, Magnin, who is a socialist and mistrusts the Communists, nevertheless recognizes, *in his thoughts*, that the Communists are the most disciplined (p. 142). However, I have included in the above list only those who actually state the thesis out loud. If we included thoughts reported in *style indirect libre*, the redundancies would be even more numerous.

29. Cf. the narrator's comment: "a militant Communist, obliged by his functions to observe a strict discipline . . . , has a good chance of being an excellent officer" (p. 149).

30. Individual variations among readers can, here as in other cases, be quite wide. We have seen, for example, that Lucien Goldmann found Malraux's thesis too simple, too "Stalinist," and for that reason unacceptable.

31. Nizan, "*Le Temps du mépris* par André Malraux," *Monde*, June 6, 1935; reprinted in *Pour une nouvelle culture*, p. 161.

32. See Genette, "Vraisemblance et motivation," pp. 78–86.

33. Suleiman, "Ideological Dissent from Works of Fiction: Toward a Rhetoric of the *roman à thèse*."

34. Drieu La Rochelle, *Gilles*, p. 387.

35. See Barthes, "Le Mythe, aujourd'hui," in *Mythologies*, pp. 191–247.

36. *Ibid.*, p. 214.

37. Indeed, from the Algerian Jew Bénédict, who appears in the first chapter (Bénédict is attractive to women, is "occasionally brave," but has a "Jewish repulsion" for war; he is also "crafty" ["rusé"]) to the Jewish antifascist Gaston Cohen, whom Gilles-Walter meets in Spain (Cohen has "the hereditary mania" of reasoning and calculating instead of trusting in "the simplicity of physical action"), the novel presents

a veritable gallery of Jewish "types" who all have at least one culturally negative trait and are associated, directly or indirectly, with a party or an ideology that the novel's own ideological system condemns. The series includes the Falkenberg family, Rébecca Simonovitch, the "disarticulated" Jew Preuss (would this be an echo of the Jew Seuss?), the "little Jew" with the high-pitched voice who is among the radical-socialist leader Clérences' entourage, as well as the "beautiful Jewess with white breasts" who is called the radical party's "Esther." Some of these characters (Myriam Falkenberg, for example) are presented with more sympathy, or less negatively, than others—but they all symbolize, each in his or her own way, a menace to French "health," they are all incarnations of "modern decadence."

38. Brooke-Rose, "The Readerhood of Man," pp. 146–147.

5. *Subversions, or the Play of Writing*

1. Kermode, *The Genesis of Secrecy. On the Interpretation of Narrative*, p. 14.

2. Barthes, "Ecrivains et écrivants," pp. 148 and 151. English trans. "Authors and Writers," Richard Howard, tr. I have modified Howard's translation, esp. by keeping the two terms in French.

3. Barthes, "Ecrivains et écrivants," p. 153.

4. Barthes, *Leçon*, pp. 14 and 16.

5. Alain Robbe-Grillet, "Sur quelques notions périmés," in *Pour un nouveau roman*, p. 36. The theoretical attack against the "dogma of expression-representation" was led above all by Jean Ricardou, both a critic and a *nouveau romancier*. See especially his "La Littérature comme critique," in *Pour une théorie du nouveau roman*.

6. An example that immediately comes to mind is the Soviet socialist realist novel, to which my models would most likely apply—as they probably would also to "official" novels under the Nazi regime in Germany. As I am not familiar with these areas, I leave the question to others—remarking only, as a qualification, that the *roman à thèse* in France (and this would be equally true of England and the United States) has represented, for the most part, ideologically minority or oppositional views, whereas the Zhdanovist or Nazi novels were expressly at the service of an official ideology. This difference may be unimportant in the long run—as Michel Beaujour has remarked: "Since conclusions, interpretations, are, like the moral of the fable, on the side of the law (or at least of some law, which may be waiting in the wings for its opportunity to become legal), even the radical *roman à thèse* (that of Nizan, for instance) is a stalking horse for the law of the father and for social dictatorship" ("Exemplary Pornography: Barrès, Loyola, and the Novel," p. 345). In the short run, however, we must recall that the social and cultural significance of a work that represents a point of view in opposition to the status quo is different from that of a work representing an official ideology backed up by the apparatus of power. The difference may be worth exploring.

7. Elizabeth W. Bruss, *Autobiographical Acts. The Changing Situation of a Literary Genre*, p. 1.

8. Jacques Derrida, "The Law of Genre," p. 59.

9. Barthes, "L'Effet de réel."

10. I should make clear that I mean here irrelevancy *with regard to the thesis*, not with regard to the work considered in other terms. Thus, if a doctor arrives, makes out a prescription, and then leaves, his actions (as well as his presence as a character) are not irrelevant on the level of the narrative micro-structures, but they are irrele-

vant for the thesis—unless the doctor *also* happens to be identified as a "horrible socialist," a "good Catholic," or by some other traits that reinforce the work's ideological supersystem.

11. Paul Bourget, *L'Etape*, 2:132. Other references to this work will be given in parentheses in the text.

12. On the other hand, one could argue that it is precisely the wealth of details that makes the thesis palatable, since the reader may accept "under cover" a thesis he or she would find objectionable when nakedly stated. In that case, irrelevant details would turn out to be not a threat to, but part of the rhetorical strategy of, the *roman à thèse*.

13. Maurice Barrès, *Les Déracinés*, p. 126. Other references to this work will be given in parentheses in the text.

14. Marin, *Le Récit est un piège*.

15. *La Nouvelle Critique* (July–August 1949), no. 8, p. 83; quoted in Roger Garaudy, *L'Itinéraire d'Aragon*, p. 335. The fact that Aragon's gloss on the novel was addressed to Communist readers (*La Nouvelle Critique* was a Communist journal) is probably not without importance.

16. Garaudy, *L'Itinéraire d'Aragon*, p. 323.

17. Louis Aragon, *Les Beaux Quartiers*, p. 497. Other references to this work will be given in parentheses in the text.

18. We find here the preferred metaphors of left-wing writers: mechanical on the one hand ("grasping the system"), theatrical on the other ("drama unfolding"). See above, ch. 3, n. 29.

19. Garaudy, *L'Itinéraire d'Aragon*, p. 335.

20. For the notion of "focalizer," see Mieke Bal, "Narration et focalisation."

21. Paul Nizan, *Antoine Bloyé*, p. 281. Other references to this work will be given in parentheses in the text.

22. Sartre, Preface to Nizan's *Aden Arabie*, p. 38. Reprinted in *Situations IV* (Paris: Gallimard, 1964), p. 161.

23. Interview in *L'Impartial de l'Est*, December 30, 1933.

24. Sartre, "Le Mur," in *Le Mur*, p. 28.

25. Using Greimas's semiotic square, one can show the difference as follows:

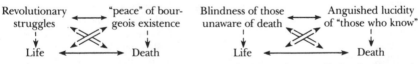

"*Correct*" *interpretation*   *What is actually suggested by the text*

Revolutionary ⟷ "peace" of bourgeois existence   Blindness of those unaware of death ⟷ Anguished lucidity of "those who know"

Life ⟷ Death   Life ⟷ Death

By superimposing the two squares, one can see the internal contradiction in the novel.

26. "Dostoïevsky, *L'Adolescent*," *Monde*, March 29, 1935, p. 8. Reprinted in Paul Nizan, *Pour une nouvelle culture*, p. 144.

27. *L'Humanité*, December 18, 1933, p. 4.

28. See Rufus W. Mathewson, Jr., *The Positive Hero in Russian Literature*, esp. ch. 12.

29. Du Bos, *François Mauriac et le problème du romancier catholique*, p. 91.

30. Flower, *Intention and Achievement. An Essay on the Novels of François Mauriac*, pp. 7 and 107.

31. Mauriac, *Le Noeud de vipères,* p. 233. Other references to this work will be given in parentheses in the text.

32. Gerald Prince has suggested that Luc is not Louis' nephew, but his illegitimate son by his sister-in-law Marinette. According to Prince, Louis does not mention this because he speaks about Luc in a section of his journal addressed to his wife. See Prince, *"Le Noeud de vipères* ou les destinations du récit."

33. Bakhtin has noted that a first-person narrative does not necessarily preclude monologism: despite the suppression of the "direct word of the author," the universe of the narrative can remain "firm and monological." See M. Bakhtin, *Problems of Dostoevsky's Poetics,* p. 46.

34. One might be led to suppose that this kind of understatement is specific to descriptions of mystical experience: since the experience itself is ineffable, it can only be described indirectly or metaphorically (as in the poetry of St. John of the Cross, for example). In that case, the idea of a novel that would "prove" the experience of divine grace becomes unthinkable. *Le Noeud de vipères,* however, is not unique in its recourse to indirection and understatement. As we shall see presently, *La Conspiration,* which is not a Catholic novel, also leaves a great deal unsaid.

35. Flower, *Intention and Achievement,* p. 29.

36. Sartre, "Qu'est-ce que la littérature?," p. 241.

37. The similarity between Rosenthal's and Pluvinage's failed apprenticeships is suggested in various ways in the novel. Rosenthal and Pluvinage are both defeated by the "Law of the father," which they have internalized: Rosenthal punishes himself for his incestuous love affair by killing himelf; as for Pluvinage, by becoming a police informer he places himself under the tutelage of Police Commissioner Massart, who is his mother's lover. His father is dead, but in the end Pluvinage feels he has been reintegrated into his father's world, from which he had tried to escape: "A horrible fatality is bringing me back to the atmosphere of my father" (Nizan, *La Conspiration,* p. 243). The similarity of the two stories is also suggested by one of Massart's remarks to Pluvinage: "Joining the police is like committing suicide. Our kind of power compensates for the visible power we lack and for our failures" (p. 212). The omniscient narrator underlines the similarity when he equates Pluvinage's betrayal with a kind of death: "He was wholly without hope; he knew that betrayal is irremediable like death, and that, like death, it can never be undone" (p. 208).

38. Nizan, *La Conspiration,* p. 249. The suspension points are in the text.

39. Such a juxtaposition is not as arbitrary as it may appear, for earlier, in a letter to Rosenthal, Laforgue had already expressed the thought that any genuine revolutionary action would have to be undertaken within the Communist Party: "Maybe if it weren't for our fear of political servitude, and for our sense that nothing is more important than to abstain from choice, the genuine solution would be, for us too, to simply join the Party, even though *intellectuals* probably don't have too easy a time of it. We'll have to see . . ." (p. 69). At the end, when he recognizes that abstention from choice is no longer possible, Laforgue is presumably ready to take the plunge.

40. As is well known, Nizan resigned from the Party after the Hitler-Stalin Pact. He died before he could explain his action in published writings, but his letters make clear that in this instance he placed individual judgment before party loyalty. For a perceptive and richly documented account of Nizan's relations with the Party, see Annie Cohen-Solal and Henriette Nizan, *Paul Nizan, communiste impossible.* Cohen-Solal's thesis is that Nizan was never well-integrated into the Party, and that after 1937

he became more and more "divorced" from it. This may provide a biographical explanation for the reticence of *La Conspiration*.

41. A note at the end of the original edition of *La Conspiration* stated that the sequel to the novel would be devoted to the years 1936 and 1937, and gave as its title: *La Soirée de Somosierra*. In a letter to his wife, written from the front in 1939, Nizan speaks of having finished "the first part of the novel, the part entitled *Les Amours de septembre*," with Laforgue as its hero. This manuscript was never found. See *Paul Nizan, intellectuel communiste. Ecrits et correspondance, 1926–1940*, Jean-Jacques Brochier, ed., p. 258.

42. J.- B. Pontalis, Preface to Xavière Gauthier, *Surréalisme et sexualité*, p. 16.

43. See, in this regard, the interesting article by Denis Ferraris, "Quaestio de legibilibus aut legendis scriptis: Sur la notion de lisibilité en littérature." Ferraris suggests that one indication of the reader's terror in the face of certain modern texts is the counterattack that consists in calling the text "unreadable." What the "unreadable" text may provoke is the fear that the reader's own self is "unreadable," unintelligible.

44. For a development of this argument, see my essay, "The Question of Readability in Avant-Garde Fiction."

6. Conclusion

1. Tomashevsky, "Thematics," p. 90.
2. Sarraute, *L'Ere du soupçon*, p. 74.
3. See Beaujour, "Exemplary Pornography: Barrès, Loyola, and the Novel," pp. 325–349.
4. Grivel, *Production de l'intérêt romanesque*, p. 318. Other page references to this work will be given in parentheses in the text.
5. Jameson, "The Ideology of the Text," p. 240. See also my remarks in "The Place of Linguistics in Contemporary Literary Theory," pp. 575–578.
6. This quotation from Julia Kristeva (from *Séméiotiké. Recherches pour une sémanalyse*, 1969), is cited by Grivel in his programmatic conclusion, p. 372.
7. Todorov, "Introduction au vraisemblable," p. 99.
8. Nadine Dormoy Savage, "Rencontre avec Roland Barthes," p. 435.
9. Sartre, "Qu'est-ce que la littérature?," p. 262.
10. Wittgenstein, *Philosophical Investigations*, p. 47.
11. Sartre, *L'Enfance d'un chef*, p. 231. Other page references to this work will be given in parentheses in the text.
12. Idt, *"Le Mur" de Jean-Paul Sartre*, p. 156.
13. A few colleagues have confirmed this experience. Although such a reading may be due to insufficient knowledge about the French cultural context and about the subtleties of *style indirect libre* (especially in translation), it would be interesting to know whether some nonspecialist French readers do not, on occasion, have a similar reaction.
14. Ducrot, *Dire et ne pas dire*, p. 268.
15. Ducrot, "La Description sémantique des énoncés français et la notion de présupposition," p. 52.
16. See, for example, the reading by Ruth Amossy and Elisheva Rosen: "Fonctions du cliché dans le récit à thèse," in *Les Discours du cliché*, pp. 86–93.
17. Sartre, *Réflexions sur la question juive*, pp. 20–21. (English title: *Anti-Semite and Jew*.)

18. Sartre, "Qu'est-ce que la littérature?," p. 137.

19. Brasillach, *Oeuvres complètes*, 12:280–282. The review appeared in *L'Action Française*, April 13, 1939.

20. Girard, *Mensonge romantique et vérité romanesque*, p. 44.

21. Sartre, *Les Mots*, p. 13.

22. Beaujour, "Exemplary Pornography," pp. 344–345.

23. Idt, "L'Autoparodie dans *Les Mots* de Sartre," pp. 74–75.

24. *Ibid.*, p. 75.

25. Sartre, "Qu'est-ce que la littérature?," p. 103.

26. Sartre, *Les Mots*, p. 210.

Works Cited

Adereth, M. *Commitment in Modern French Literature. A Brief Study of "Littéra-ture engagée" in the Works of Péguy, Aragon, and Sartre.* London: Victor Gollancz, 1967.

Amossy, Ruth and Elisheva Rosen. *Les Discours du cliché.* Paris: Sedes, 1982.

Aragon, Louis. *Les Cloches de Bâle.* Paris: Hachette, Livre de Poche, 1970 (first ed. 1934).

—— *Les Beaux Quartiers.* Paris: Hachette, Livre de Poche, 1963 (first ed. 1936).

—— *Les Communistes.* 5 vols. Paris: La Bibliothèque Française, 1949–1951.

Aristotle. *Rhetoric.* W. Rhys Roberts, tr. New York: Modern Library, 1954.

Bakhtin, Mikhail. *Problems of Dostoevsky's Poetics.* R. W. Rotsel, tr. Ann Arbor, Mich.: Ardis, 1973.

—— *The Dialogic Imagination: Four Essays.* Michael Holquist, ed.; Caryl Emerson, tr. Austin; University of Texas Press, 1981.

Bal, Mieke. "Narration et focalisation." *Poétique* (1977), 29:107–126.

Barbéris, Pierre. *Le Père Goriot de Balzac.* Paris: Larousse, 1972.

Barrès, Maurice. *Les Déracinés.* Paris: Hachette, Livre de Poche, 1967 (first ed. 1897).

—— *L'Appel au Soldat.* Paris: Hachette, Livre de Poche, 1975 (first ed. 1900).

—— *Leurs Figures.* Paris: Hachette, Livre de Poche, 1967 (first ed. 1902).

—— *Mes Cahiers,* Vols. 1 and 2 (1896–1902). Paris: Plon, 1929 and 1930.

—— *L'Oeuvre de Maurice Barrès.* Philippe Barrès, ed. 20 vols. Paris: Au Club de l'Honnête Homme, 1965–1968.

Barrès, Philippe. Introduction to *Les Déracinés.* In *L'Oeuvre de Maurice Barrès,* 3:3–9.

Barthelme, Donald. *The Dead Father.* New York: Farrar, Straus and Giroux, 1975.

Barthes, Roland. *Mythologies.* Paris: Seuil, Collection "Points," 1970 (first ed. 1957).

—— "Ecrivains et écrivants." In *Essais Critiques.* Paris: Seuil, 1964. English translation: "Authors and Writers." In *Critical Essays.* Richard Howard, tr. Evanston: Northwestern University Press, 1972.

—— "Rhétorique de l'image." *Communications* (1964), 4:40–51.

—— "Introduction à l'analyse structurale des récits." *Communications* (1966), 8:1–27. English translation: "Introduction to the Structural Analysis of Narratives." Lionel Duisit, tr. *New Literary History* (1975), 6:237–272.

—— "L'*Effet* de réel." *Communications* (1968), 11:84–89.

—— "L'Ancienne Rhétorique." *Communications* (1970), 16:172–229.

—— *S/Z.* Paris: Seuil, 1970. English translation: *S/Z,* Richard Miller, tr. New York: Hill and Wang, 1974.

—— *Leçon.* Paris: Seuil, 1978.

Barthes, R., F. Bovon, et al. *Analyse structurale et exégèse biblique.* Geneva: Delachaux et Niestlé, 1971.

Barthes, R. et al. *Poétique de récit.* Paris: Seuil, collection "Points," 1977.

Beardsley, Monroe C. *Aesthetics: Problems in the Philosophy of Criticism.* 2d edition. Indianapolis: Hackett, 1981.

Beaujour, Michel. "Exemplary Pornography: Barrès, Loyola, and the Novel." In *The Reader in the Text. Essays on Audience and Interpretation.* Susan R. Suleiman and Inge Crosman, eds.

Beloff, Max. *The Intellectual in Politics.* New York: Library Press, 1970.

Benveniste, Emile. *Problèmes de linguistique générale.* Paris: Gallimard, 1966.

Blanchot, Maurice. "Les Romans de Sartre." *L'Arche,* October 1945, pp. 121–134. Reprinted in *La Part du feu.* Paris: Gallimard, 1949.

Bleich, David. *Subjective Criticism.* Baltimore: Johns Hopkins University Press, 1978.

Booth, W. C. *The Rhetoric of Fiction.* Chicago: University of Chicago Press, 1960.

Bourget, Paul. *Le Disciple.* Paris: Plon, 1901 (first ed. 1889).

——. *L'Etape.* 2 vols. Paris: Plon, 1902.

—— Author's preface to *La Terre promise.* Paris: Plon, 1902.

—— Preface to Henry Bordeaux's *Les Pierres du foyer.* Paris: Plon, 1918.

Brasillach, Robert. *Notre Avant-Guerre.* Paris: Plon, 1941.

—— Review of J.-P. Sartre's *Le Mur. Oeuvres complètes,* vol. 12. Paris: Au Club de l'Honnête Homme, 1964.

Bremond, Claude. *Logique du récit.* Paris: Seuil, 1973.

Brochier, Jean-Jacques, ed. *Paul Nizan, intellectuel communiste. Ecrits et correspondance, 1926–1940.* Paris: Maspero, 1967.

Brombert, Victor. *The Intellectual Hero. Studies in the French Novel, 1880–1955.* Chicago: University of Chicago Press, 1960.

Brooke-Rose, Christine. "Historical Genres/Theoretical Genres: A Discussion of Todorov on the Fantastic." *New Literary History* (1976), 8:145–158.

—— "The Readerhood of Man." In *The Reader in the Text. Essays on Audience and Interpretation.* Susan R. Suleiman and Inge Crosman, eds.

Brun, Charles. *Le Roman social en France au XIXe siècle.* Paris: V. Giard and E. Bière, 1910.

Bruss, Elizabeth W. "L'Autobiographie considérée comme acte littéraire." *Poétique* (1974), 17:14–26.

—— *Autobiographical Acts. The Changing Situation of a Literary Genre.* Baltimore: Johns Hopkins University Press, 1976.

Caute, David. *Communism and the French Intellectuals.* New York: Macmillan, 1964.

Chatman, Seymour. *Story and Discourse. Narrative Structure in Fiction and Film.* Ithaca: Cornell University Press, 1978.

Cohen-Solal, Annie and Henriette Nizan. *Paul Nizan, communiste impossible.* Paris: Grasset, 1980.

Culler, Jonathan. *Structuralist Poetics.* London: Routledge and Kegan Paul, 1975.

Danto, Arthur C. *Analytical Philosophy of History.* Cambridge: Cambridge University Press, 1968.

Decottignies, Jean. *L'Ecriture de la fiction. Situation idéologique du roman.* Paris: Presses Universitaires de France, 1979.

Derrida, Jacques. "The Law of Genre." *Critical Inquiry* (1980), 7(1):55–82.

Desanti, Dominique. *Drieu La Rochelle ou la séduction mystifiée.* Paris: Flammarion, 1978.

Drieu La Rochelle, Pierre. *Gilles.* Paris: Gallimard, 1939.

Dubief, Henri. *Le Déclin de la IIIe République, 1929–1938.* Paris: Seuil, collection "Points," 1976.

Dubois, J. *Grammaire structurale du français: nom et pronom.* Paris: Larousse, 1965.

Dubois, J., et al. *Dictionnaire de linguistique.* Paris: Larousse, 1973.

Du Bos, Charles. *François Mauriac et le problème du romancier catholique.* Paris: Corrêa, 1933.

Duchet, Claude. "Une Écriture de la socialité." *Poétique* (1973), 16:446–454.

Ducrot, Oswald. "La Description sémantique des énoncés français et la notion de présupposition." *L'Homme* (1968), 1:37–53.

—— *Dire et ne pas dire.* Paris: Hermann, 1972.

Ferraris, Denis. "Quaestio de legibilibus aut legendis scriptis: sur la notion de lisibilité en littérature." *Poétique* (1980), 43:282–292.

Feuillerat, Albert. *Paul Bourget. Histoire d'un esprit sous la Troisième République.* Paris: Plon, 1938.

Field, Frank. *Three French Writers and the Great War. Studies in the Rise of Communism and Fascism.* Cambridge: Camgridge University Press, 1975.

Flower, J. E. *Intention and Achievement. An Essay on the Novels of François Mauriac.* Oxford: Oxford University Press, 1969.

Forster, E. M. *Aspects of the Novel.* New York: Harcourt, Brace and World, 1927.

Fréville, Jean. Review of Nizan's *Antoine Bloyé.* *L'Humanité*, Dec. 18, 1933.

Frohock, W. M. *André Malraux and the Tragic Imagination*. Stanford: Stanford University Press, 1952.

Frye, Northrop. *The Antomy of Criticism*. New York: Atheneum, 1967.

Garaudy, Roger. *L'Itinéraire d'Aragon*. Paris: Gallimard, 1961.

Genette, Gérard. "Structuralisme et critique littéraire." In *Figures*. Paris: Seuil, 1966. English translation in *Figures of Literary Discourse*. New York: Columbia University Press, 1982.

—— "Frontières du récit." In *Figures II*. Paris: Seuil, 1969.

—— "Vraisemblance et motivation." In *Figures II*. Paris: Seuil, 1969.

—— "Discours du récit." In *Figures III*. Paris: Seuil, 1972. English translation: *Narrative Discourse: An Essay in Method*. Jane E. Lewin, tr. Ithaca: Cornell University Press, 1979.

—— "Genres, 'types,' modes." *Poétique* (1977), 32:389–421.

Gide, André. "A propos des *Déracinés*." In *Prétextes*. Paris: Mercure de France, 1919

—— *Le Retour de l'Enfant Prodigue*. In *Romans, Récits et Soties*. Paris: Gallimard, Bibliothèque de la Pléiade, 1958.

Gilbert, Sandra and Susan Gubar. *The Madwoman in the Attic. The Woman Writer and the Nineteenth-Century Literary Imagination*. New Haven: Yale University Press, 1979.

Girard, René. *Mensonge romantique et vérité romanesque*. Paris: Grasset, 1961. English translation: *Deceit, Desire and the Novel*. Baltimore: Johns Hopkins University Press, 1965.

Goguel, François. *La Politique des Partis sous la Troisième République*. Paris: Seuil, 1946.

Goldmann, Lucien. *Pour une sociologie du roman*. Paris: Gallimard, collection "Idées," 1964.

Greimas, A. J. *Sémantique structurale*. Paris: Larousse, 1966.

—— *Du Sens*. Paris: Seuil, 1970.

—— *Maupassant: la sémiotique du texte*. Paris: Seuil, 1976.

Grivel, Charles. *Production de l'intérêt romanesque*. The Hague: Mouton, 1973.

Grover, Frédéric and Pierre Andrieu. *Drieu La Rochelle*. Paris: Hachette, 1979.

Hamon, Philippe. "Qu'est-ce qu'une description?" *Poétique* (1972), 12:465–485.

—— "Un Discours contraint." *Poétique* (1973), 16:411–445.

—— "Pour un statut sémiologique du personnage." In *Poétique du récit*. R. Barthes et al., eds. 1977.

Heath, Stephen. *The Nouveau Roman: A Study in the Practice of Writing*. Philadelphia: Temple University Press, 1972.

Holland, Norman. *Five Readers Reading*. New Haven: Yale University Press, 1975.

Howe, Irving. *Politics and the Novel*. Cleveland and New York: World, 1957.

Huizinga, J. *Homo Ludens. A Study of the Play Element in Culture.* Boston: Beacon, 1955.

Hutcheon, Linda. *Narcissistic Narrative. The Metafictional Paradox.* Waterloo, Ontario: Wilfrid Laurier University Press, 1980.

Idt, Geneviève. *"Le Mur" de Jean-Paul Sartre: techniques et contexte d'une provocation.* Paris: Larousse, 1972.

—— "L'Autoparodie dans *Les Mots* de Sartre." *Cahiers du 20e Siècle* (1976), 6:53–85.

"Intertextualités." *Poétique* (1976). No. 27. Special issue.

Jakobson, Roman. "Closing Statement: Linguistics and Poetics." In *Style in Language.* Thomas A. Sebeok, ed. Cambridge, Mass.: M.I.T. Press, 1960.

Jameson, Fredric. "Magical Narratives: Romance as Genre." *New Literary History* (1975), 7:135–164.

—— "The Ideology of the Text." *Salmagundi* (1975–76), No. 31–32, pp. 204–246.

—— *The Political Unconscious.* Ithaca: Cornell University Press, 1981.

Jolles, A. *Formes simples.* A. M. Buguet, tr. Paris: Seuil, 1972.

Jost, François. "La Tradition du *Bildungsroman.*" *Comparative Literature* (1969), 21:97–115.

Kermode, Frank. *The Genesis of Secrecy. On the Interpretation of Narrative.* Cambridge, Mass.: Harvard University Press, 1979.

Kibédi-Varga, A. "L'Invention de la fable." *Poétique* (1976), 25:107–115.

Klinkenberg, J. M. "Le Concept d'isotopie en sémantique et en sémiotique littéraire." *Le Français Moderne* (1973), 41:285–290.

Kristeva, Julia. *Séméiotiké: recherches pour une sémanalyse.* Paris: Seuil, 1969.

—— *Le Texte du roman.* The Hague: Mouton, 1970.

LaFontaine, Jean de. *Fables.* Paris: Garnier Flammarion, 1966.

Laqueur, Walter and George L. Mosse, eds. *The Left-Wing Intellectuals Between the Wars, 1919–1939.* New York: Harper Torchbooks, 1966.

Larousse du XIXe Siècle. Paris: Administration du Grand Dictionnaire Universel, 1866.

Leenhardt, Jacques and Pierre Józsa. *Lire la lecture. Essai de sociologie de la lecture.* Paris: Editions du Sycomore, 1982.

Lévi-Strauss, Claude. *Anthropologie structurale.* Paris: Plon, 1958. English translation: *Structural Anthropology.* Claire Jacobson and Brooke Grundfest Schoepf, trs. New York: Basic Books, 1963.

Lubbock, Percy. *The Craft of Fiction.* London: Cape, 1921.

Lukács, György. *The Theory of the Novel.* Anna Bostock, tr. Cambridge, Mass.: M.I.T. Press, 1971.

Macherey, Pierre. *Pour une théorie de la production littéraire.* Paris: Maspero, 1971.

Malraux, André. *Le Temps du mépris.* Paris: Gallimard, 1935.

—— *L'Espoir.* Paris: Gallimard, 1937.

Mander, John. *The Writer and Commitment.* London: Secker and Warburg, 1961.

Marin, Louis. *Le Récit évangélique.* Paris: Desclée de Brouwer, 1974.

—— *Le Récit est un piège.* Paris: Minuit, 1978.

Mathewson, Rufus W., Jr. *The Positive Hero in Russian Literature.* 2d ed. Stanford: Stanford University Press, 1975.

Mauriac, François. *Le Noeud de vipères.* Paris: Hachette, Livre de Poche, 1963 (first ed. 1933).

May, Georges. *Le Dilemme du roman au dix-huitième siècle.* Paris: Presses Universitaires de France, 1963.

Mayeur, J.-M. *Les Débuts de la IIIe République, 1871–1898.* Paris: Seuil, collection "Points," 1973.

Miller, Nancy K. *The Heroine's Text. Readings in the French and English Novel, 1722–1782.* New York: Columbia University Press, 1980.

Mitterand, Henri. *Le Discours du roman.* Paris: Presses Universitaires de France, 1980.

Mosher, J. *The Exemplum in the Early Religious and Didactic Literature of England.* New York: Columbia University Press, 1911.

Mukařovsky, J. *Aesthetic Function, Norm and Value as Social Facts.* Mark Suino, tr. Ann Arbor: University of Michigan Slavic Contributions, 1970.

Murdoch, Iris. *Sartre: Romantic Rationalist.* New Haven: Yale University Press, 1953.

The New English Bible. New York: Oxford University Press, 1971.

Nizan, Paul. *Aden Arabie.* Paris: Maspero, 1960 (first ed. 1930).

—— Interview about *Antoine Bloyé. L'Impartial de L'Est,* December 30, 1933.

—— *Antoine Bloyé.* Paris: Hachette, Livre de Poche, 1971 (first ed. 1933).

—— *Le Cheval de Troie.* Paris: Gallimard, 1935.

—— *La Conspiration.* Paris: Gallimard, 1938.

—— *Pour une nouvelle culture.* Susan Suleiman, ed. Paris: Grasset, 1971.

Orwell, George. *Homage to Catalonia.* London: Secker and Warburg, 1938.

Polanyi, Livia. "So What's The Point?" *Semiotica* (1979), 25:207–241.

Pontalis, J. B. Preface to Xavière Gauthier, *Surréalisme et sexualité.* Paris: Gallimard, 1971.

Prince, Gerald. "Introduction à l'étude du narrataire." *Poétique* (1973), 14:178–196.

—— "*Le Noeud de vipères* ou les destinations du récit." *Orbis Literarum* (1976), 31:72–78.

Popp, Vladimir. *Morphologie du conte.* M. Derrida, T. Todorov, and C. Kahn, trs. Paris: Seuil, 1965 (first Russian ed. 1928).

Rastier, François. "Les Niveaux d'ambiguïté des structures narratives." *Semiotica* (1971), 3:289–342.

Redfern, W. D. *Paul Nizan. Committed Literature in a Conspiratorial World.* Princeton: Princeton University Press, 1972.

Ricardou, Jean. *Problèmes du nouveau roman*. Paris: Seuil, 1967.

—— *Pour une théorie du nouveau roman*. Paris: Seuil, 1971.

Rieuneau, Maurice. *Guerre et révolution dans le roman français, 1919–1939*. Paris: Klincksieck, 1974.

Riffaterre, Michael. "Système d'un genre descriptif." *Poétique* (1972), 9:15–30.

—— *Typology and Intertextuality*. Bloomington: Indiana University Press (forthcoming).

Rimmon, Shlomith. *The Concept of Ambiguity: The Example of James*. Chicago: University of Chicago Press, 1977.

Rimmon-Kenan, Shlomith. "The Paradoxical Status of Repetition." *Poetics Today* (1980), 1(4):151–160.

Robbe-Grillet, Alain. *Pour un nouveau roman*. Paris: Minuit, 1963.

Sacks, Sheldon. "Golden Birds and Dying Generations." *Comparative Literature Studies* (1969), 6:274–291.

Sarraute, Nathalie. *L'Ere du soupçon*. Paris: Gallimard, collection "Idées," 1956.

Sartre, Jean-Paul. *Le Mur*. Paris: Gallimard, Collection "Folio," 1980 (first ed. 1939).

—— "L'Enfance d'un chef." In *Le Mur*.

—— "Qu'est-ce que la littérature?" In *Situations II*. Paris: Gallimard, 1948.

—— *Réflexions sur la question juive*. Paris: Gallimard, collection "Idées," 1954.

—— Preface to Paul Nizan, *Aden Arabie*. Paris: Maspero, 1960.

—— *Les Mots*. Paris: Gallimard, 1964.

Savage, Catharine. *Malraux, Sartre, and Aragon as Political Novelists*. University of Florida Monographs in the Humanitites, No. 17, 1964.

Savage, Nadine Dormoy. "Rencontre avec Roland Barthes." *French Review* (1979), 52:432–439.

Schalk, David L. *The Spectrum of Political Engagement: Mounier, Benda, Nizan, Brasillach, Sartre*. Princeton: Princeton University Press, 1979.

Schor, Naomi. *Zola's Crowds*. Baltimore: Johns Hopkins University Press, 1978.

Searle, John R. *Speech Acts: An Essay in the Philosophy of Language*. Cambridge: Cambridge University Press, 1969.

Sennett, Richard. *Authority*. New York: Knopf, 1980.

Serres, Michel. "Connaissez-vous René Girard?" *Le Nouvel Observateur*, 17–23 avril 1978.

Shils, Edward A. "Authoritarianism: 'Right' and 'Left.'" In Richard Christie and Marie Jahoda, eds. *Studies in the Scope and Method of "The Authoritarian Personality."* Glencoe Ill.: Free Press, 1954.

Soucy, Robert. *Fascism in France. The Case of Maurice Barrès*. Berkeley: University of California Press, 1979.

Sternhell, Zeev. *Maurice Barrès et le nationalisme français*. Paris: Armand Colin, 1972.

—— *La Droite révolutionnaire*. Paris: Seuil, 1978.

Stierle, K. "L'Histoire comme Exemple, l'Exemple comme Histoire." *Poétique* (1972), 10:176–195.

Suleiman, Susan R. "Ideological Dissent from Works of Fiction: Toward a Rhetoric of the *roman à thèse*." *Neophilologus* (1976), 60:162–177.

—— "Reading Robbe-Grillet: Sadism and Text in *Projet pour une révolution à New York*." *Romanic Review* (1977), 68:43–62.

—— "The Place of Linguistics in Contemporary Literary Theory." *New Literary History* (1981), 12:571–584.

—— "The Question of Readability in Avant-Garde Fiction." *Studies in Twentieth Century Literature* (1981–1982), 6(1–2):17–36.

Suleiman, Susan R. and Inge Crosman, eds. *The Reader in the Text: Essays on Audience and Interpretation*. Princeton: Princeton University Press, 1980.

Thibaudet, Albert. *La Vie de Maurice Barrès*. Paris: NRF, 1921.

Thomas, Hugh. *The Spanish Civil War*. New York: Harper and Row, 1961.

Tison-Braun, Micheline. *La Crise de l'humanisme. Le Conflit de l'individu et de la société dans la littérature française moderne*. 2 vols. Paris: Nizet, 1958 and 1967.

Todorov, Tzvetan. *Introduction à la littérature fantastique*. Paris: Seuil, 1970. English translation: *The Fantastic: A Structural Approach to a Literary Genre*. Ithaca: Cornell University Press, 1975.

—— "Introduction au vraisemblable." In *Poétique de la prose*. Paris: Seuil, 1971. English translation: *The Poetics of Prose*. Ithaca: Cornell University Press, 1977.

—— "The Origin of Genres." Richard W. Berrong, tr. *New Literary History* (1976), 8:159–170. In French: "L'Origine des genres." In *Les Genres du discours*. Paris: Seuil, 1978.

—— *Symbolisme et interprétation*. Paris: Seuil, 1978.

Tomashevsky, Boris. "Thematics." In *Russian Formalist Criticism: Four Essays*. Lee T. Lemon and Marion J. Reis, eds. Lincoln: University of Nebraska Press, 1965.

Vierne, Simone. *Jules Verne et le roman initiatique*. Paris: Editions du Sirac, 1973.

—— *Rite Roman Initiation*. Grenoble: Presses Universitaires de Grenoble, 1973.

Welter, J.-Th. *L'Exemplum dans la littérature religieuse et didactique du Moyen Age*. Paris: E-H Guitard, 1927.

Williams, Raymond. *Marxism and Literature*. New York: Oxford University Press, 1977.

Wittgenstein, Ludwig. *Philosophical Investigations*. G. E. M. Anscombe, tr. 3rd ed. Oxford: Blackwell, 1972.

Wright, Gordon. *France in Modern Times*. Chicago: Rand McNally, 1960.

Zola, Emile. *Vérité*. Paris: F. Bernouard, 1928 (first ed. 1903).

Zumthor, Paul. *Essai de poétique médiévale*. Paris: Editions du Seuil, 1972.

Index